Dynamic Models of Energy, Robotic, and Biological Systems

Jose de Jesus Rubio · Alejandro Zacarias ·
Jaime Pacheco

Dynamic Models of Energy, Robotic, and Biological Systems

Systems, Design, and Validation

Springer

Jose de Jesus Rubio
ESIME Azcapotzalco
Instituto Politécnico Nacional
Mexico City, Distrito Federal, Mexico

Alejandro Zacarias
ESIME Azcapotzalco
Instituto Politécnico Nacional
Mexico City, Distrito Federal, Mexico

Jaime Pacheco
ESIME Azcapotzalco
Instituto Politécnico Nacional
Mexico City, Distrito Federal, Mexico

ISBN 978-3-031-85440-8 ISBN 978-3-031-85438-5 (eBook)
https://doi.org/10.1007/978-3-031-85438-5

This Springer imprint is published by the registered company Springer Nature Switzerland AG
The registered company address is: Gewerbestrasse 11, 6330 Cham, Switzerland

Preface

The goal of this book is to provide a detailed presentation of the dynamic models of systems. Dynamic model is a very interesting investigation field, since there are many applications of dynamic models in energy, robotic, and biological systems.

Each system has a different dynamic model; however, there are some characteristics in the dynamic model of each kind of system. The energy systems of this book contain the dynamic model of the device structure to convert the air energy, magnets movements, wheel movement, or hydrogen to mechanical energy, and the dynamic model of an electric generator to convert the mechanical energy to electrical energy. The robotic systems of this book contain the dynamic model of the actuators to convert electrical energy in mechanical energy, and the dynamic model of the structure to convert the mechanical energy in robot movements. The biological systems of this book contain the acquisition system to obtain the brain, eye, or nose signals, and the dynamic model of the neural network to approximate the obtained signals for modeling, pattern recognition, or classification.

This book is expected to be used primary by researchers and secondary by students and in the areas of control, robotics, energy, biological, mechanical, mechatronics, and computing systems.

The suggested use of the book is to be focused on each kind of system because they are different each other, Chaps. "Dynamic Model of a Wind Turbine for the Electric Energy Generation"–"Modeling and Control of a Fuel Cell" for the energy systems, Chaps. "Dynamic Model with Sensor and Actuator for a Transelevator"–"Inverse Dynamics Model of a Delta-Type Parallel Robot" for the rebotic systems, and Chaps. "Acquisition System and Approximation of Brain Signals"–"A Method with Neural Networks for the Classification of Fruits and Vegetables" for the biological systems.

Mexico City, Mexico
2024

Jose de Jesus Rubio

Acknowledgments The author thanks the Hindawi Publishing Corporation for permission to re-use portions of the work of [1] in Chap. "Dynamic Model of a Wind Turbine for the Electric Energy Generation" of this work.

The author thanks the Institute of Electrical and Electronics Engineers for permission to re-use portions of the work of [2] in Chap. "An Electricity Generator Based on the Interaction of Static and Dynamic Magnets" of this work.

The author thanks the Springer-Verlag Berlin Heidelberg for permission to re-use portions of the work of [3, 4, 5, 6] in Chaps. "Dynamic Model with Sensor and Actuator for a Transelevator", "Dynamic Model with Sensor and Actuator for an Articulated Robotic Arm", "A Method for Online Pattern Recognition of Abnormal Eye Movements", and "A Method with Neural Networks for the Classification of Fruits and Vegetables" of this work.

The author thanks the Institution of Engineering and Technology for permission to re-use portions of the work of [5] in Chap. "Acquisition System and Approximation of Brain Signals" of this work.

The author thanks the Instituto Politécnico Nacional, Consejo Nacional de Humanidades Ciencias y Tecnologías, Secretaría de Investigación y Posgrado, and Comisión de Operación y Fomento de Actividades Académicas for their help in this study.

References

1. J.J. Rubio, L.A. Soriano, W. Yu, Dynamic model of a wind turbine for the electric energy generation. Math. Probl. Eng. 1–8 (2014)
2. J.J. Rubio, A. Aguilar, J.A. Meda-Campaña, G. Ochoa, R. Balcazar, J. Lopez, An electricity generator based on the interaction of static and dynamic magnets. IEEE Trans. Magn. **55**(8), 8204511 (2019)
3. J.J. Rubio, J. Pacheco, J.H. Perez-Cruz, F. Torres, Mathematical model with sensor and actuator for a transelevator. Neural Comput. Appl. **24**(2), 277–285 (2014)
4. J.J. Rubio, J. Serrano, M. Figueroa, C.F. Aguilar-Ibañez, Dynamic model with sensor and actuator for an articulated robotic arm. Neural Comput. Appl. **24**(3–4), 573–581 (2014)
5. J.J. Rubio, D.M. Vazquez, D. Mujica-Vargas, Acquisition system and approximation of brain signals. IET Sci. Meas. Technol. **7**(4), 232–239 (2013)
6. J.J. Rubio, F. Ortiz, C.R. Mariaca, J.C. Tovar, A method for online pattern recognition for abnormal eye movements. Neural Comput. Appl. **22**(3–4), 597–605 (2013)
7. J.J. Rubio, A method with neural networks for the classification of fruits and vegetables. Soft. Comput. **21**(23), 7207–7220 (2017)

Competing Interests The authors have no competing interests to declare that are relevant to the content of this manuscript.

Introduction

Dynamic models are essential for understanding the system dynamics in open-loop (manual mode) or closed-loop (automatic) control. It is of importance because one mistake in experiments on prototypes could cause accidents or damage in prototypes or devices, while one mistake in the simulation of dynamic models could cause nothing. It helps in the method designs by considering dynamic models as a first stage of design before the experiments. Each system has a different dynamic model; hence, this book presents the designs of 10 dynamic models corresponding to 10 different systems. They are mainly classified into two kind of dynamic models.

The first kind of dynamic models of this book are mainly obtained by the Euler-Lagrange method and are described by differential equations; they are either derived from data (empirical) and from more fundamental relationships (first principles, physics-based) that rely on knowledge of the process. A combination of the two approaches is often used in practice where fundamental balance equations are adjusted to fit process data. The second kind of dynamic models in this book are mainly obtained by the neural networks and are described by difference equations; they are either derived from data (empirical) and from more fundamental relationships (their structure, their learning) that rely on knowledge of the process. A combination of the two approaches is often used in practice where unknown or uncertain parameters are adjusted to fit process data.

This book contains three main kind of dynamic models: Chaps. "Dynamic Model of a Wind Turbine for the Electric Energy Generation"–"Modeling and Control of a Fuel Cell" contains the dynamic models of energy systems, Chaps. "Dynamic Model with Sensor and Actuator for a Transelevator"–"Inverse Dynamics Model of a Delta-Type Parallel Robot" contains the dynamic models of robotic systems, and Chaps. "Acquisition System and Approximation of Brain Signals"–"A Method with Neural Networks for the Classification of Fruits and Vegetables" contains the dynamic models of biological systems. In this book, the dynamic models of energy systems and robotic systems are mainly obtained by the Euler–Lagrange method and are described by differential equations, while the dynamic models of biological systems are mainly obtained by neural networks and are described by difference equations.

The coverage of the chapters in this book is as follows.

In Chap. "Dynamic Model of a Wind Turbine for the Electric Energy Generation", a novel dynamic model is introduced for the modeling of wind turbine behavior. The objective of the wind turbine is electric energy generation. The analytic model has the characteristic that considers a rotatory tower. Experiments show the validity of the proposed method. This work is also published in [1].

In Chap. "An Electricity Generator Based on the Interaction of Static and Dynamic Magnets", the dynamic model of an electricity generator with four static magnets and four dynamic magnets is suggested for electricity generation. The introduced electricity generator is based on the electricity generator with two static magnets and two dynamic magnets, but it has three main advantages: it has more interactions between the static and dynamic magnets, it generates more electricity, and it generates smoother signals. Electricity generators are compared for the electricity generation. This work is also published in [2].

In Chap. "Dynamic Model of an Electric Vehicle with Energy Recovery", a dynamic model which describes the energy recovery for an electric vehicle is introduced. Generators connected with the wheels are used for the energy recovery during vehicle transportation. A prototype of the electric vehicle is used to validate the proposed approach. The stability analysis of the dynamic model is presented.

In Chap. "Modeling and Control of a Fuel Cell", the experimental control to obtain the maximum output voltage and the minimum input supplies in a real proton exchange membrane fuel cell is considered. The introduced technique employs a novel dynamic model that considers an outside resistor as other loss, and the experimental control which utilizes a novel law with an adaptive equation. The proposed dynamic model and control are validated by experiments and simulations.

In Chap. "Dynamic Model with Sensor and Actuator for a Transelevator", the structural, sensor, and actuator dynamic models of a transelevator are presented; subsequently, the combined dynamic model of the transelevator is obtained by using the combination of the structural, sensor, and actuator dynamic models. The proposed dynamic model is validated by comparing the simulation results against the experimental results. Finally, the stability analysis of the aforementioned model is studied. This work is also published in [3].

In Chap. "Dynamic Model with Sensor and Actuator for an Articulated Robotic Arm", the combined dynamic model for the articulated robotic arm is obtained using the combination of the structural, the sensor, and the actuator dynamic models. The proposed approach is validated by comparing the simulation results against the experimental results. This work is also published in [4].

In Chap. "Inverse Dynamics Model of a Delta-Type Parallel Robot", the inverse dynamics model of a delta-type parallel robot is introduced with the goal of relating the dynamic behavior of the torque with the dynamic behavior of the position, velocity, and acceleration. Results obtained from the programming of this inverse dynamics model of the delta-type parallel robot are compared for two kinds of simulation software (Simulink and Working Model) with the goal of reaching its validation.

In Chap. "Acquisition System and Approximation of Brain Signals", the acquisition system of one channel is introduced to obtain the biological brain signals. Such a system consists of a low pass filter, an amplifier, a high pass filter, and a data acquisition board. A novel slopes algorithm with bounded output is proposed for approximation of the brain signals. The proposed method is compared with both the least squares and nearest neighbor algorithms. This work is also published in [5].

In Chap. "A Method for Online Pattern Recognition of Abnormal Eye Movements", a method for the pattern recognition is used to provide a better diagnosis for patients with abnormal eye movements. The real data of signals of two eye movements (up and down) of patients are obtained using a mindset ms-100 system. A new method which uses one intelligent algorithm for online pattern recognition is proposed. The difference between the proposed method and the previous works is that in other works, both behaviors (up and down) are trained with one intelligent algorithm, while in this work, up behavior is trained with one intelligent algorithm and down behavior is trained with another intelligent algorithm; this is because the multi-output system can always be decomposed into a collection of single-output systems with the advantage of using different parameters for each one if necessary. The comparison results of the proposed method using the adaline network, multilayer network, or Sugeno fuzzy inference system are presented for online pattern recognition of two eye movements. This work is also published in [6].

In Chap. "A Method with Neural Networks for the Classification of Fruits and Vegetables", a novel method for the classification of fruits and vegetables is introduced. This technique is divided into two parts: the electronic nose and the classification method. First, an electronic nose is designed with an arduino microcontroller and with some electronic sensors to obtain real data of the smells of fruits or vegetables. Second, a classification method is introduced with a neural network to detect between three kind of objects: fruits or vegetables. The introduced strategy is validated by three experiments with the adaline, multilayer, and radial basis function neural networks. This work is also published in [7].

References

1. J.J. Rubio, L.A. Soriano, W. Yu, Dynamic model of a wind turbine for the electric energy generation. Math. Probl. Eng. 1–8 (2014)
2. J.J. Rubio, A. Aguilar, J.A. Meda-Campaña, G. Ochoa, R. Balcazar, J. Lopez, An electricity generator based on the interaction of static and dynamic magnets. IEEE Trans. Magn. **55**(8), 8204511 (2019)
3. J.J. Rubio, J. Pacheco, J.H. Perez-Cruz, F. Torres, Mathematical model with sensor and actuator for a transelevator. Neural Comput. Appl. **24**(2), 277–285 (2014)
4. J.J. Rubio, J. Serrano, M. Figueroa, C.F. Aguilar-Ibañez, Dynamic model with sensor and actuator for an articulated robotic arm. Neural Comput. Appl. **24**(3–4), 573–581 (2014)

5. J.J. Rubio, D.M. Vazquez, D. Mujica-Vargas, Acquisition system and approximation of brain signals. IET Sci. Meas. Technol. **7**(4), 232–239 (2013)
6. J.J. Rubio, F. Ortiz, C.R. Mariaca, J.C. Tovar, A method for online pattern recognition for abnormal eye movements. Neural Comput. Appl. **22**(3–4), 597–605 (2013)
7. J.J. Rubio, A method with neural networks for the classification of fruits and vegetables. Soft. Comput. **21**(23), 7207–7220 (2017)

Contents

Dynamic Model of a Wind Turbine for the Electric Energy Generation ... 1
1 Introduction ... 1
2 Dynamic Model of the Wind Turbine with a Rotatory Tower ... 2
2.1 The Mechanic Model ... 2
2.2 The Aerodynamic Model ... 5
2.3 The Electric Model ... 6
2.4 The Final Dynamic Model ... 7
3 Experiments to Validate the Dynamic Model ... 8
3.1 Example 1: The First Behavior ... 9
3.2 Example 2: The Second Behavior ... 11
4 Concluding Remarks ... 12
References ... 13

An Electricity Generator Based on the Interaction of Static and Dynamic Magnets ... 15
1 Introduction ... 15
2 Dynamic Model of the Electricity Generator with Two Static Magnets and Two Dynamic Magnets ... 16
2.1 The Euler-Lagrange Method to Obtain the Dynamic Models of Electricity Generators with Two Dynamic Magnets ... 16
2.2 Prototype of the Electricity Generator with Two Static Magnets and Two Dynamic Magnets ... 17
2.3 The Mechanic Model of the Electricity Generator ... 17
2.4 The Electric Model of the Electricity Generator ... 23
2.5 The Dynamic Model in State Space for the Electricity Generator ... 23

3 Dynamic Model of the Electricity Generator with Four Static Magnets and Four Dynamic Magnets ... 23
3.1 The Euler-Lagrange Method to Obtain the Dynamic Models of Electricity Generators with Four Dynamic Magnets ... 24
3.2 Prototype of the Electricity Generator with Four Static Magnets and Four Dynamic Magnets ... 24
3.3 The Mechanic Model of the Electricity Generator ... 26
3.4 The Electric Model of the Electricity Generator ... 32
3.5 The Dynamic Model in State Space for the Electricity Generator ... 32
4 Comparisons of the Electricity Generators ... 33
4.1 Comparison 1 ... 34
4.2 Comparison 2 ... 36
5 Concluding Remarks ... 38
References ... 38

Dynamic Model of an Electric Vehicle with Energy Recovery ... 41
1 Introduction ... 41
2 Prototype Description ... 42
3 Dynamic Model of the Electric Vehicle with Energy Recovery ... 42
3.1 Modified Dynamic Model of LuGre ... 43
3.2 Dynamic Model of the Wheels ... 44
3.3 Dynamic Model of the Electric Motor ... 46
3.4 Dynamic Model of the Electric Generator ... 47
3.5 Final Dynamic Model of the Electric Vehicle with Energy Recovery ... 47
4 Validation of the Proposed Dynamic Model ... 48
5 Stability Analysis ... 51
6 Concluding Remarks ... 53
References ... 53

Modeling and Control of a Fuel Cell ... 55
1 Introduction ... 55
2 Platform of the Fuel Cell ... 56
3 Dynamic Model of the Fuel Cell with an Outside Resistor ... 56
3.1 Theoretical Voltage of the Fuel Cell ... 58
3.2 Pressure Effect in the Theoretical Voltage ... 58
3.3 Voltage Losses ... 59
3.4 Output Voltage Equation of the Fuel Cell with the Outside Resistor ... 61
3.5 Basic Reactions ... 61
3.6 State Equations ... 62
3.7 The Complete System ... 62

4 Experimental Control of the Fuel Cell 63
5 Experimental Results 64
5.1 Experiment 1 64
5.2 Experiment 2 65
6 Concluding Remarks 68
References 68

Dynamic Model with Sensor and Actuator for a Transelevator 71
1 Introduction 71
2 Preliminaries 72
3 Dynamic Model of Elements of the Transelevator 73
3.1 Structural Dynamic Model 73
3.2 Actuator Dynamic Model 76
3.3 Sensor Dynamic Model 77
4 Dynamic Model with Sensor and Actuator for a Transelevator 78
5 Validation of the Dynamic Model 81
6 Stability Analysis 84
7 Concluding Remarks 86
References 86

Dynamic Model with Sensor and Actuator for an Articulated Robotic Arm 87
1 Introduction 87
2 Preliminaries 88
3 Dynamic Model of the Articulated Robotic Arm 89
3.1 Structural Dynamic Model 89
4 Actuator Dynamic Model 93
4.1 Sensor Dynamic Model 95
5 Dynamic Model with Sensor and Actuator for the Articulated Robotic Arm 96
6 Validation of the Proposed Dynamic Model 99
7 Concluding Remarks 103
References 103

Inverse Dynamics Model of a Delta-Type Parallel Robot 105
1 Introduction 105
2 Direct Kinematics 106
3 Inverse Dynamics 108
4 Simulations 112
5 Concluding Remarks 119
References 120

Acquisition System and Approximation of Brain Signals 121
1 Introduction 121
2 Acquisition of the EEG Signals 122
2.1 EEG Signals 122
2.2 Instrumentation Amplifier 123

2.3 High Pass Filter ... 124
2.4 Amplification ... 124
2.5 Low Pass Filter ... 124
2.6 Final Electronic Circuit ... 125
2.7 Data Acquisition ... 125
3 Slopes Algorithm ... 126
3.1 Detailed Description of the Algorithm ... 127
3.2 Boundedness of the Slopes Algorithm Output ... 128
3.3 The Proposed Algorithm ... 129
4 Results and Discussions ... 129
4.1 Example 1: The First Brain Behavior ... 130
4.2 Example 2: The Second Brain Behavior ... 131
4.3 Comparison of the Algorithms ... 131
5 Concluding Remarks ... 134
References ... 135

A Method for Online Pattern Recognition of Abnormal Eye Movements ... 137
1 Introduction ... 137
2 The Communication System ... 139
3 The Logical Combinations ... 140
4 Differences Between the Proposed Method for Online Pattern Recognition and Previous Works ... 141
5 Intelligent Algorithms ... 142
5.1 The Adaline Network ... 142
5.2 The Multilayer Neural Network ... 143
5.3 The Sugeno Fuzzy Inference System ... 144
6 Description of the Proposed Method for Online Pattern Recognition ... 145
7 The Proposed Method for Online Pattern Recognition ... 148
8 Experimental Results ... 148
9 Concluding Remarks ... 150
References ... 150

A Method with Neural Networks for the Classification of Fruits and Vegetables ... 153
1 Introduction ... 153
2 Electronic Nose ... 154
2.1 Sensors ... 155
2.2 Microcontroller ... 156
3 Concentrations for the Objects ... 156
4 Intelligent Algorithms ... 161
4.1 Adaline Neural Network ... 162
4.2 Multilayer Neural Network ... 163
4.3 Radial Basis Function Neural Network ... 163

5 Final Intelligent Algorithms 165
5.1 Adaline Neural Network 165
5.2 Multilayer Neural Network 165
5.3 Radial Basis Function Neural Network 166
6 Classification Method with the Neural Networks 166
6.1 Training 166
6.2 Testing 166
7 Experimental Results 168
7.1 Experiment 1 168
7.2 Experiment 2 172
7.3 Experiment 3 176
8 Concluding Remarks 180
References 180

About the Authors

Jose de Jesus Rubio is a full-time professor at the Sección de Estudios de Posgrado e Investigación, ESIME Azcapotzalco, Instituto Politécnico Nacional. He has published over 182 international journal papers with 4,115 cites from Scopus. He has been Senior Editor of *IEEE Transactions on Neural Networks and Learning Systems*. He has been Associate Editor of *IEEE Transactions on Fuzzy Systems Neural Networks*, *Neural Computing and Applications*, and *Frontiers in Neurorobotics*. He has been Guest Editor of *Neurocomputing*, *Applied Soft Computing*, *Journal of Supercomputing*, *Mathematics*, *Sensors*, *Machines*, *Computational Intelligence and Neuroscience*, *Frontiers in Psychology*, *Journal of Real-Time Image Processing*, and *Computer Science and Information Systems*. He has been tutor of four Postdoctoral students, 26 Ph.D. students, 48 M.S. students, four S. students, and 17 B.S. students. His fields of interest are robotic systems, energy systems, modeling, intelligent systems, and control.

Publications: https://www.scopus.com/authid/detail.uri?authorId=56002688600.

Alejandro Zacarias is a full-time professor at the Sección de Estudios de Posgrado e Investigación, ESIME Azcapotzalco, Instituto Politécnico Nacional. He has published 31 papers in international journals with 591 cites from Scopus. He has been tutor of nine Ph.D. students, 21 M.S. students, and 30 B.S. students. His fields of interest are solar energy, biofuels, boiling heat, and control.

Publications: https://www.scopus.com/authid/detail.uri?authorId=55363829900.

Jaime Pacheco is a full-time professor at the Sección de Estudios de Posgrado e Investigación, ESIME Azcapotzalco, Instituto Politécnico Nacional. He has published 56 papers in international journals with 989 cites from Scopus. He has been tutor of 12 Ph.D. students, 47 M.S. students, three S. students, and six B.S. students. His fields of interest are robotic systems, modeling, intelligent systems, and control.

Publications: https://www.scopus.com/authid/detail.uri?authorId=6507891870.

Dynamic Model of a Wind Turbine for the Electric Energy Generation

Abstract In this chapter, a novel dynamic model is introduced for the modeling of the wind turbine behavior. The objective of the wind turbine is the electric energy generation. The analytic model has the characteristic that considers a rotatory tower. Experiments show the validity of the proposed method.

1 Introduction

Researchers are often trying to improve the total power of a wind turbine. The dynamic model of a wind turbine plays an important role in some applications as the control, classification, or prediction.

Some authors have proposed the equations to model the dynamic behavior of the wind turbine such as in [1–5].

This chapter presents a novel dynamic model of a wind turbine: the first dynamic is for the wind turbine, the second is for the tower, and both are related. Because the rotatory tower can turn, it may help the wind turbine to increase the air intake. Some companies propose wind turbines that contain rotatory blades; however, in this study a rotatory tower is proposed instead of rotatory blades because the first dynamic model is easier to obtain than the second.

The proposed model is linear in the states as the works analyzed by [6–10]. The technique provides an acceptable approximation of the wind turbine behavior.

The chapter is structured as follows. In Sect. 2, the dynamic model of a windward wind turbine of three blades with a rotatory tower is introduced. In Sect. 3, the simulations of the dynamic model are compared with the real data obtained by a real wind turbine prototype. Finally, in Sect. 4, the conclusion and future research are detailed.

J. de J. Rubio et al., *Dynamic Models of Energy, Robotic, and Biological Systems*,
https://doi.org/10.1007/978-3-031-85438-5_1

2 Dynamic Model of the Wind Turbine with a Rotatory Tower

This section is divided into four parts: the first is the description of the mechanic model, the second is the description of the aerodynamic model, the third is the description of the electric model, and finally, the fourth is the combination of the aforementioned models to obtain the final dynamic model.

The dynamic model of the wind turbine is, first, the equations that represent the change between the wind energy and mechanic energy, and, second, the equations that represent the change between the mechanic energy and electric energy.

2.1 *The Mechanic Model*

A windward wind turbine of three blades with a rotatory tower is considered. First, the Euler Lagrangian method [11, 12] is used to obtain the model that represents the change from the wind energy to mechanic energy for the wind turbine, and the change from the electric energy to mechanic energy for the tower. The masses are concentrated at the center of mass. Consider the lateral view of Fig. 1 and the upper view of Fig. 2.

From Figs. 1 and 2, it can be seen that:

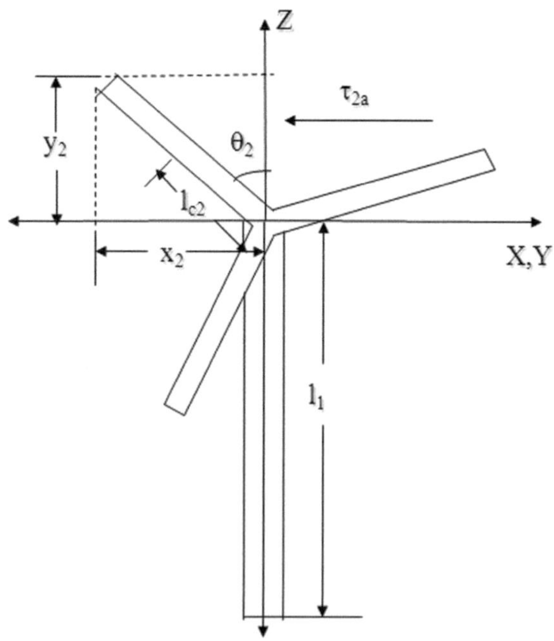

Fig. 1 Lateral view of the wind turbine

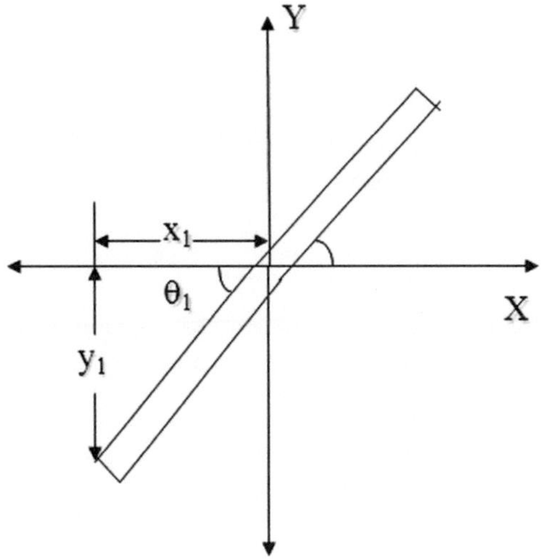

Fig. 2 Upper view of the wind turbine

$$\begin{aligned} x_2 &= -l_{c2}S_2(-C_1) = l_{c2}S_2C_1, \\ y_2 &= -l_{c2}S_2(-S_1) = l_{c2}S_2S_1, \end{aligned} \tag{1}$$

where $S_1 = \sin(\theta_1)$, $S_2 = \sin(\theta_2)$, $C_1 = \cos(\theta_1)$, $C_2 = \cos(\theta_2)$, θ_1 is the angular position of the tower motor in rad, θ_2 is the angular position of a wind turbine blade in rad, and l_{c2} is the length to the center of the wind turbine blade in m. Consequently, the kinetic energy K_1, K_2, and potential energy P_1, P_2 are given as follows:

$$\begin{aligned} K_1 &= 0, \\ K_2 &= \tfrac{1}{2}m_2 l_{c2}^2 S_2^2 \dot{\theta}_1^2 + \tfrac{1}{2}m_2 l_{c2}^2 \dot{\theta}_2^2, \\ P_1 &= m_1 g l_{c1}, \\ P_2 &= l_1 + m_2 g l_{c2} C_2, \end{aligned} \tag{2}$$

where m_1 is the tower mass in kg, m_2 is the blade mass in kg, g is the acceleration gravity in m/s^2, l_1 is the constant length of the tower in m, and l_{c1} is the length to the center of the tower in m. The torque τ_{T1a} and τ_{T2a} are given as follows:

$$\begin{aligned} \tau_{T1a} &= \tau_{1a} - k_{b1}\theta_1 - b_{b1}\dot{\theta}_1, \\ \tau_{T2a} &= \tau_{2a} - k_{b2}\theta_2 - b_{b2}\dot{\theta}_2, \end{aligned} \tag{3}$$

where τ_{2a} is the torque of the generator moved by the blade in kgm^{2}rad/s^2, τ_{1a} is the torque of the motor used to move the tower in kgm^{2}rad/s^2, k_{b1} and k_{b2} are the spring effect presented when the blade is near to stop in kgm^2/s^2, b_{b1} and b_{b2} are the shock absorber in kgm^{2}rad/s. Using the Euler-Lagrange method in [11, 12] gives the following equations:

$$\begin{aligned} & m_2 l_{c2}^2 S_2^2 \ddot{\theta}_1 + 2 m_2 l_{c2}^2 S_2 C_2 \dot{\theta}_1 \dot{\theta}_2 + b_{b1} \dot{\theta}_1 + k_{b1} \theta_1 = \tau_{1a}, \\ & m_2 l_{c2}^2 \ddot{\theta}_2 + m_2 g l_{c2} S_2 + b_{b2} \dot{\theta}_2 + k_{b2} \theta_2 = \tau_{2a}, \end{aligned} \tag{4}$$

The angular position of the blade 1 is related with the angular position of the blades 2 and 3 as follows:

$$\begin{aligned} \theta_3 &= \theta_2 + \tfrac{2}{3}\pi \text{rad}, \\ \theta_4 &= \theta_2 + \tfrac{4}{3}\pi \text{rad}, \end{aligned} \tag{5}$$

where θ_3 and θ_4 are the angular position for the blades 2 and 3, respectively. Then, using Eq. (4), it yields the equations for blades 2 and 3 as a function of θ_2 as follows:

$$\begin{aligned} & m_2 l_{c2}^2 S_{2+\frac{2}{3}\pi}^2 \ddot{\theta}_1 + 2 m_2 l_{c2}^2 S_{2+\frac{2}{3}\pi} C_{2+\frac{2}{3}\pi} \dot{\theta}_1 \dot{\theta}_2 + b_{b1} \dot{\theta}_1 + k_{b1} \theta_1 = \tau_{1b}, \\ & m_2 l_{c2}^2 \ddot{\theta}_2 + m_2 g l_{c2} S_{2+\frac{2}{3}\pi} + b_{b2} \dot{\theta}_2 + k_{b2} (\theta_2 + \tfrac{2}{3}\pi) = \tau_{2b}, \end{aligned} \tag{6}$$

$$\begin{aligned} & m_2 l_{c2}^2 S_{2+\frac{4}{3}\pi}^2 \ddot{\theta}_1 + 2 m_2 l_{c2}^2 S_{2+\frac{4}{3}\pi} C_{2+\frac{4}{3}\pi} \dot{\theta}_1 \dot{\theta}_2 + b_{b1} \dot{\theta}_1 + k_{b1} \theta_1 = \tau_{1c}, \\ & m_2 l_{c2}^2 \ddot{\theta}_2 + m_2 g l_{c2} S_{2+\frac{4}{3}\pi} + b_{b2} \dot{\theta}_2 + k_{b2} (\theta_2 + \tfrac{4}{3}\pi) = \tau_{2c}, \end{aligned} \tag{7}$$

where τ_{1b}, τ_{2b}, τ_{1c}, and τ_{2c} are the torques applied to move the blades 2 and 3, respectively. Adding $S_2^2 + S_{2+\frac{2}{3}\pi}^2 + S_{2+\frac{4}{3}\pi}^2$, $S_2 C_2 + S_{2+\frac{2}{3}\pi} C_{2+\frac{2}{3}\pi} + S_{2+\frac{4}{3}\pi} C_{2+\frac{4}{3}\pi}$, and $S_2 + S_{2+\frac{2}{3}\pi} + S_{2+\frac{4}{3}\pi}$, respectively gives:

$$S_2^2 + S_{2+\frac{2}{3}\pi}^2 + S_{2+\frac{4}{3}\pi}^2 = 1.5, \tag{8}$$

$$S_2 C_2 + S_{2+\frac{2}{3}\pi} C_{2+\frac{2}{3}\pi} + S_{2+\frac{4}{3}\pi} C_{2+\frac{4}{3}\pi} = 0, \tag{9}$$

$$S_2 + S_{2+\frac{2}{3}\pi} + S_{2+\frac{4}{3}\pi} = 0, \tag{10}$$

Now, adding the three equations of (4), (6), and (7) and using (8), (9), and (10) gives:

$$\begin{aligned} & 4.5 m_2 l_{c2}^2 \ddot{\theta}_1 + 3 b_{b1} \dot{\theta}_1 + 3 k_{b1} \theta_1 = \tau_1, \\ & 3 m_2 l_{c2}^2 \ddot{\theta}_2 + 3 b_{b2} \dot{\theta}_2 + 3 k_{b2} \theta_2 + 2\pi k_{b2} = \tau_2, \end{aligned} \tag{11}$$

where $\tau_1 = \tau_{1a} + \tau_{1b} + \tau_{1c}$ and $\tau_2 = \tau_{2a} + \tau_{2b} + \tau_{2c}$. From Figs. 1 and 2, τ_2 of (11) is defined as follows:

$$\begin{aligned} \tau_2 &= C_1 F_2, \\ F_2 &= F_{2a} + F_{2b} + F_{2c}, \end{aligned} \tag{12}$$

where $C_1 = \cos(\theta_1)$, F_{2a}, F_{2b}, and F_{2c} are the force of the air received by the three blades. Equation (12) describes the assumption that the air goes in one direction, if $\theta_1 = 0$, then the maximum air intake moves the blades of the wind turbine, but if the tower turns to the left or to the right and θ_1 changes, then the wind turbine turns, and the air intake decreases. From Figs. 1 and 2, [12], τ_1 of (11) is defined as follows:

$$\tau_1 = k_m i_1, \tag{13}$$

where k_m is a motor magnetic flux constant of the tower in Wb, and i_1 is the motor armature current of the tower in A. Equations (11), (12), and (13) are the main equations of the mechanic model that represents the wind turbine and tower.

2.2 *The Aerodynamic Model*

The aerodynamic model is the dynamic model of the torque applied to the blades. The mechanic power captured by the wind turbine P_a is given by [2–5]:

$$P_a = F_{2a}\dot{\theta}_2 = \frac{1}{2}\rho A C_p(\lambda, \beta) V_\omega^3, \tag{14}$$

where ρ is the air density in Kg/m^3, $A = \pi R^2$ is the area swept by the rotor blades in m^2 with radius R in m, V_ω is the wind speed in m/s, and $C_p(\lambda, \beta)$ is the performance coefficient of the wind turbine, whose value is a function of the tip speed ratio λ, defined as follows [2–5]:

$$\lambda = \frac{\dot{\theta}_2 R}{V_\omega}, \tag{15}$$

For the purposes of simulation, the following model of $C_p(\lambda, \beta)$ is presented as follows [2–5]:

$$C_p(\lambda, \beta) = c_1\left(\frac{c_2}{\lambda_i} - c_3\beta - c_4\right)e^{-c_5/\lambda_i} + c_6\lambda, \tag{16}$$

where:

$$\frac{1}{\lambda_i} = \frac{1}{\lambda + 0.08\beta} - \frac{0.035}{\beta^3 + 1}, \tag{17}$$

and the coefficients are $c_1 = 0.5176$, $c_2 = 116$, $c_3 = 0.4$, $c_4 = 5$, $c_5 = 21$, $c_6 = 0.0068$, and β is the blade pitch angle in rad. Using Eqs. (12), (14), (15), (16), and (17) gives the dynamic model of the torque applied to the wind turbine blades as follows:

$$\begin{aligned}
\tau_2 &= C_1\left(F_{2a} + F_{2b} + F_{2c}\right), \\
F_{2a} &= \frac{1}{2\dot{\theta}_2}\rho A C_p(\lambda, \beta) V_\omega^3, \\
F_{2b} &= \frac{1}{2\dot{\theta}_2}\rho A C_p(\lambda, \beta) V_\omega^3, \\
F_{2c} &= \frac{1}{2\dot{\theta}_2}\rho A C_p(\lambda, \beta) V_\omega^3,
\end{aligned} \tag{18}$$

where C_1 is defined in (12), λ is defined in (15), $C_p(\lambda, \beta)$ is defined in (16), and λ_i is defined in (17).

2.3 The Electric Model

Now, analyze the change from the mechanic to electric energy for the wind turbine generator, and the electric energy to mechanic energy for the tower motor. Figure 3 shows the wind turbine generator and Fig. 4 shows the tower motor.

In [12, 13], they presented the model of a motor; similarly, from Fig. 3 a model for the generator is obtained by using the Kirchhoff voltage law. Therefore, the dynamic models of the motor and generator are as follows:

$$\begin{aligned} V_1 &= R_1 i_1 + L_1 \dot{i}_1 + k_1 \dot{\theta}_1, \\ k_2 \dot{\theta}_2 &= R_2 i_2 + L_2 \dot{i}_2 + V_2, \end{aligned} \tag{19}$$

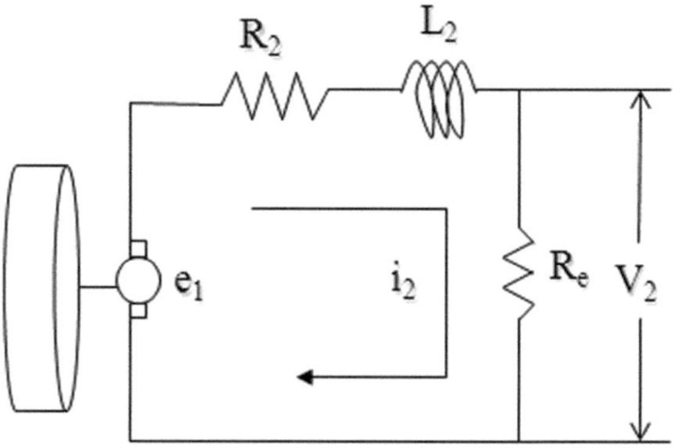

Fig. 3 The wind turbine generator

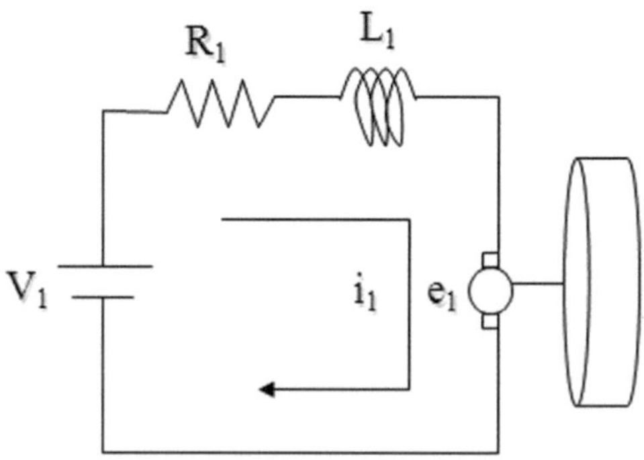

Fig. 4 The tower motor

where k_1 is the motor back emf constant in Vs/rad, k_2 is the generator back emf constant in Vs/rad, R_1 is the motor armature resistance in Ω, R_2 is the generator armature resistance in Ω, L_1 is the motor armature inductance in H, L_2 is the generator armature inductance in H, V_1 is the motor armature voltage in V, V_2 is the generator armature voltage in V, i_1 is the motor armature current in A, and i_2 is the generator armature current in A. For the generator of this chapter $V_2 = R_e i_2$. Thus, (19) becomes:

$$\begin{aligned} V_1 &= R_1 i_1 + L_1 \dot{i}_1 + k_1 \dot{\theta}_1, \\ k_2 \dot{\theta}_2 &= (R_2 + R_e)\, i_2 + L_2 \dot{i}_2, \\ V_2 &= R_e i_2. \end{aligned} \tag{20}$$

2.4 The Final Dynamic Model

Thus, Eqs. (11), (13), and (18) that represent the change between the wind energy and mechanic energy, and Eq. (20) that represents the change between the mechanic energy and electric energy are considered to be the wind turbine dynamic model with a rotatory tower.

Define the state variables as $x_1 = i_2, x_2 = \theta_2, x_3 = \dot{\theta}_2, x_4 = i_1, x_5 = \theta_1, x_6 = \dot{\theta}_1$, the inputs as $u_1 = F_2, u_2 = V_1$, and the output as $y = V_2$. Consequently, the dynamic model of Eqs. (11), (13), (15), (18), and (20) becomes:

$$\begin{aligned} \dot{x}_1 &= -\tfrac{(R_2+R_e)}{L_2} x_1 + \tfrac{k_2}{L_2} x_3, \\ \dot{x}_2 &= x_3, \\ \dot{x}_3 &= -\tfrac{k_{b2}}{m_2 l_{c2}^2} x_2 - \tfrac{b_{b2}}{m_2 l_{c2}^2} x_3 - \tfrac{2\pi k_{b2}}{3 m_2 l_{c2}^2} + \tfrac{\cos(x_5)}{3 m_2 l_{c2}^2} u_1, \\ \dot{x}_4 &= -\tfrac{R_1}{L_1} x_4 - \tfrac{k_1}{L_1} x_6 + \tfrac{1}{L_1} u_2, \\ \dot{x}_5 &= x_6, \\ \dot{x}_6 &= -\tfrac{3 k_{b1}}{4.5 m_2 l_{c2}^2} x_5 - \tfrac{3 b_{b1}}{4.5 m_1 l_{c2}^2} x_6 + \tfrac{k_m}{4.5 m_2 l_{c2}^2} x_4, \\ y &= R_e x_1, \\ u_1 &= F_{2a} + F_{2b} + F_{2c}, \\ F_{2a} &= \tfrac{1}{2x_3} \rho A C_p(\lambda, \beta) V_\omega^3, \\ F_{2b} &= \tfrac{1}{2x_3} \rho A C_p(\lambda, \beta) V_\omega^3, \\ F_{2c} &= \tfrac{1}{2x_3} \rho A C_p(\lambda, \beta) V_\omega^3, \\ \lambda &= \tfrac{x_3 R}{V_\omega}, \end{aligned} \tag{21}$$

where $C_p(\lambda, \beta)$ is defined in (16), and λ_i is defined in (17).

Remark 1 The model of this research considers a direct current motor and a direct current generator. This wind turbine is proposed to be used on the house roof for the daily usage to feed a light as a renewable source. If more than one wind turbine is used, more electricity is generated. The proposed model could be extended to other kind of machines by changing Eq. (20).

Remark 2 Note that the dynamic model states of the wind turbine with a rotatory tower (21) is a linear system [6–10].

3 Experiments to Validate the Dynamic Model

Figure 5 shows the prototype of a wind turbine with a rotatory tower which is considered for the simulations of the dynamic model. This prototype has three blades with a rotatory tower which does not use a gear box. Table 1 shows the parameters of the prototype. The parameters m_2 and l_{c2}, are obtained from the wind turbine blades. The parameters R_1, L_1, and k_1, are obtained from the tower motor. The parameters k_2, R_2, R_e, and L_2, are obtained from the wind turbine generator. The parameters R, ρ, V_ω, and β, are obtained from [2–5].

The dynamic model of the wind turbine with a rotatory tower is given by Eq. (21) with the parameters of Table 1. 1×10^{-5} are considered as the initial conditions for the plant states $x_1 = i_2$, $x_2 = \theta_2$, $x_3 = \dot{\theta}_2$, $x_4 = i_1$, $x_5 = \theta_1$, and $x_6 = \dot{\theta}_1$. The root mean square error (RMSE) is used is given as follows [13, 14]:

$$RMSE = \left(\frac{1}{T} \int_0^T e^2 d\tau \right)^{\frac{1}{2}} \tag{22}$$

Fig. 5 Prototype of a wind turbine with a rotatory tower

Table 1 Parameters of the prototype

Parameter	Value	Parameter	Value
l_{c2}	0.5 m	R_e	30 Ω
m_2	0.5 kg	k_m	0.09 Wb
k_{b2}	1×10^{-6} kgm^2/s^2	k_{b1}	1×10^{-6} kgm^2/s^2
b_{b2}	1×10^{-1} kgm^{2}rad/s	b_{b1}	1×10^{-1} kgm^{2}rad/s
k_2	0.45 Vs/rad	k_1	0.0045 Vs/rad
R_2	6.96 Ω	R_1	18 Ω
L_2	6.031×10^{-1} H	L_1	6.031×10^{-1} H
R	l_{c2} m	V_ω	5 m/s
ρ	1.225 kg/m^3	β	0.5 rad
g	9.81 m/s^2		

where $e^2 = e_{uj}^2 = (u_{jr} - u_j)^2$, $e^2 = e_{xi}^2 = (x_{ir} - x_i)^2$, or $e^2 = e_y^2 = (y_r - y)^2$, u_{jr}, x_{ir}, and y_r are the real data of u_j, x_i, and y, respectively, $i = 1, 2, \ldots, 6$, $j = 1, 2$.

3.1 Example 1: The First Behavior

Figures 6 and 7, show the wind turbine inputs, outputs, and states. Table 2 shows the RMSE for the errors.

From Figs. 6 and 7, it can be seen that the dynamic model has good behavior described as follows: (1) from 0 s to 2 s, both inputs are fed; consequently, the tower moves far to the maximum air intake, the generator current is decreased, and the wind turbine blades stop to move; (2) from 2 s to 4 s, both inputs are not fed; consequently, current is not generated, both the tower and wind turbine blades do no move; (3) from 4 s to 6 s, both inputs are fed, but the air intake is positive and the tower voltage is negative; consequently, the tower returns to the maximum air intake, the generator current is increased, and the wind turbine blades move; (4) from 6 s to 8 s, both inputs are not fed; consequently, current is not generated, the tower and wind turbine blades do no move. The dynamic model is a good approximation of the wind turbine behavior because the signals of the first are near to the signals of the second. In Table 2, it is shown that the dynamic model is a good approximation of the real process because the RMSE is near to zero.

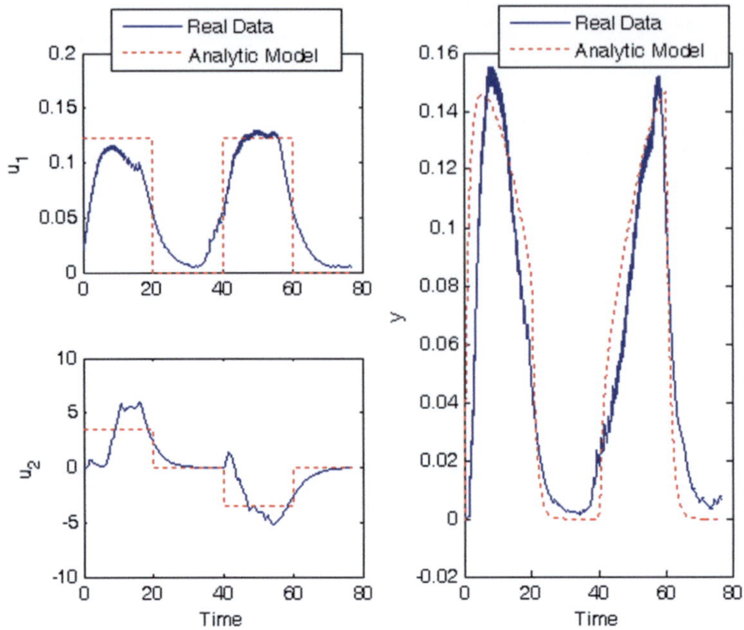

Fig. 6 Inputs and output of the wind turbine of Example 1

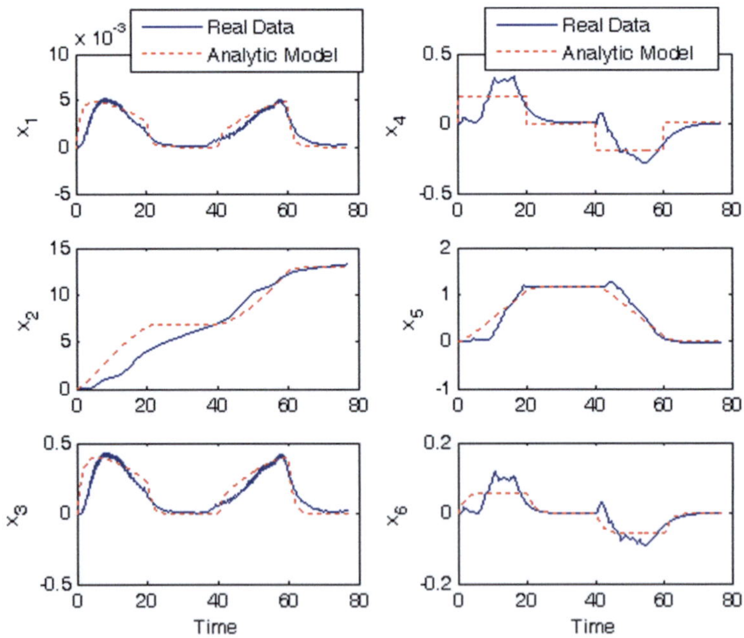

Fig. 7 States of the wind turbine of Example 1

Table 2 RMSE for Example 1

	RMSE		RMSE		RMSE
e_{u1}^2	0.0204	e_{x1}^2	5.7158×10^{-4}	e_{x4}^2	0.0658
e_{u2}^2	1.1835	e_{x2}^2	0.9843	e_{x5}^2	0.0872
e_y^2	0.0171	e_{x3}^2	0.0470	e_{x6}^2	0.0163

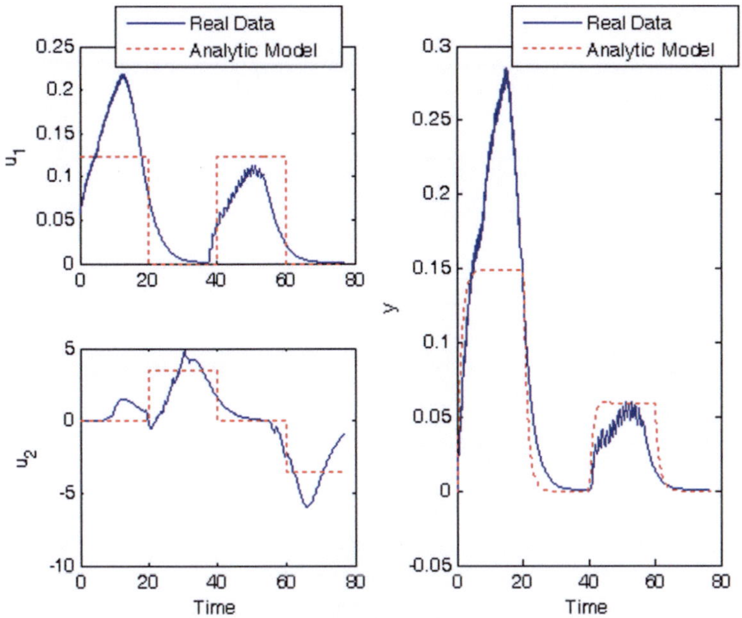

Fig. 8 Inputs and output of the wind turbine of Example 2

3.2 *Example 2: The Second Behavior*

Figures 8 and 9 show the wind turbine inputs, outputs, and states. Table 3 shows the RMSE for the errors.

From Figs. 8 and 9, it can be seen that the dynamic model has good behavior described as follows: (1) from 0 s to 2 s, the input air is fed and the tower input is not fed; consequently, the tower remain in the maximum air intake, the generator current is maximum, and the wind turbine blades have motion; (2) from 2 s to 4 s, the air is not fed and the tower input is fed; consequently, current is not generated, the tower moves far to the maximum air intake, and the wind turbine blades do not have motion; (3) from 4 s to 6 s, the air is fed and the tower input is not fed; consequently, the tower does not move, the generator current is minimum, and the wind turbine blades almost do not move; (4) from 6 s to 8 s, the air is not fed and the tower input is fed with a negative voltage; consequently, current is not generated, the tower return

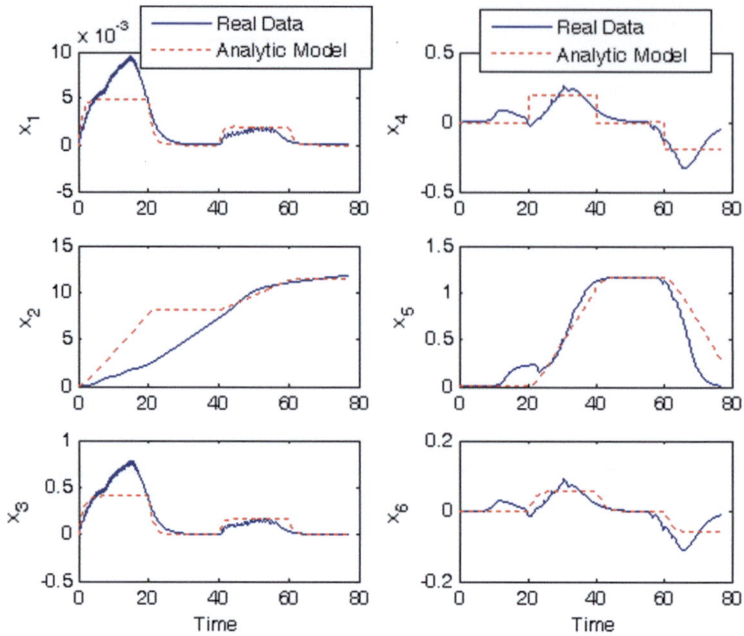

Fig. 9 States of the wind turbine of Example 2

Table 3 RMSE for Example 2

	RMSE		RMSE		RMSE
e_{u1}^2	0.0288	e_{x1}^2	9.3212×10^{-4}	e_{x4}^2	0.0523
e_{u2}^2	0.9423	e_{x2}^2	1.7209	e_{x5}^2	0.1324
e_{y}^2	0.0280	e_{x3}^2	0.0766	e_{x6}^2	0.0162

to the maximum air intake, and the wind turbine blades do not have motion. The dynamic model is a good approximation of the wind turbine behavior because the signals of the first are near to the signals of the second. From Table 3, it is shown that the dynamic model is a good approximation of the real process because the RMSE is near to zero.

4 Concluding Remarks

In this chapter, a dynamic model of a wind turbine with a rotatory tower was introduced, and the simulations using the parameters of a prototype showed that the proposed dynamic model has an acceptable approximation of the wind turbine behavior.

The proposed dynamic model could be used on control, prediction, or classification. As future research, the modeling will be improved using other interesting methods such as the least squares, neural networks, or fuzzy systems.

References

1. L.L. Fan, Y.D. Song, Neuro-adaptive model-reference fault-tolerant control with application to wind turbines. IET Control. Theory & Appl. **6**(4), 475–486 (2012)
2. A. Zertek, G. Verbic, M. Pantos, Optimised control approach for frequency-control contribution of variable speed wind turbines. IET Renew. Power Gener. **6**(1), 17–23 (2012)
3. E.B. Muhando, T. Senjyu, A. Yona, H. Kinjo, T. Funabashi, Disturbance rejection by dual pitch control and self-tuning regulator for wind turbine generator parametric uncertainty compensation. IET Control. Theory & Appl. **1**(5), 1431–1440 (2007)
4. C.Y. Tang, Y. Guo, J.N. Jiang, Nonlinear dual-mode control of variable-speed wind turbines with doubly fed induction generators. IEEE Trans. Control. Syst. Technol. **19**(4), 744–756 (2011)
5. R. Vepa, Nonlinear optimal control of a wind turbine generator. IEEE Trans. Energy Convers. **26**(2), 468–478 (2011)
6. M. Dehghan, M. Hajarian, Modied AOR iterative methods to solve linear systems. J. Vib. Control. **20**(5), 661–669 (2012)
7. M. Hajarian, Matrix form of the Bi-CGSTAB method for solving the coupled Sylvester matrix equations. IET Control. Theory & Appl. **7**(14), 1828–1833 (2013)
8. M. Hajarian, Efficient iterative solutions to general coupled matrix equations. Int. J. Autom. Comput. **10**(5), 481–486 (2013)
9. M. Hajarian, Matrix iterative methods for solving the Sylvester-transpose and periodic Sylvester matrix equations. J. Frankl. Inst. **350**(10), 3328–3341 (2013)
10. J.J. Rubio, G. Ordaz, M. Jimenez-Lizarraga, R.I. Cabrera, General solution to the Navier-Stokes equation to describe the dynamics of a homogeneous viscous fluid in an open pipe. Revista Mexicana de Fisica **59**(3), 217–223 (2013)
11. F.L. Lewis, D.M. Dawson, C.T. Abdallah, *Control of Robot Manipulators, Theory and Practice* (2004). ISBN: 0-8247-4072-6
12. M.W. Spong, S. Hutchinson, M. Vidyasagar, *Robot Modeling and Control* (John Wiley & Sons, 2006). ISBN-13: 978-0-471-64990-8
13. J.J. Rubio, J. Pacheco, J.H. Pérez-Cruz, F. Torres, Mathematical model with sensor and actuator for a transelevator. Neural Comput. Appl. **24**, 277–285 (2014)
14. J.J. Rubio, Evolving intelligent algorithms for the modelling of brain and eye signals. Appl. Soft Comput. **14**(B), 259–268 (2014)

An Electricity Generator Based on the Interaction of Static and Dynamic Magnets

Abstract In this chapter, the dynamic model of an electricity generator with four static magnets and four dynamic magnets is suggested for the electricity generation. The introduced electricity generator is based on the electricity generator with two static magnets and two dynamic magnets, but it has three main advantages: it has more interactions between the static and dynamic magnets, it generates more electricity, and it generates smoother signals. Electricity generators are compared for the electricity generation.

1 Introduction

Recently, the term free-energy is utilized in systems which can obtain energy from the environment, avoiding the necessity of a kind of fuel. Some of the most important free-energy systems can be classified as: electricity generators with magnets, wind turbines, or solar generators. This research is concentrated on the electricity generators with magnets. The electricity generator of this study uses the interactions between their static and dynamic magnets for the electricity generation.

There is interesting research focused on systems with magnets. In [1–5], permanent generators are designed. Permanent motors are discussed in [6–10]. In [11–15], permanent machines are proposed. Permanent rotors are studied in [16–20]. In [21–25] several properties of components in magnets are studied. Important characteristics of magnet cores are investigated in [26–29]. The aforementioned investigation shows that the systems with magnets are welcomed as recent and interesting issues, and in some cases it could be concentrated in electricity generators with magnets.

The disadvantage in the electricity generators with magnets is that they need the electricity as a fuel, or in the other case, the electricity generators with magnets generate electricity during some time until they stop. In this chapter, the dynamic model of an electricity generator with magnets is proposed in which the number of static and dynamic magnets is increased with the target to increase the electricity generation. The suggested dynamic model is described by differential equations and it is based on the parallel axis theorem to obtain the inertia model, the Euler-Lagrange

J. de J. Rubio et al., *Dynamic Models of Energy, Robotic, and Biological Systems*,
https://doi.org/10.1007/978-3-031-85438-5_2

method to obtain the mechanic model, and the Kirchhoff voltage law to obtain the electric model.

The electricity generators with magnets could be used for two possible applications: (a) to feed the lights in the homes, offices, or vehicles; (b) to feed the batteries of the portable phones or computers.

The other sections are detailed as follows. The dynamic model of the electricity generator with two static magnets and two dynamic magnets is explained in Sect. 2. Section 3 suggests the dynamic model of the electricity generator with four static magnets and four dynamic magnets. The comparisons between the two electricity generators are shown in Sect. 4. In Sect. 5, the conclusion and forthcoming research are described.

2 Dynamic Model of the Electricity Generator with Two Static Magnets and Two Dynamic Magnets

In this section, the Euler-Lagrange method, the prototype, the mechanic model, the electric model, and the state space model for an electricity generator with two static and two dynamic magnets are described.

2.1 *The Euler-Lagrange Method to Obtain the Dynamic Models of Electricity Generators with Two Dynamic Magnets*

The equation to be solved by the Euler-Lagrange method to obtain the dynamic model of an electricity generator with two static and two dynamic magnets is as follows:

$$\begin{aligned} \tau &= \tfrac{d}{dt}\left(\frac{\partial L_1}{\partial \dot{\theta}}\right) - \left(\tfrac{\partial L_1}{\partial \theta}\right) + \tfrac{d}{dt}\left(\frac{\partial L_2}{\partial \dot{\theta}}\right) - \left(\tfrac{\partial L_2}{\partial \theta}\right) + b\dot{\theta}, \\ L_1 &= K_1 - P_1, \\ L_2 &= K_2 - P_2, \end{aligned} \tag{1}$$

where τ is the torque produced by the interaction of magnets, L_1 and L_2 are the Lagrangian produced by the dynamic magnet 1 and 2, K_1 and K_2 are the kinetic energy produced by the dynamic magnet 1 and 2, P_1 and P_2 are the potential energy produced by the dynamic magnet 1 and 2, and b is the damping coefficient of dynamic magnets.

The procedure to obtain the dynamic model of the electricity generator is as follows:

1. Energies K_1, K_2, P_1, P_2 are obtained as: (a) the interactions of all static magnets and the dynamic magnet 1 are utilized to obtain K_1, P_1; (b) the interactions of all static magnets and the dynamic magnet 2 are utilized to obtain K_2, P_2.
2. Energies K_1, P_1 are substituted in the second part of Eq. (1) to obtain L_1.
3. Energies K_2, P_2 are substituted in the third part of Eq. (1) to obtain L_2.
4. Lagrangians L_1, L_2 are substituted in first part of Eq. (1) to obtain τ.

2.2 Prototype of the Electricity Generator with Two Static Magnets and Two Dynamic Magnets

The dynamic model of the electricity generator of this section is based on the interaction of two dynamic magnets with two static magnets to obtain a mechanic motion, and the mechanic motion is converted to electricity via an electric generator.

Figure 1 shows the full electricity generator with two static magnets and two dynamic magnets. Figure 2 shows four views of motions in two dynamic magnets with respect to two static magnets. The operation of this mechanism is discussed as follows. Static is for all parts which do not present motion, and Dynamic is for all parts which present motion. The static platform is to hold the dynamic and static magnets, dynamic links, and dynamic arrow, while the static structure is to hold the static stator and dynamic arrow. Dynamic magnets have motion because they interact with static magnets. Dynamic link 1 and dynamic link 2 have rotations around their joint because on one side they are joined to each other, and on the other side they are joined to the two dynamic magnets. The dynamic arrow is joined to the joint of dynamic link 1 and dynamic link 2; consequently, the rotation of the dynamic link 1 and dynamic link 2 yields the rotation of the dynamic arrow. The dynamic arrow is the first part of the electric generator, the the second part of the electric generator is the static stator. The rotation of the dynamic arrow yields electricity inside of the static stator. Then, the operation of the discussed mechanism starts with the magnetism produced by interaction between the static and dynamic magnets and it finishes with the electricity produced by the static stator.

2.3 The Mechanic Model of the Electricity Generator

Figure 1 shows the electricity generator with magnets.

By using the inertia, the kinetic energy of the dynamic magnet 1 K_1 is as follows:

$$K_1 = \frac{1}{2} I_1 \dot{\theta}^2, \tag{2}$$

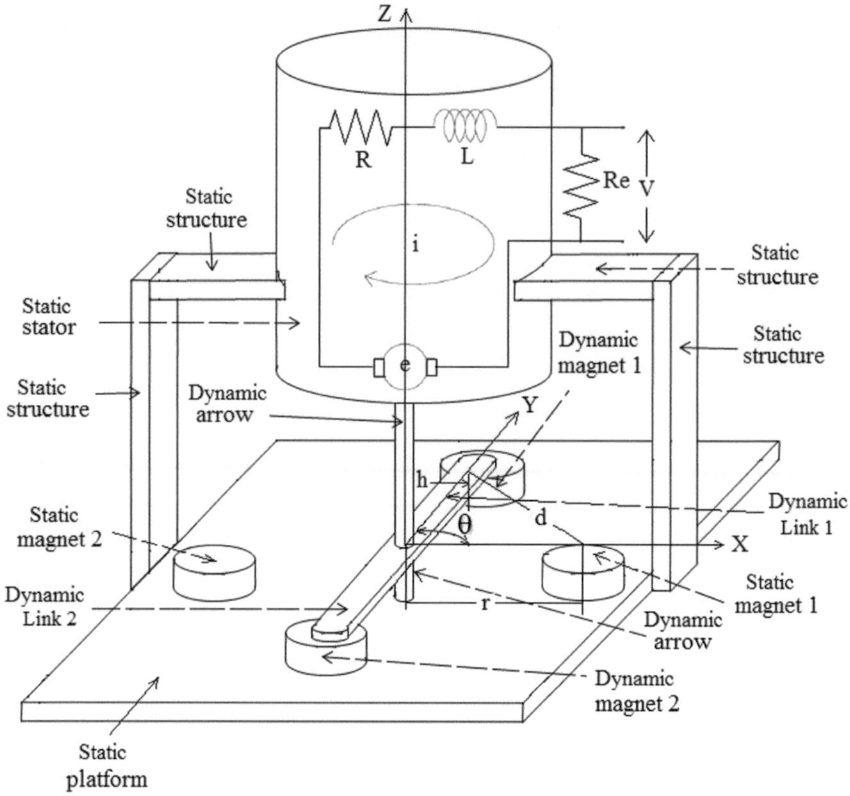

Fig. 1 Electricity generator with two static magnets and two dynamic magnets

where I_1 is the inertia produced by the dynamic magnet 1 and $\dot{\theta}$ is the angular velocity of the dynamic magnet 1. Utilizing the section with the dynamic magnet 1, the inertia produced by the link 1 $\overline{I}_{e1}$ is as follows:

$$I_{e1} = \frac{1}{12} m_{e1} \left(a_1^2 + c_1^2 \right), \tag{3}$$

where m_{e1} is the mass of the link 1, a_1 is the width of the link 1, and c_1 is the length of the link 1. The inertia of the dynamic magnet 1 $\overline{I}_{i1}$ is as follows:

$$I_{i1} = \frac{1}{2} m_i r_i^2, \tag{4}$$

where m_i is the mass of the dynamic magnet 1, and r_i is the radius of dynamic magnet 1. Utilizing the parallel axis theorem, the inertia is as follows:

$$I = \overline{I} + m r_g^2, \tag{5}$$

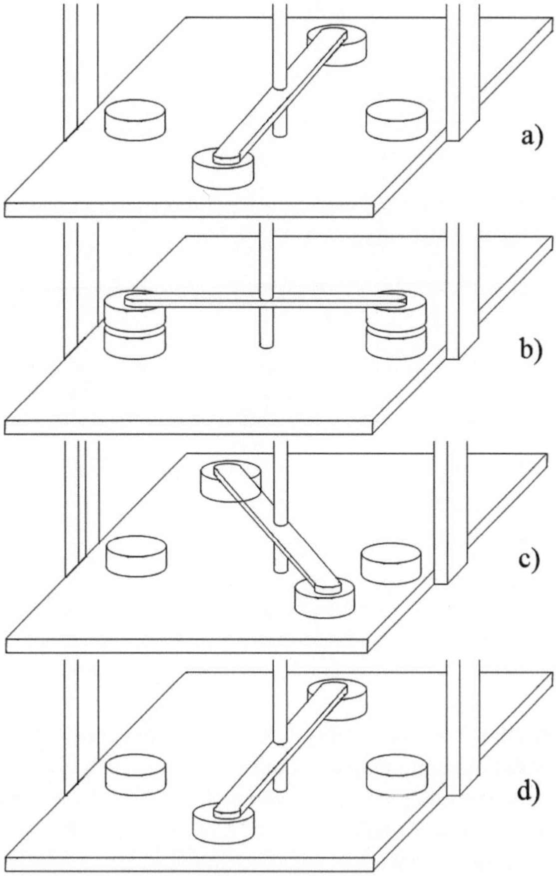

Fig. 2 Motions in two dynamic magnets with respect to two static magnets

where $\overline{I}$ is the inertia of Eq. (3) or (4), m is the mass of Eq. (3) or (4), and r_g is the radius of the body rotation. Applying Eq. (5) to Eq. (3) and (4) yields:

$$\begin{aligned} I_{eu} &= \tfrac{1}{12} m_{e1} \left(a_1^2 + c_1^2\right) + m_{e1} r_g^2, \\ I_{iu} &= \tfrac{1}{2} m_i r_i^2 + m_i r_g^2, \end{aligned} \tag{6}$$

where I_{eu} is the inertia produced in the link 1, and I_{iu} is the inertia produced in the dynamic magnet 1. The inertia produced for the dynamic magnet 1 I_1 is:

$$
\begin{aligned}
I_1 &= I_{eu} + I_{iu} \\
&= \frac{1}{12} m_{e1} \left(a_1^2 + c_1^2\right) + m_{e1} r_g^2 \\
&+ \frac{1}{2} m_i r_i^2 + m_i r_g^2,
\end{aligned} \tag{7}
$$

Substituting the inertia produced for the dynamic magnet 1 in the kinetic energy of the dynamic magnet 1 K_1 yields:

$$
\begin{aligned}
K_1 = &\left(\frac{1}{24} m_{e1} \left(a_1^2 + c_1^2\right) + \frac{1}{2} m_{e1} r_g^2\right) \dot{\theta}^2 \\
&+ \left(\frac{1}{4} m_i r_i^2 + \frac{1}{2} m_i r_g^2\right) \dot{\theta}^2,
\end{aligned} \tag{8}
$$

For obtaining the Lagrangian L_1, the potential energy P_1 for the dynamic magnet 1 is obtained by the Fig. 1:

$$
\begin{aligned}
P_1 &= \frac{B_{11}^2}{2\mu} V_{11} + \frac{B_{12}^2}{2\mu} V_{12} \\
&= \frac{B^2}{2\mu} V_{11} + \frac{B^2}{2\mu} V_{12},
\end{aligned} \tag{9}
$$

where $B_{11} = B_{m1} + B_{f1}$ is the magnet flux density presented in the volume generated by the dynamic magnet 1 and static magnet 1, $B_{12} = B_{m1} + B_{f2}$ is the magnet flux density presented in the volume of the dynamic magnet 1 and static magnet 2, since all magnets are equal $B_{11} = B_{12} = B$, V_{11} is the volume of the dynamic magnet 1 and static magnet 1, V_{12} is the volume of the dynamic magnet 1 and static magnet 2, and μ is the magnet permeability constant in magnets. From Fig. 1, the volumes are:

$$
\begin{aligned}
V_{11} &= \pi r_i^2 d_{11}, \\
V_{12} &= \pi r_i^2 d_{12},
\end{aligned} \tag{10}
$$

where r_i is the radius of the magnet surface, d_{11} is the centers distance between the dynamic magnet 1 and static magnet 1, d_{12} is the centers distance between the dynamic magnet 1 and static magnet 2. From Fig. 1, the distances are:

$$
\begin{aligned}
d_{11} &= \left(x_{11}^2 + y_{11}^2 + z_{11}^2\right)^{0.5}, \\
d_{12} &= \left(x_{12}^2 + y_{12}^2 + z_{12}^2\right)^{0.5},
\end{aligned} \tag{11}
$$

x_{11}, y_{11}, z_{11} are parts of the distance d_{11}, and x_{12}, y_{12}, z_{12} are parts of the distance d_{12}, where:

$$\begin{aligned} x_{11} &= r_g(1-\cos\theta), \\ y_{11} &= y_{12} = r_g \sin\theta, \\ z_{11} &= z_{12} = h, \\ x_{12} &= r_g(1+\cos\theta), \end{aligned} \tag{12}$$

where r_g is the radius of dynamic magnets, and h is the distance of a dynamic magnet and a static magnet on the axis z. Substituting Eq. (12) in Eq. (11) gives:

$$\begin{aligned} d_{11} &= \left[r_g^2(1-\cos\theta)^2 + r_g^2(\sin\theta)^2 + h^2\right]^{0.5} \\ &= \left[2r_g^2(1-\cos\theta) + h^2\right]^{0.5}, \\ d_{12} &= \left[r_g^2(1+\cos\theta)^2 + r_g^2(\sin\theta)^2 + h^2\right]^{0.5} \\ &= \left[2r_g^2(1+\cos\theta) + h^2\right]^{0.5}, \end{aligned} \tag{13}$$

Substituting Eq. (13) in Eq. (10) gives:

$$\begin{aligned} V_{11} &= \pi r_i^2 \left[2r_g^2(1-\cos\theta) + h^2\right]^{0.5}, \\ V_{12} &= \pi r_i^2 \left[2r_g^2(1+\cos\theta) + h^2\right]^{0.5}, \end{aligned} \tag{14}$$

Substituting Eq. (14) in the potential energy P_1 of Eq. (9) gives:

$$\begin{aligned} P_1 = &\frac{B^2}{2\mu}\pi r_i^2 \left[2r_g^2(1-\cos\theta) + h^2\right]^{0.5} \\ &+ \frac{B^2}{2\mu}\pi r_i^2 \left[2r_g^2(1+\cos\theta) + h^2\right]^{0.5}, \end{aligned} \tag{15}$$

Substituting the potential energy P_1 of Eq. (15) and kinetic energy K_1 of Eq. (8) into the Lagrangian L_1 of Eq. (1) gives:

$$\begin{aligned} L_1 &= K_1 - P_1 \\ &= \left(\frac{1}{24}m_{e1}\left(a_1^2 + c_1^2\right) + \frac{1}{2}m_{e1}r_g^2\right)\dot{\theta}^2 \\ &+ \left(\frac{1}{4}m_i r_i^2 + \frac{1}{2}m_i r_g^2\right)\dot{\theta}^2 \\ &- \frac{B^2}{2\mu}\pi r_i^2 \left[2r_g^2(1-\cos\theta) + h^2\right]^{0.5} \\ &- \frac{B^2}{2\mu}\pi r_i^2 \left[2r_g^2(1+\cos\theta) + h^2\right]^{0.5}, \end{aligned} \tag{16}$$

Utilizing a similar procedure, L_2 of Eq. (1) gives:

$$
\begin{aligned}
L_2 &= K_2 - P_2, \\
&= \left(\frac{1}{24}m_{e2}\left(a_2^2 + c_2^2\right) + \frac{1}{2}m_{e2}r_g^2\right)\dot{\theta}^2 \\
&+ \left(\frac{1}{4}m_i r_i^2 + \frac{1}{2}m_i r_g^2\right)\dot{\theta}^2 \\
&- \frac{B^2}{2\mu}\pi r_i^2\left[2r_g^2(1+\cos\theta) + h^2\right]^{0.5} \\
&- \frac{B^2}{2\mu}\pi r_i^2\left[2r_g^2(1-\cos\theta) + h^2\right]^{0.5},
\end{aligned}
\tag{17}
$$

Substituting L_1 of Eq. (16) and L_2 of Eq. (17) into Eq. (1) yields the torque of magnets τ as follows:

$$
\begin{aligned}
\tau &= \left(\frac{1}{12}m_{e1}\left(a_1^2 + c_1^2\right) + m_{e1}r_g^2\right)\ddot{\theta} \\
&+ \left(\frac{1}{2}m_i r_i^2 + m_i r_g^2\right)\ddot{\theta} \\
&+ \frac{\pi B^2 r_g^2 r_i^2 \sin\theta}{2\mu\left[h^2 + 2r_g^2(1-\cos\theta)\right]^{0.5}} - \frac{\pi B^2 r_g^2 r_i^2 \sin\theta}{2\mu\left[h^2 + 2r_g^2(1+\cos\theta)\right]^{0.5}} \\
&+ \left(\frac{1}{12}m_{e2}\left(a_2^2 + c_2^2\right) + m_{e2}r_g^2\right)\ddot{\theta} \\
&+ \left(\frac{1}{2}m_i r_i^2 + m_i r_g^2\right)\ddot{\theta} + b\dot{\theta} \\
&- \frac{\pi B^2 r_g^2 r_i^2 \sin\theta}{2\mu\left[h^2 + 2r_g^2(1+\cos\theta)\right]^{0.5}} + \frac{\pi B^2 r_g^2 r_i^2 \sin\theta}{2\mu\left[h^2 + 2r_g^2(1-\cos\theta)\right]^{0.5}},
\end{aligned}
\tag{18}
$$

Finally, utilizing $2m_{e1} = 2m_{e2} = m_e$, $2a_1 = 2a_2 = a$, $2c_1 = 2c_2 = c$, the torque of magnets τ is as follows:

$$
\begin{aligned}
\tau &= m_e\left(\frac{1}{24}a^2 + \frac{1}{24}c^2 + r_g^2\right)\ddot{\theta} \\
&+ m_i\left(r_i^2 + 2r_g^2\right)\ddot{\theta} + b\dot{\theta} \\
&+ \frac{\pi B^2 r_g^2 r_i^2 \sin\theta}{\mu\left[h^2 + 2r_g^2(1-\cos\theta)\right]^{0.5}} - \frac{\pi B^2 r_g^2 r_i^2 \sin\theta}{\mu\left[h^2 + 2r_g^2(1+\cos\theta)\right]^{0.5}}.
\end{aligned}
\tag{19}
$$

2.4 The Electric Model of the Electricity Generator

Now, the conversion from the mechanic movement to electricity of the electricity generator is discussed.

From Fig. 1, and utilizing the Kirchhoff voltage law, the electric model of the generator is as follows:

$$e = V_R + V_L + V, \tag{20}$$

where $e = K_m\dot{\theta}$ is the electromotive force, $V_R = Ri$ is the voltage in the resistance, $V_L = L\dot{i}$ is the voltage in the inductance, $V = R_e i$ is the voltage in the load, K_m is the electromotive force constant, $\dot{\theta}$ is the derivative of angle, R is the resistance, i is the current, L is the inductance, and R_e is the load resistance. Then, Eq. (20) is written as follows:

$$K_m\dot{\theta} = Ri + L\dot{i} + R_e i. \tag{21}$$

2.5 The Dynamic Model in State Space for the Electricity Generator

Thus, Eq. (19) is the conversion between the magnetism and mechanic motions, and Eq. (21) is the conversion between the mechanic motions and electricity; they are known as the dynamic model of the electricity generator.

States are selected as $z_1 = i$, $z_2 = \theta$, $z_3 = \dot{\theta}$ and the input is selected as $v = \tau$. Finally, the dynamic model of Eqs. (19) and (21) is as follows:

$$\begin{aligned}
\dot{z}_1 &= -\frac{(R+R_e)}{L} z_1 + \frac{K_m}{L} z_3,\\
\dot{z}_2 &= z_3,\\
\dot{z}_3 &= \left(\frac{1}{m_e(\frac{1}{24}a^2+\frac{1}{24}c^2+r_g^2)+m_i(r_i^2+2r_g^2)}\right)\\
&* \left(v - \frac{\pi B^2 r_i^2 r_g^2 \sin z_2}{\mu\left[h^2+2r_g^2(1-\cos z_2)\right]^{0.5}}\right.\\
&\left. + \frac{\pi B^2 r_i^2 r_g^2 \sin z_2}{\mu\left[h^2+2r_g^2(1+\cos z_2)\right]^{0.5}} - b z_3\right).
\end{aligned} \tag{22}$$

3 Dynamic Model of the Electricity Generator with Four Static Magnets and Four Dynamic Magnets

In this section, the Euler-Lagrange method, the prototype, the mechanic model, the electric model, and the state space model for an electricity generator with four static and four dynamic magnets are described.

3.1 The Euler-Lagrange Method to Obtain the Dynamic Models of Electricity Generators with Four Dynamic Magnets

The equation to be solved by the Euler-Lagrange method to obtain the dynamic model of the electricity generator with four static and four dynamic magnets is as follows:

$$\begin{aligned}
&\tau = \frac{d}{dt}\left(\frac{\partial L_1}{\partial \dot{\theta}}\right) - \left(\frac{\partial L_1}{\partial \theta}\right) + \frac{d}{dt}\left(\frac{\partial L_2}{\partial \dot{\theta}}\right) - \left(\frac{\partial L_2}{\partial \theta}\right)\\
&+\frac{d}{dt}\left(\frac{\partial L_3}{\partial \dot{\theta}}\right) - \left(\frac{\partial L_3}{\partial \theta}\right) + \frac{d}{dt}\left(\frac{\partial L_4}{\partial \dot{\theta}}\right) - \left(\frac{\partial L_4}{\partial \theta}\right) + b\dot{\theta},\\
&L_1 = K_1 - P_1,\\
&L_2 = K_2 - P_2,\\
&L_3 = K_3 - P_3,\\
&L_4 = K_4 - P_4,
\end{aligned} \tag{23}$$

where τ is the torque produced by the interaction of magnets, L_1, L_2, L_3, and L_4 are the Lagrangian produced by the dynamic magnet 1, 2, 3, and 4, K_1, K_2, K_3, and K_4 are the kinetic energy produced by the dynamic magnet 1, 2, 3, and 4, P_1, P_2, P_3, and P_4 are the potential energy produced by the dynamic magnet 1, 2, 3, and 4, b is the damping coefficient of dynamic magnets.

The procedure to obtain the dynamic model of the electricity generator is as follows:

1. Energies K_1, K_2, K_3, K_4, P_1, P_2, P_3, P_4 are obtained as: (a) the interactions of all static magnets and the dynamic magnet 1 are utilized to obtain K_1, P_1; (b) the interaction between all static magnets and the dynamic magnet 2 are utilized to obtain K_2, P_2; (c) the interaction between all static magnets and the dynamic magnet 3 are utilized to obtain K_3, P_3; (d) the interaction between all static magnets and the dynamic magnet 4 are utilized to obtain K_4, P_4.
2. Energies K_1, P_1 are substituted in the second part of Eq. (23) to obtain L_1.
3. Energies K_2, P_2 are substituted in the third part of Eq. (23) to obtain L_2.
4. Energies K_3, P_3 are substituted in the fourth part of Eq. (23) to obtain L_3.
5. Energies K_4, P_4 are substituted in the fifth part of Eq. (23) to obtain L_4.
6. Lagrangians L_1, L_2, L_3, L_4 are substituted in first part of Eq. (23) to obtain τ.

3.2 Prototype of the Electricity Generator with Four Static Magnets and Four Dynamic Magnets

The dynamic model of the electricity generator of this section is based on the interaction of two dynamic magnets with four static magnets to obtain a mechanic motion, and the mechanic motion is converted to electricity via an electric generator.

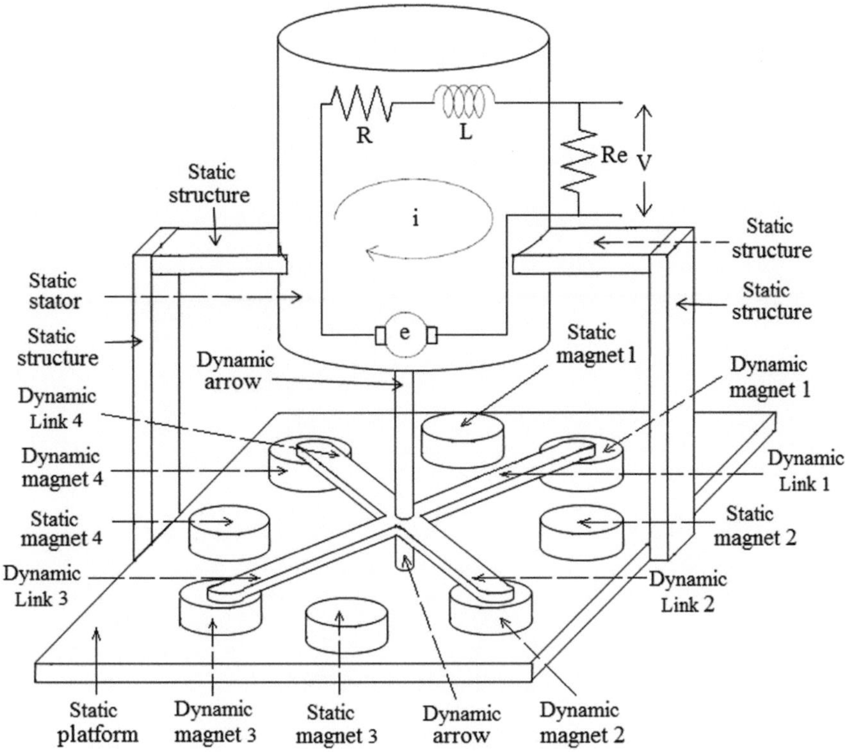

Fig. 3 Electricity generator with four static magnets and four dynamic magnets

Figure 3 shows the full electricity generator with four static magnets and four dynamic magnets. Figure 4 shows three views of motions in four dynamic magnets with respect to four static magnets. The operation of this mechanism is discussed as follows. Static is for all parts which do not present motion, and Dynamic is for all parts which present motion. The static platform is to hold the dynamic and static magnets, dynamic links, and dynamic arrow, while the static structure is to hold the static stator and dynamic arrow. Dynamic magnets have motion because they interact with static magnets. Dynamic link 1 and dynamic link 2 have rotations around their joint because on one side they are joined each other, and on the other side they are joined to the two dynamic magnets. The dynamic arrow is joined to the joint of dynamic link 1 and dynamic link 2; consequently, the rotation of the dynamic link 1 and dynamic link 2 yields the rotation of the dynamic arrow. Dynamic link 3 and dynamic link 4 have rotations around their joint because on one side they are joined to each other, and on the other side they are joined to the two dynamic magnets. The dynamic arrow is joined to the joint of dynamic link 3 and dynamic link 4; consequently, the rotation of the dynamic link 3 and dynamic link 4 also yields the rotation of the dynamic arrow. The dynamic arrow is the first part of the

Fig. 4 Motions in four dynamic magnets with respect to four static magnets

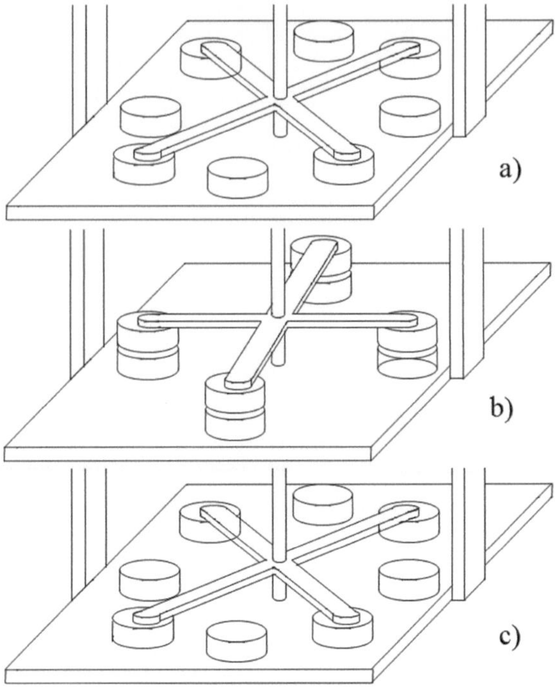

electric generator, while the second part of the electric generator is the static stator. The rotation of the dynamic arrow yields electricity inside of the static stator. Then, the operation of the explained mechanism starts with the magnetism produced by interaction between the static and dynamic magnets and it finishes with the electricity produced by the static stator.

3.3 *The Mechanic Model of the Electricity Generator*

Figure 3 shows the electricity generator with magnets.

By using the inertia, the kinetic energy of the dynamic magnet 1 K_1 is as follows:

$$K_1 = \frac{1}{2} I_1 \dot{\theta}^2, \tag{24}$$

where I_1 is the inertia produced by the dynamic magnet 1 and $\dot{\theta}$ is the angular velocity of the dynamic magnet 1. Utilizing the section with the dynamic magnet 1, the inertia produced by the link 1 $\overline{I}_{e1}$ is as follows:

$$I_{e1} = \frac{1}{12} m_{e1} \left(a_1^2 + c_1^2\right), \tag{25}$$

where m_{e1} is the mass of the link 1, a_1 is the width of the link 1, and c_1 is the length of the link 1. The inertia of the dynamic magnet 1 $\overline{I}_{i1}$ is as follows:

$$I_{i1} = \frac{1}{2} m_i r_i^2, \tag{26}$$

where m_i is the mass of the dynamic magnet 1, and r_i is the radius of dynamic magnet 1. Utilizing the parallel axis theorem, the inertia is as follows:

$$I = \overline{I} + m r_g^2, \tag{27}$$

where $\overline{I}$ is the inertia of Eq. (25) or (26), m is the mass of Eq. (25) or (26), and r_g is the radius of the body rotation. Applying Eq. (27) to Eq. (25) and (26) yields:

$$\begin{aligned} I_{eu} &= \tfrac{1}{12} m_{e1} \left(a_1^2 + c_1^2\right) + m_{e1} r_g^2, \\ I_{iu} &= \tfrac{1}{2} m_i r_i^2 + m_i r_g^2, \end{aligned} \tag{28}$$

where I_{eu} is the inertia produced in the link 1, I_{iu} is the inertia produced in the dynamic magnet 1. The inertia produced for the dynamic magnet 1 I_1 is as follows:

$$\begin{aligned} I_1 &= I_{eu} + I_{iu} \\ &= \frac{1}{12} m_{e1} \left(a_1^2 + c_1^2\right) + m_{e1} r_g^2 + \frac{1}{2} m_i r_i^2 + m_i r_g^2, \end{aligned} \tag{29}$$

Substituting the inertia produced for the dynamic magnet 1 in the kinetic energy of the dynamic magnet 1 K_1 yields:

$$\begin{aligned} K_1 &= \left(\frac{1}{24} m_{e1} \left(a_1^2 + c_1^2\right) + \frac{1}{2} m_{e1} r_g^2\right) \dot{\theta}^2 \\ &+ \left(\frac{1}{4} m_i r_i^2 + \frac{1}{2} m_i r_g^2\right) \dot{\theta}^2, \end{aligned} \tag{30}$$

For the Lagrangian L_1, the potential energy P_1 for the dynamic magnet 1 is obtained by the Fig. 3 as follows:

$$\begin{aligned} P_1 &= \frac{B_{11}^2}{2\mu} V_{11} + \frac{B_{12}^2}{2\mu} V_{12} + \frac{B_{13}^2}{2\mu} V_{13} + \frac{B_{14}^2}{2\mu} V_{14} \\ &= \frac{B^2}{2\mu} V_{11} + \frac{B^2}{2\mu} V_{12} + \frac{B^2}{2\mu} V_{13} + \frac{B^2}{2\mu} V_{14}, \end{aligned} \tag{31}$$

where $B_{11} = B_{m1} + B_{f1}$ is the magnet flux density presented in the volume generated by the dynamic magnet 1 and static magnet 1, $B_{12} = B_{m1} + B_{f2}$ is the magnet flux density presented in the volume of the dynamic magnet 1 and static magnet 2, $B_{13} = B_{m1} + B_{f3}$ is the magnet flux density presented in the volume of the dynamic magnet 1 and static magnet 3, $B_{14} = B_{m1} + B_{f4}$ is the magnet flux density presented in the volume of the dynamic magnet 1 and static magnet 4, since all magnets are equal $B_{11} = B_{12} = B_{13} = B_{14} = B$, V_{11} is the volume of the dynamic magnet 1 and static magnet 1, V_{12} is the volume of the dynamic magnet 1 and static magnet 2, V_{13} is the volume of the dynamic magnet 1 and static magnet 3, V_{14} is the volume of the dynamic magnet 1 and static magnet 4, and μ is the magnet permeability constant in magnets. From Fig. 3, the volumes are:

$$\begin{aligned} V_{11} &= \pi r_i^2 d_{11}, \\ V_{12} &= \pi r_i^2 d_{12}, \\ V_{13} &= \pi r_i^2 d_{13}, \\ V_{14} &= \pi r_i^2 d_{14}, \end{aligned} \tag{32}$$

where r_i is the radius of the surface in the magnet, d_{11} is the centers distance between the dynamic magnet 1 and static magnet 1, d_{12} is the centers distance between the dynamic magnet 1 and static magnet 2, d_{13} is the centers distance between the dynamic magnet 1 and static magnet 3, d_{14} is the centers distance between the dynamic magnet 1 and static magnet 4. From Fig. 3, the distances are:

$$\begin{aligned} d_{11} &= \left(x_{11}^2 + y_{11}^2 + z_{11}^2\right)^{0.5}, \\ d_{12} &= \left(x_{12}^2 + y_{12}^2 + z_{12}^2\right)^{0.5}, \\ d_{13} &= \left(x_{13}^2 + y_{13}^2 + z_{13}^2\right)^{0.5}, \\ d_{14} &= \left(x_{14}^2 + y_{14}^2 + z_{14}^2\right)^{0.5}, \end{aligned} \tag{33}$$

where x_{11}, y_{11}, z_{11} are parts of the distance d_{11}, x_{12}, y_{12}, z_{12} are parts of the distance d_{12}, x_{13}, y_{13}, z_{13} are parts of the distance d_{13}, and x_{14}, y_{14}, z_{14} are parts of the distance d_{14}, where:

$$\begin{aligned} x_{11} &= r_g(1 - \cos\theta), \\ y_{11} &= y_{13} = r_g \sin\theta, \\ z_{11} &= z_{12} = z_{13} = z_{14} = h, \\ x_{12} &= x_{14} = r_g \cos\theta, \\ y_{12} &= r_g(1 - \sin\theta), \\ x_{13} &= r_g(1 + \cos\theta), \\ y_{14} &= r_g(1 + \sin\theta), \end{aligned} \tag{34}$$

where r_g is the radius of dynamic magnets, h is the distance of a dynamic magnet and a static magnet on the axis z. Substituting Eq. (34) in Eq. (33) gives:

$$
\begin{aligned}
d_{11} &= \left[r_g^2(1-\cos\theta)^2 + r_g^2(\sin\theta)^2 + h^2\right]^{0.5} \\
&= \left[2r_g^2(1-\cos\theta) + h^2\right]^{0.5}, \\
d_{12} &= \left[r_g^2(\cos\theta)^2 + r_g^2(1-\sin\theta)^2 + h^2\right]^{0.5} \\
&= \left[2r_g^2(1-\sin\theta) + h^2\right]^{0.5}, \\
d_{13} &= \left[r_g^2(1+\cos\theta)^2 + r_g^2(\sin\theta)^2 + h^2\right]^{0.5} \\
&= \left[2r_g^2(1+\cos\theta) + h^2\right]^{0.5}, \\
d_{14} &= \left[r_g^2(\cos\theta)^2 + r_g^2(1+\sin\theta)^2 + h^2\right]^{0.5} \\
&= \left[2r_g^2(1+\sin\theta) + h^2\right]^{0.5}.
\end{aligned} \tag{35}
$$

Substituting Eq. (35) in Eq. (32) gives:

$$
\begin{aligned}
V_{11} &= \pi r_i^2\left[2r_g^2(1-\cos\theta) + h^2\right]^{0.5}, \\
V_{12} &= \pi r_i^2\left[2r_g^2(1-\sin\theta) + h^2\right]^{0.5}, \\
V_{13} &= \pi r_i^2\left[2r_g^2(1+\cos\theta) + h^2\right]^{0.5}, \\
V_{14} &= \pi r_i^2\left[2r_g^2(1+\sin\theta) + h^2\right]^{0.5}.
\end{aligned} \tag{36}
$$

Substituting Eq. (36) in the potential energy P_1 of Eq. (31) gives:

$$
\begin{aligned}
P_1 &= \tfrac{B^2}{2\mu}\pi r_i^2\left[2r_g^2(1-\cos\theta) + h^2\right]^{0.5} \\
&+ \tfrac{B^2}{2\mu}\pi r_i^2\left[2r_g^2(1-\sin\theta) + h^2\right]^{0.5} \\
&+ \tfrac{B^2}{2\mu}\pi r_i^2\left[2r_g^2(1+\cos\theta) + h^2\right]^{0.5} \\
&+ \tfrac{B^2}{2\mu}\pi r_i^2\left[2r_g^2(1+\sin\theta) + h^2\right]^{0.5}.
\end{aligned} \tag{37}
$$

Substituting the potential energy P_1 of Eq. (37) and kinetic energy K_1 of Eq. (30) into the Lagrangian L_1 of Eq. (23) gives:

$$
\begin{aligned}
L_1 &= K_1 - P_1 \\
&= \left(\tfrac{1}{24}m_{e1}\left(a_1^2 + c_1^2\right) + \tfrac{1}{2}m_{e1}r_g^2\right)\dot{\theta}^2 \\
&+ \left(\tfrac{1}{4}m_i r_i^2 + \tfrac{1}{2}m_i r_g^2\right)\dot{\theta}^2 \\
&- \tfrac{B^2}{2\mu}\pi r_i^2\left[2r_g^2(1-\cos\theta) + h^2\right]^{0.5} \\
&- \tfrac{B^2}{2\mu}\pi r_i^2\left[2r_g^2(1-\sin\theta) + h^2\right]^{0.5} \\
&- \tfrac{B^2}{2\mu}\pi r_i^2\left[2r_g^2(1+\cos\theta) + h^2\right]^{0.5} \\
&- \tfrac{B^2}{2\mu}\pi r_i^2\left[2r_g^2(1+\sin\theta) + h^2\right]^{0.5}.
\end{aligned} \tag{38}
$$

Utilizing a similar procedure, L_2 of Eq. (23) gives:

$$\begin{aligned} L_2 &= K_2 - P_2 \\ &= \left(\tfrac{1}{24} m_{e2}\left(a_2^2 + c_2^2\right) + \tfrac{1}{2} m_{e2} r_g^2\right) \dot{\theta}^2 \\ &+ \left(\tfrac{1}{4} m_i r_i^2 + \tfrac{1}{2} m_i r_g^2\right) \dot{\theta}^2 \\ &- \tfrac{B^2}{2\mu} \pi r_i^2 \left[2 r_g^2 (1 - \cos\theta) + h^2\right]^{0.5} \\ &- \tfrac{B^2}{2\mu} \pi r_i^2 \left[2 r_g^2 (1 - \sin\theta) + h^2\right]^{0.5} \\ &- \tfrac{B^2}{2\mu} \pi r_i^2 \left[2 r_g^2 (1 + \cos\theta) + h^2\right]^{0.5} \\ &- \tfrac{B^2}{2\mu} \pi r_i^2 \left[2 r_g^2 (1 + \sin\theta) + h^2\right]^{0.5}. \end{aligned} \tag{39}$$

Utilizing a similar procedure, L_3 of (23) gives:

$$\begin{aligned} L_3 &= K_3 - P_3 \\ &= \left(\tfrac{1}{24} m_{e1}\left(a_3^2 + c_3^2\right) + \tfrac{1}{2} m_{e3} r_g^2\right) \dot{\theta}^2 \\ &+ \left(\tfrac{1}{4} m_i r_i^2 + \tfrac{1}{2} m_i r_g^2\right) \dot{\theta}^2 \\ &- \tfrac{B^2}{2\mu} \pi r_i^2 \left[2 r_g^2 (1 - \cos\left(\theta - \tfrac{\pi}{4}\right)) + h^2\right]^{0.5} \\ &- \tfrac{B^2}{2\mu} \pi r_i^2 \left[2 r_g^2 (1 - \sin\left(\theta - \tfrac{\pi}{4}\right)) + h^2\right]^{0.5} \\ &- \tfrac{B^2}{2\mu} \pi r_i^2 \left[2 r_g^2 (1 + \cos\left(\theta - \tfrac{\pi}{4}\right)) + h^2\right]^{0.5} \\ &- \tfrac{B^2}{2\mu} \pi r_i^2 \left[2 r_g^2 (1 + \sin\left(\theta - \tfrac{\pi}{4}\right)) + h^2\right]^{0.5}. \end{aligned} \tag{40}$$

Utilizing a similar procedure, L_4 of (23) gives:

$$\begin{aligned} L_4 &= K_4 - P_4 \\ &= \left(\tfrac{1}{24} m_{e4}\left(a_4^2 + c_4^2\right) + \tfrac{1}{2} m_{e4} r_g^2\right) \dot{\theta}^2 \\ &+ \left(\tfrac{1}{4} m_i r_i^2 + \tfrac{1}{2} m_i r_g^2\right) \dot{\theta}^2 \\ &- \tfrac{B^2}{2\mu} \pi r_i^2 \left[2 r_g^2 (1 - \cos\left(\theta - \tfrac{\pi}{4}\right)) + h^2\right]^{0.5} \\ &- \tfrac{B^2}{2\mu} \pi r_i^2 \left[2 r_g^2 (1 - \sin\left(\theta - \tfrac{\pi}{4}\right)) + h^2\right]^{0.5} \\ &- \tfrac{B^2}{2\mu} \pi r_i^2 \left[2 r_g^2 (1 + \cos\left(\theta - \tfrac{\pi}{4}\right)) + h^2\right]^{0.5} \\ &- \tfrac{B^2}{2\mu} \pi r_i^2 \left[2 r_g^2 (1 + \sin\left(\theta - \tfrac{\pi}{4}\right)) + h^2\right]^{0.5}. \end{aligned} \tag{41}$$

Substituting L_1 of Eq. (38), L_2 of Eq. (39), L_3 of Eq. (40), and L_4 of Eq. (41) into Eq. (23) yields the torque of magnets τ as follows:

$$
\begin{aligned}
\tau &= \left(\tfrac{1}{12}m_{e1}\left(a_1^2+c_1^2\right)+m_{e1}r_g^2\right)\ddot{\theta} \\
&+\left(\tfrac{1}{2}m_i r_i^2+m_i r_g^2\right)\ddot{\theta}+b\dot{\theta} \\
&+\frac{\pi B^2 r_g^2 r_i^2\sin\theta}{2\mu\left[h^2+2r_g^2(1-\cos\theta)\right]^{0.5}}-\frac{\pi B^2 r_g^2 r_i^2\cos\theta}{2\mu\left[h^2+2r_g^2(1-\sin\theta)\right]^{0.5}} \\
&-\frac{\pi B^2 r_g^2 r_i^2\sin\theta}{2\mu\left[h^2+2r_g^2(1+\cos\theta)\right]^{0.5}}+\frac{\pi B^2 r_g^2 r_i^2\cos\theta}{2\mu\left[h^2+2r_g^2(1+\sin\theta)\right]^{0.5}} \\
&+\left(\tfrac{1}{24}m_{e2}\left(a_2^2+c_2^2\right)+\tfrac{1}{2}m_{e2}r_g^2\right)\dot{\theta}^2 \\
&+\left(\tfrac{1}{4}m_i r_i^2+\tfrac{1}{2}m_i r_g^2\right)\dot{\theta}^2 \\
&-\frac{\pi B^2 r_g^2 r_i^2\sin\theta}{2\mu\left[h^2+2r_g^2(1+\cos\theta)\right]^{0.5}}+\frac{\pi B^2 r_g^2 r_i^2\cos\theta}{2\mu\left[h^2+2r_g^2(1+\sin\theta)\right]^{0.5}} \\
&+\frac{\pi B^2 r_g^2 r_i^2\sin\theta}{2\mu\left[h^2+2r_g^2(1-\cos\theta)\right]^{0.5}}-\frac{\pi B^2 r_g^2 r_i^2\cos\theta}{2\mu\left[h^2+2r_g^2(1-\sin\theta)\right]^{0.5}} \\
&+\left(\tfrac{1}{12}m_{e3}\left(a_3^2+c_3^2\right)+m_{e3}r_g^2\right)\ddot{\theta} \\
&+\left(\tfrac{1}{2}m_i r_i^2+m_i r_g^2\right)\ddot{\theta}+b\dot{\theta} \\
&+\frac{\pi B^2 r_g^2 r_i^2\sin\left(\theta-\frac{\pi}{4}\right)}{2\mu\left[h^2+2r_g^2\left(1-\cos\left(\theta-\frac{\pi}{4}\right)\right)\right]^{0.5}}-\frac{\pi B^2 r_g^2 r_i^2\cos\left(\theta-\frac{\pi}{4}\right)}{2\mu\left[h^2+2r_g^2\left(1-\sin\left(\theta-\frac{\pi}{4}\right)\right)\right]^{0.5}} \\
&-\frac{\pi B^2 r_g^2 r_i^2\sin\left(\theta-\frac{\pi}{4}\right)}{2\mu\left[h^2+2r_g^2\left(1+\cos\left(\theta-\frac{\pi}{4}\right)\right)\right]^{0.5}}+\frac{\pi B^2 r_g^2 r_i^2\cos\left(\theta-\frac{\pi}{4}\right)}{2\mu\left[h^2+2r_g^2\left(1+\sin\left(\theta-\frac{\pi}{4}\right)\right)\right]^{0.5}} \\
&+\left(\tfrac{1}{24}m_{e4}\left(a_4^2+c_4^2\right)+\tfrac{1}{2}m_{e4}r_g^2\right)\dot{\theta}^2 \\
&+\left(\tfrac{1}{4}m_i r_i^2+\tfrac{1}{2}m_i r_g^2\right)\dot{\theta}^2 \\
&-\frac{\pi B^2 r_g^2 r_i^2\sin\left(\theta-\frac{\pi}{4}\right)}{2\mu\left[h^2+2r_g^2\left(1+\cos\left(\theta-\frac{\pi}{4}\right)\right)\right]^{0.5}}+\frac{\pi B^2 r_g^2 r_i^2\cos\left(\theta-\frac{\pi}{4}\right)}{2\mu\left[h^2+2r_g^2\left(1+\sin\left(\theta-\frac{\pi}{4}\right)\right)\right]^{0.5}} \\
&+\frac{\pi B^2 r_g^2 r_i^2\sin\left(\theta-\frac{\pi}{4}\right)}{2\mu\left[h^2+2r_g^2\left(1-\cos\left(\theta-\frac{\pi}{4}\right)\right)\right]^{0.5}}-\frac{\pi B^2 r_g^2 r_i^2\cos\left(\theta-\frac{\pi}{4}\right)}{2\mu\left[h^2+2r_g^2\left(1-\sin\left(\theta-\frac{\pi}{4}\right)\right)\right]^{0.5}}
\end{aligned}
\tag{42}
$$

Finally, utilizing $2m_{e1}=2m_{e2}=2m_{e3}=2m_{e4}=m_e, 2a_1=2a_2=2a_3=2a_4=a, 2c_1=2c_2=2c_3=2c_4=c$, the torque of magnets τ is as follows:

$$
\begin{aligned}
\tau &= m_e\left(\tfrac{1}{24}a^2+\tfrac{1}{24}c^2+r_g^2\right)\ddot{\theta} \\
&+m_i\left(r_i^2+2r_g^2\right)\ddot{\theta}+b\dot{\theta} \\
&+\frac{\pi B^2 r_g^2 r_i^2\sin\theta}{\mu\left[h^2+2r_g^2(1-\cos\theta)\right]^{0.5}}+\frac{\pi B^2 r_g^2 r_i^2\cos\theta}{\mu\left[h^2+2r_g^2(1+\sin\theta)\right]^{0.5}} \\
&-\frac{\pi B^2 r_g^2 r_i^2\sin\theta}{\mu\left[h^2+2r_g^2(1+\cos\theta)\right]^{0.5}}-\frac{\pi B^2 r_g^2 r_i^2\cos\theta}{\mu\left[h^2+2r_g^2(1-\sin\theta)\right]^{0.5}} \\
&+\frac{\pi B^2 r_g^2 r_i^2\sin\left(\theta-\frac{\pi}{4}\right)}{\mu\left[h^2+2r_g^2\left(1-\cos\left(\theta-\frac{\pi}{4}\right)\right)\right]^{0.5}}+\frac{\pi B^2 r_g^2 r_i^2\cos\left(\theta-\frac{\pi}{4}\right)}{\mu\left[h^2+2r_g^2\left(1+\sin\left(\theta-\frac{\pi}{4}\right)\right)\right]^{0.5}} \\
&-\frac{\pi B^2 r_g^2 r_i^2\sin\left(\theta-\frac{\pi}{4}\right)}{\mu\left[h^2+2r_g^2\left(1+\cos\left(\theta-\frac{\pi}{4}\right)\right)\right]^{0.5}}-\frac{\pi B^2 r_g^2 r_i^2\cos\left(\theta-\frac{\pi}{4}\right)}{\mu\left[h^2+2r_g^2\left(1-\sin\left(\theta-\frac{\pi}{4}\right)\right)\right]^{0.5}}.
\end{aligned}
\tag{43}
$$

3.4 The Electric Model of the Electricity Generator

Now, the conversion from the mechanic movement to electricity of the electricity generator is discussed.

From Fig. 3, and utilizing the Kirchhoff voltage law, the electric model of the generator is as follows:

$$e = V_R + V_L + V, \tag{44}$$

where $e = K_m\dot{\theta}$ is the electromotive force, $V_R = Ri$ is the voltage in the resistance, $V_L = L\dot{i}$ is the voltage in the inductance, $V = R_e i$ is the voltage in the load, K_m is the electromotive force constant, $\dot{\theta}$ is the derivative of angle, R is the resistance, i is the current, L is the inductance, and R_e is the load resistance. Then, Eq. (44) is written as follows:

$$K_m\dot{\theta} = Ri + L\dot{i} + R_e i. \tag{45}$$

3.5 The Dynamic Model in State Space for the Electricity Generator

Thus, Eq. (43) is the conversion between the magnetism and mechanic motions, and Eq. (45) is the conversion between the mechanic motions and electricity; they are known as the dynamic model of the electricity generator.

States are selected as $z_1 = i$, $z_2 = \theta$, $z_3 = \dot{\theta}$ and the input is selected as $\upsilon = \tau$. Finally, the dynamic model of Eqs. (43) and (45) is as follows:

$$\begin{aligned}
\dot{z}_1 &= -\frac{(R+R_e)}{L} z_1 + \frac{K_m}{L} z_3, \\
\dot{z}_2 &= z_3, \\
\dot{z}_3 &= \left(\frac{1}{m_e\left(\frac{1}{24}a^2+\frac{1}{24}c^2+r_g^2\right)+m_i\left(r_i^2+2r_g^2\right)}\right) \\
&* \left(\upsilon - \frac{\pi B^2 r_i^2 r_g^2 \sin z_2}{\mu\left[h^2+2r_g^2(1-\cos z_2)\right]^{0.5}}\right. \\
&- \frac{\pi B^2 r_i^2 r_g^2 \cos z_2}{\mu\left[h^2+2r_g^2(1+\sin z_2)\right]^{0.5}} + \frac{\pi B^2 r_i^2 r_g^2 \sin z_2}{\mu\left[h^2+2r_g^2(1+\cos z_2)\right]^{0.5}} \\
&+ \frac{\pi B^2 r_i^2 r_g^2 \cos z_2}{\mu\left[h^2+2r_g^2(1-\sin z_2)\right]^{0.5}} - \frac{\pi B^2 r_i^2 r_g^2 \sin\left(z_2-\frac{\pi}{4}\right)}{\mu\left[h^2+2r_g^2\left(1-\cos\left(z_2-\frac{\pi}{4}\right)\right)\right]^{0.5}} \\
&- \frac{\pi B^2 r_i^2 r_g^2 \cos\left(z_2-\frac{\pi}{4}\right)}{\mu\left[h^2+2r_g^2\left(1+\sin\left(z_2-\frac{\pi}{4}\right)\right)\right]^{0.5}} + \frac{\pi B^2 r_i^2 r_g^2 \sin\left(z_2-\frac{\pi}{4}\right)}{\mu\left[h^2+2r_g^2\left(1+\cos\left(z_2-\frac{\pi}{4}\right)\right)\right]^{0.5}} \\
&\left.+ \frac{\pi B^2 r_i^2 r_g^2 \cos\left(z_2-\frac{\pi}{4}\right)}{\mu\left[h^2+2r_g^2\left(1-\sin\left(z_2-\frac{\pi}{4}\right)\right)\right]^{0.5}} - b z_3\right).
\end{aligned} \tag{46}$$

Remark 1 Most of the existing dynamic models are about permanent generators which consider electromagnetic coils which require electricity for their functioning, i.e., in permanent generators the electricity is used to generate electricity. The dynamic models of suggested electricity generators are different from the permanent generators because the interaction between magnets is used for their functioning, i.e., in suggested electricity generators the magnets are used to generate electricity. Thus, the electricity generators proposed in this chapter are new.

4 Comparisons of the Electricity Generators

Figure 5 shows the electricity generator prototype with two static magnets and two dynamic magnets of Eq. (22). In the first part of this comparison, real data of the electricity generator prototype with two static magnets and two dynamic magnets of Fig. 5, and the electricity generator model with two static magnets and two dynamic magnets of Eq. (22) are compared for two different inputs denoted as Comparison 1 and Comparison 2. The target of the electricity generator model with two static magnets and two dynamic magnets is to generate the same quantity of electricity as the electricity generator prototype with two static magnets and two dynamic magnets.

In the second part of this comparison, the electricity generator model with two static magnets and two dynamic magnets of Eq. (22), and the electricity generator model of four static magnets and four dynamic magnets of Eq. (46) are compared for two different inputs denoted as Comparison 1 and Comparison 2. The target of the suggested electricity generator model of four static magnets and four dynamic magnets is to generate more electricity than the electricity generator model with two static magnets and two dynamic magnets.

In this section, the electricity generator prototype with two static magnets and two dynamic magnets of the prototype of Fig. 5 is called Real Data, the electricity generator model with two static magnets and two dynamic magnets of Eq. (22), [30] is called 2DynamicMagnets, and the electricity generator model of four static magnets and four dynamic magnets of (46) is called 4DynamicMagnets.

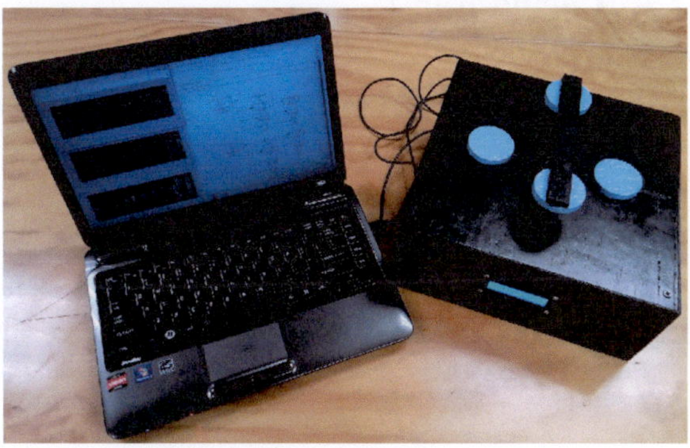

Fig. 5 Prototype of the electricity generator

Table 1 Parameters of electricity generators

Parameter	Value
m_i	9.2×10^{-2} kg
μ	9.42×10^{-5} Hm^{-1}
B	8.4×10^{-1} T
L	6.03×10^{-1} H
K_m	45×10^{-2} Vsrad^{-1}
b	1×10^{-1} kgm^{2}rads^{-1}
m_e	5×10^{-3} kg
h	4×10^{-2} m
R	$6.96\ \Omega$
R_e	$30\ \Omega$
r_g	7.5×10^{-2} m
r_i	2.9×10^{-2} m
a	1.5×10^{-1} m
c	1.5×10^{-2} m

In the next two subsections, the root mean square error (RMSE) will be used in comparisons, which is as follows:

$$RMSE = \left(\frac{1}{T} \int_0^T z^2 d\tau \right)^{\frac{1}{2}}, \tag{47}$$

where $z^2 = z_1^2$ is for state 1, $z^2 = z_2^2$ is for state 2, $z^2 = z_3^2$ is for state 3 in the electricity generators, T is the final time.

In the electricity generators, parameter values for dynamic models are shown in Table 1.

4.1 Comparison 1

In this comparison, the next input is utilized for Real Data, 2DynamicMagnets, and 4DynamicMagnets:

$$v = \begin{cases} 1 \text{ for } t = [0, 5]\,\text{s} \\ 0 \text{ for } t = [5, 10]\,\text{s} \end{cases} \tag{48}$$

Figure 6 shows inputs and states of Real Data, 2DynamicMagnets, and 4DynamicMagnets for a time from 0 s to 10 s. Table 2 shows the RMSE of Eq. (47).

From Fig. 6, it can be observed that the 2DynamicMagnets obtains almost the same performance as Real Data because the 2DynamicMagnets generates almost

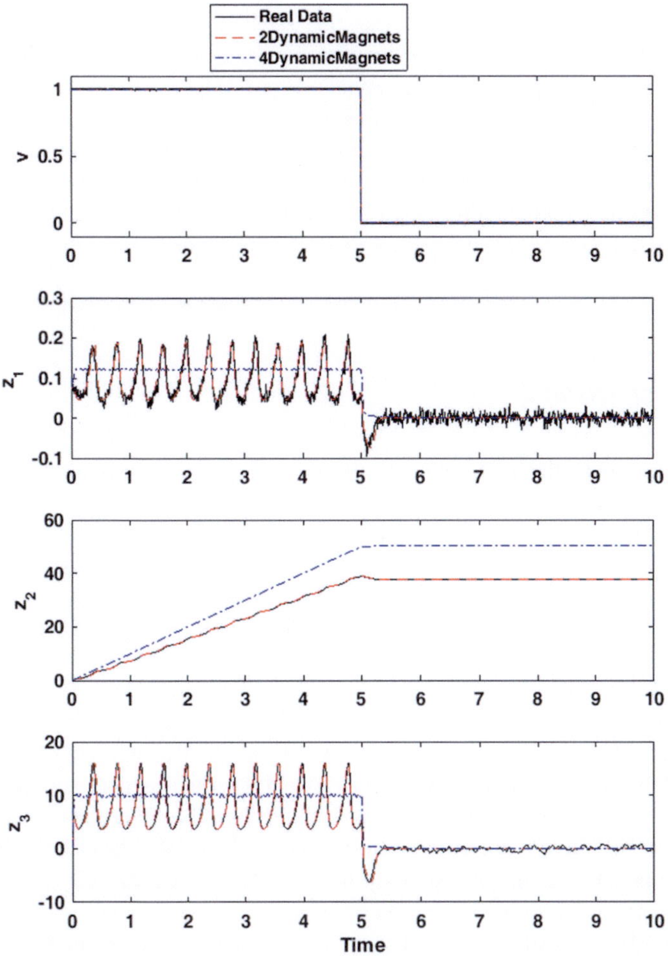

Fig. 6 Comparison 1 between Real Data, 2DynamicMagnets, and 4DynamicMagnets

Table 2 RMSE for comparison 1

Generators	RMSE z_1	RMSE z_2	RMSE z_3
Real data	0.0535	21.9333	4.4045
2DynamicMagnets	0.0531	21.9468	4.4019
4DynamicMagnets	0.0608	28.9676	4.9931

the same electricity as Real Data. From Table 2, it can be observed that 2Dynamic-Magnets obtains almost the same performance as Real Data because the RMSE for the 2DynamicMagnets is almost equal to Real Data. Then, the 2DynamicMagnets obtains its target, the same generation of electricity as Real Data.

From Fig. 6, it can be observed that the 4DynamicMagnets obtains better performance than 2DynamicMagnets because the 4DynamicMagnets generates more electricity and generates smoother signals. From Table 2, it can be observed that 4DynamicMagnets obtains better performance than 2DynamicMagnets because the RMSE for the 4DynamicMagnets is bigger than for 2DynamicMagnets. Then, the 4DynamicMagnets obtains its target, the generation of more electricity with smoother signals. Even that not any of the magnets generator in this investigation achieves the generation of a constant electricity, more electricity is generated with the incorporation of more magnets.

4.2 Comparison 2

In this comparison, the next input is utilized for Real Data, 2DynamicMagnets, and 4DynamicMagnets:

$$v = \begin{cases} 1 \text{ for } t = [0, 2.5]\,\text{s} \\ 0 \text{ for } t = [2.5, 5]\,\text{s} \\ 1 \text{ for } t = [5, 7.5]\,\text{s} \\ 0 \text{ for } t = [7.5, 10]\,\text{s} \end{cases} \tag{49}$$

Figure 7 shows inputs and states of Real Data, 2DynamicMagnets, and 4DynamicMagnets for a time from 0 s to 10 s. Table 3 shows the RMSE of Eq. (47).

From Fig. 7, it can be observed that the 2DynamicMagnets obtains almost the same performance as Real Data because the 2DynamicMagnets generates almost the same electricity as Real Data. From Table 3, it can be observed that 2DynamicMagnets obtains almost the same performance as Real Data because the RMSE for the 2DynamicMagnets is almost equal to Real Data. Then, the 2DynamicMagnets obtains its target, the same generation of electricity as Real Data.

From Fig. 7, it can be observed that the 4DynamicMagnets obtains better performance than 2DynamicMagnets because the 4DynamicMagnets generates more electricity and generates smoother signals. From Table 3, it can be observed that 4DynamicMagnets obtains better performance than 2DynamicMagnets because the RMSE for the 4DynamicMagnets is bigger than for 2DynamicMagnets. Then, the 4DynamicMagnets obtains its target, the generation of more electricity with smoother signals. Despite not any of the magnets generator in this investigation achieves the generation of a constant electricity, more electricity is generated with the incorporation of more magnets.

Remark 2 The generation of more electricity by magnets is important because these generators can obtain energy from the environment, avoiding the necessity of a kind of fuel. Therefore, using four dynamic magnets produces better results than using two magnets because even two more magnets are required, using four dynamic magnets produces the generation of more electricity with smoother signals than using two magnets.

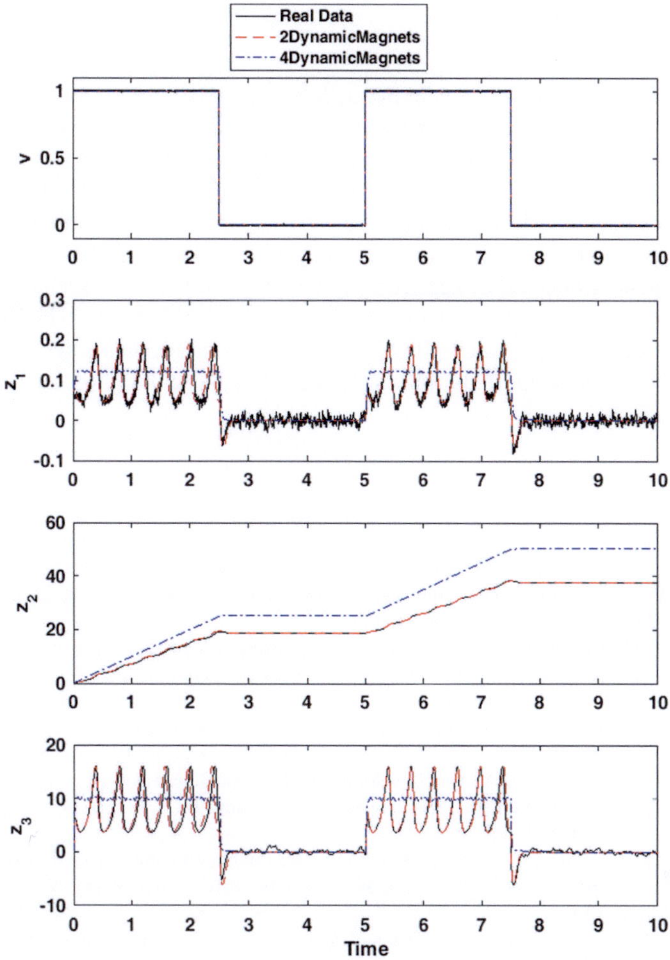

Fig. 7 Comparison 2 between Real Data, 2DynamicMagnets, and 4DynamicMagnets

Table 3 RMSE for comparison 2

Generators	RMSE z_1	RMSE z_2	RMSE z_3
Real Data	0.0533	18.4638	4.4113
2DynamicMagnets	0.0531	18.4762	4.4076
4DynamicMagnets	0.0607	24.5505	4.9872

5 Concluding Remarks

In this chapter, the dynamic model of an electricity generator with four static magnets and four dynamic magnets was proposed. The introduced electricity generator was compared with the electricity generator with two static magnets and two dynamic magnets producing that the suggested electricity generator obtained better performance in comparison with the other electricity generator because the proposed electricity generator generates more electricity with smoother signals. The suggested electricity generator could be applied as a fuel for several kind of mechanic systems. In the forthcoming research, other kinds of electricity generators will be studied, the discussed electricity generator will be applied in several mechanic systems, and the optimization of the suggested electricity generator will be designed.

References

1. Y. Gritli, A. Tani, C. Rossi, D. Casadei, Assessment of current and voltage signature analysis for the diagnosis of rotor magnet demagnetization in five-phase ac permanent magnet generator drives. Math. Comput. Simul. **158**, 91–106 (2019)
2. A. Laczko, S. Brisset, M. Radulescu, Design of a brushless dc permanent-magnet generator for use in micro-wind turbine applications. Int. J. Appl. Electromagn. Mech. **56**(S1), 3–15 (2018)
3. K.S. Lee, S.H. Lee, J.H. Park, J.Y. Choi, K.H. Sim, Design and experimental analysis of a 3 kW single-phase linear permanent magnet generator for stirling engines. IEEE Trans. Magn. **54**(11), 8204205 (2018)
4. P. Liu, H. Zhang, S. Ma, Y. Shi, Development of compact seed source with high-precision discharge switch for magnetic flux compression generator. Int. J. Appl. Electromagn. Mech. **58**(1), 15–25 (2018)
5. T. Xia, H. Yu, Z. Chen, L. Huang, X. Liu, M. Hu, Design and analysis of a field-modulated tubular linear permanent magnet generator for direct-drive wave energy conversion. IEEE Trans. Magn. **53**(6), 8103904 (2017)
6. C. Du, D. Meng, D. Meng, Analysis and optimization of a new double- sided permanent magnet linear synchronous motor for electromagnetic launching. Int. J. Appl. Electromagn. Mech. **57**(2), 147–164 (2018)
7. R. Ilka, Y. Alinejad-Beromi, H. Yaghobi, Cogging torque reduction of permanent magnet synchronous motor using multi-objective optimization. Math. Comput. Simul. **153**, 83–95 (2018)
8. D. Fu, Y. Xu, F. Gillon, J. Gong, N. Bracikowski, Presentation of a novel transverse-flux permanent magnet linear motor and its magnetic field analysis based on Schwarz-Christoffel mapping method. IEEE Trans. Magn. **54**(3), 6000204 (2018)
9. W. Jiang, S. Feng, Z. Zhang, J. Zhang, Z. Zhang, Study of efficiency characteristics of interior permanent magnet synchronous motors. IEEE Trans. Magn. **54**(11), 8108005 (2018)
10. B. Li, S. Zhang, G. Li, H. Li, Synthesis strategy for stator magnetic field of permanent magnet spherical motor. IEEE Trans. Magn. **54**(10), 8203105 (2018)
11. H. Lan, J. Zou, Y. Xu, M. Liu, Investigation of unbalanced magnetic force in permanent magnet synchronous machines with asymmetric design. IEEE Trans. Magn. **54**(11), 8203305 (2018)
12. I. Petrov, P. Lindh, J. Pyrhonen, Importance of accurate iron permeability in saturated condition on performance evaluation of flux-switching permanent magnet synchronous machines. IEEE Trans. Magn. **54**(6), 8103607–8103607 (2018)

13. S. Wu, W. Tong, R. Sun, R. Tang, A generalized method of electromagnetic vibration analysis of amorphous alloy permanent magnet synchronous machines. IEEE Trans. Magn. **54**(11), 8108405 (2018)
14. Y. Yang, G. Liu, X.T. Yang, X. Wang, Analytical electromagnetic performance calculation of Vernier hybrid permanent magnet machine. IEEE Trans. Magn. **54**(6), 8202612–8202612 (2018)
15. D. Zeng, J. Zou, Y. Xu, Analysis and discussion of the indirect testing method for the losses of permanent magnet synchronous machines. IEEE Trans. Magn. **54**(11), 8106205 (2018)
16. T.A. Huynh, M.F. Hsieh, Performance analysis of permanent magnet motors for electric vehicles (ev) traction considering driving cycles. Energies **11**(1385), 1–24 (2018)
17. T.A. Huynh, M.F. Hsieh, Performance evaluation of interior permanent magnet motors using thin electrical steels. IEEJ J. Ind. Appl. **6**(6), 422–428 (2018)
18. M. Tian, W. Zhao, X. Wang, D. Wang, Y. Yang, J. Diao, X. Ma, Analysis on a novel flux adjustable permanent magnet coupler with a double-layer permanent magnet rotor. IEEE Trans. Magn. **54**(11), 8109205 (2018)
19. M.S. Wang, M.F. Hsieh, I.N. Syamsiana, W.C. Fang, Fuzzy maximum torque per ampere and maximum torque per voltage control of interior permanent magnet synchronous motor drive. Sens. Mater. **29**(4), 461–472 (2017)
20. I.P. Wiltuschnig, P.R. Eckert, A.F. Flores Filho, D.G. Dorrell, Comparison of traditional, quasi-Halbach array and interior permanent magnet configurations for outer rotor brushless ac machines. Int. J. Appl. Electromagn. Mech. **57**(S1), 217–225 (2018)
21. T.A. Huynh, M.F. Hsieh, K.J. Shih, H.F. Kuo, An investigation into the effect of PM arrangements on PMa-SynRM performance. IEEE Trans. Ind. Appl. **54**(6), 5856–5868 (2018)
22. D.G. Dorrell, J. Shek, M.F. Hsieh, The development of an indexing method for the comparison of unbalanced magnetic pull in electrical machines. IEEE Trans. Ind. Appl. **52**(1), 145–153 (2016)
23. M. Han, W. Zhou, Unusual negative permeability of single magnetic nanowire excited by the spin transfer torque effect. J. Magn. Magn. Mater. **457**, 52–56 (2018)
24. X. Luo, Y. Wu, M. Han, L. Deng, High frequency permeability of Fe-Cu-Nb-Si-B nanocrystalline flakes with the distribution of shape anisotropy fields. J. Magn. Magn. Mater. **451**, 5–10 (2018)
25. H. Zheng, M. Han, L. Zheng, J. Deng, P. Zheng, Q. Wu, L. Deng, H. Qin, Magnetic properties of hexagonal barium ferrite films on Pt/Mgo (111) substrates annealed at different temperatures. J. Magn. Magn. Mater. **413**, 25–29 (2016)
26. N. Denis, M. Inoue, K. Fujisaki, H. Itabashi, T. Yano, Iron loss reduction in permanent magnet synchronous motor by using stator core made of nanocrystalline magnetic material. IEEE Trans. Magn. **53**(11), 8110006 (2017)
27. N. Denis, S. Takeda, K. Fujitani, K. Fujisaki, S. Odawara, Anisotropic magnetic core for the iron loss reduction of permanent magnet synchronous motor. J. Magn. Soc. Jpn. **42**(3), 62–71 (2018)
28. P. Rasilo, W. Martinez, K. Fujisaki, J. Kyyra, A. Ruderman, Simulink model for PWM-supplied laminated magnetic cores including hysteresis, eddy-current, and excess losses. IEEE Trans. Power Electron. **34**(2), 1683–1695 (2019)
29. A. Yao, T. Sugimoto, S. Odawara, K. Fujisaki, Core loss properties of a motor with nanocrystalline rotor and stator cores under inverter excitation. IEEE Trans. Magn. **54**(11), 8203205 (2018)
30. J.J. Rubio, J. Pieper, J.A. Meda-Campaña, A. Aguilar, V.I. Rangel, G.J. Gutierrez, Modeling and regulation of two mechanical systems. IET Sci. Meas. & Technol. **12**(5), 657–665 (2018)

Dynamic Model of an Electric Vehicle with Energy Recovery

Abstract In this chapter, a dynamic model which describes the energy recovery for an electric vehicle is introduced. Generators connected to the wheels are used for the energy recovery during the vehicle transportation. A prototype of the electric vehicle is used to validate the proposed approach. The stability analysis of the dynamic model is presented.

1 Introduction

As a result of increasing environmental concern, the impact of conventional electricity generation on the environment is being minimized and efforts are being made to generate electricity from renewable sources.

When the gasoline is not obtained because of the high costs, the electric vehicles are a good alternative for the transportation of people and load. Some interesting works of vehicles are [1–5]. However, the energy recovery of an electric vehicle would be useful for large distance transportation.

On the other hand, there are many methods used in electric vehicles as are the controllers [6, 7], observers [8], or identifiers [9–11]. However, the above methods need a dynamic model of electric vehicle for the design, there are not many results about dynamic models of electric vehicles with a validation, a validation is the comparison between the real measures and simulations. A dynamic model without a validation only is mathematical equations, but with a validation can describe a real process.

There are some results about dynamic models with validation such as in [6] for fuel cells, [12] for quadrotors, [13, 14] for gasoline vehicles, and [15] for wind turbines. Therefore, the validation of the dynamic model of energy recovery for an electric vehicle would be of great importance.

Finally, if the stability analysis is guaranteed, then for bounded inputs on the vehicle bounded outputs are also obtained [6, 16]. The aforementioned fact shows that the dynamic behavior of the proposed vehicle would be acceptable for present and future research.

In this chapter, a dynamic model of an electric vehicle with energy recovery is presented. Generators connected to the wheels are used for the electric energy

J. de J. Rubio et al., *Dynamic Models of Energy, Robotic, and Biological Systems*,
https://doi.org/10.1007/978-3-031-85438-5_3

recovery during the vehicle movement. The money spent on the generators is an inversion because the recovered energy could be used to feed the vehicle lights. Thus, the system with generators expends less electric energy than the system without generators, and this fact is considered as a renewable source.

This chapter is organized as follows. In Sect. 2, the electric vehicle with energy recovery is described. In Sect. 3, the dynamic models of the wheels, motors, generators, and electric vehicle with energy recovery are presented. In Sect. 4, the validation of the proposed dynamic model is shown. In Sect. 5, the stability of the proposed model is analyzed. Section 6 presents conclusions and suggests future research directions.

2 Prototype Description

Figure 1 shows the explosive isometric of the electric vehicle with energy recovery where (1) are two along beams, (2) are two short beams, (3) is a thin plate, (4) are eight electric motors, (5) are eight shafts, (6) are eight wheels, (7) are eight electric generators, (8) are eight plate supports of generators, and (9) are two batteries. Figure 2 shows the electric vehicle prototype, which has 8 independent electric motors, each electric motor is mechanically connected to an electric generator using a drive shaft, and the same drive shaft is connected to the wheels; the motors, generators, and wheels are connected to the thin plate. The electric motors work at the same time and go in one direction. Batteries could be used to save the electricity taken by the electric generators or the lights could be considered to reuse the recovered energy.

Remark 1 There are some machines that can be used as motors or generators; however, they cannot be used as motor and generator at the same time because they have some cables which must be fed by a source in the motor case and must be measured by a scope in the generator case. Consequently, a motor may be used to move the electric vehicle, and a generator may be used to recover some part of the electrical energy.

3 Dynamic Model of the Electric Vehicle with Energy Recovery

Figure 3 shows the dynamic behavior of the wheels, an electric motor, and an electric generator which are combined to obtain the dynamic model of the electric vehicle with energy recovery. The proposed dynamic model considers that the electric motor is directly connected to the electric generator, and the electric motor is also directly connected to the wheel.

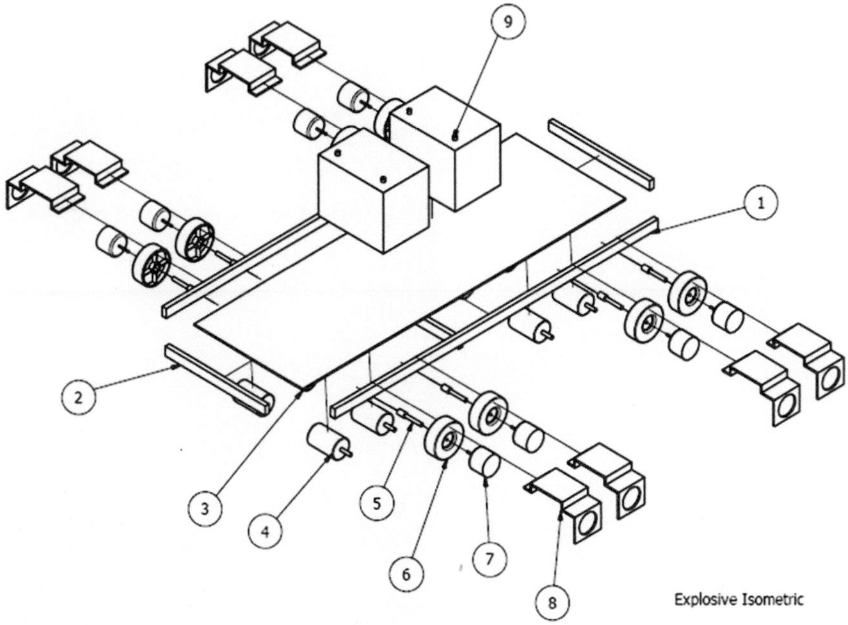

Fig. 1 Explosive isometric of the electric vehicle with energy recovery

3.1 Modified Dynamic Model of LuGre

The LuGre dynamic model describes the braking of a vehicle [8, 13, 14, 17]. The sliding and pre-sliding are considered in the same dynamic equations. The equations are described as follows:

$$\frac{dz}{dt} = v - \sigma_0 \frac{|v|}{s(v)} z, \tag{1}$$

$$s(v) = F_c + (F_s - F_c) \exp\left(-\left|\frac{v}{V_s}\right|^{\delta}\right), \tag{2}$$

$$F_f = \sigma_0 z + \sigma_1 \frac{dz}{dt} + \sigma_2 v, \tag{3}$$

The dynamic model is based in the bustle effect. The authors introduce an internal state variable z, and use one first order differential equation to describe a delay in the friction stage for the sliding and hysteresis. The LuGre dynamic model is determined for the parameters σ_i called coefficient of micro-viscous friction.

Selecting the friction micro-viscous coefficients (σ_0 and σ_1) equal to zero, the Coulomb force F_c equal to the static force F_s, and a factor n equal to 1 in the LuGre

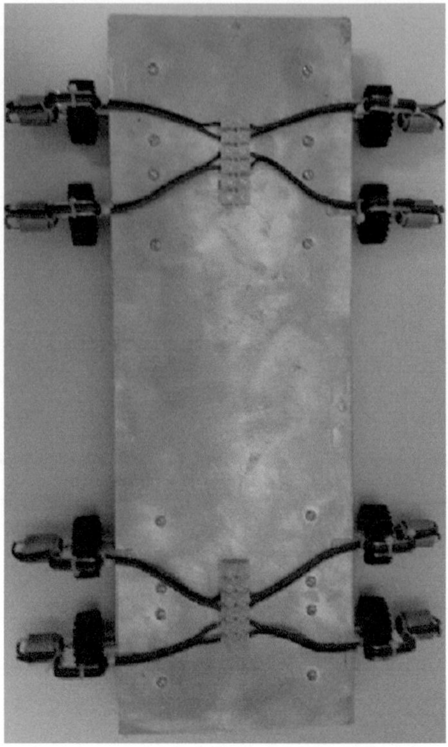

Fig. 2 Prototype of the electric vehicle with energy recovery

model gives the Dahl model. The LuGre model is popular in control; it is used for the identifiers, observers, and controllers designs, and the passivity analysis.

Remark 2 The LuGre model in this chapter is modified because only the dynamic behavior of a wheel is considered and the friction equations are not taken into account. The friction is not important during the movement of an electric wheel due to this variable being commonly used only during the vehicle braking. Furthermore, the proposed electric vehicle does not use friction because if the electric energy is fed into the vehicle, it moves, whereas if the electric energy is not fed, it does not move.

3.2 Dynamic Model of the Wheels

Figure 4 is used to obtain the dynamic model of a wheel using the fact that the wheel is directly connected to the electric motor.

Using the LuGre model (3), the vehicle velocity is given as follows:

$$\dot{v} = -\frac{8}{m} F_n \sigma_2 v + \frac{8}{m} F_n \sigma_2 r \omega_m, \tag{4}$$

Fig. 3 Motor, generator, and wheel

where r is the wheel radius, v is the linear velocity, ω is the angular velocity, F_n is the normal force, m is the total mass of the electric vehicle, and σ_2 is the viscous relative damping coefficient.

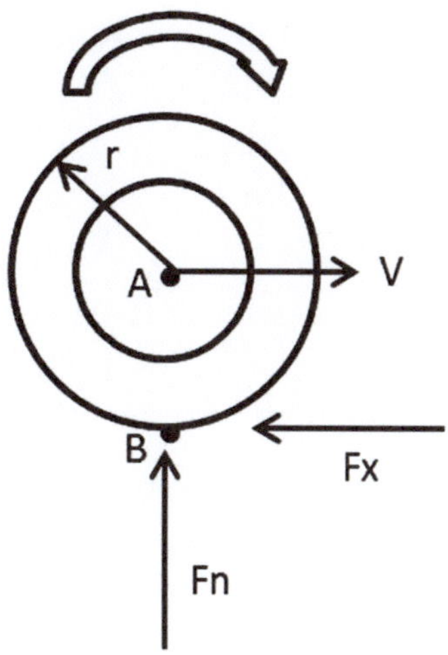

Fig. 4 Wheel dynamic

3.3 Dynamic Model of the Electric Motor

Figure 5 shows the electric motor which is connected to the electric generator.

The dynamic model of the electric motor is obtained using the voltage Kirchoff law, which is as follows [7, 15]:

$$\dot{i}_m = -\frac{R_m}{L_m}i_m - \frac{K_{1m}}{L_m}\omega_m + \frac{1}{L_m}V_{em}, \tag{5}$$

where i_m is the motor armature current, L_m is the motor armature inductance, R_m is the motor armature resistance, V_{am} is the motor armature voltage, V_{em} is the motor back emf, K_{1m} is the back emf constant, and ω_m is the motor angular velocity which is given as follows:

$$J\dot{\omega} = T_m - T_{om} - B_m\omega_m, \tag{6}$$

where $T_m = K_{aux}i_m\phi_m$, ϕ_m is the magnetic flux on the motor stator, considering that ϕ_m =constant, $T_{om} = 0$; therefore, the aforementioned equation changes to:

$$\dot{\omega}_m = \frac{K_{2m}}{J_m}\dot{i}_m - \frac{B_m}{J_m}\omega_m, \tag{7}$$

where J_m is the motor inertia moment, B_m is the viscous friction coefficient, and $K_{2m} = K_{aux}\phi_m$, K_{2m} is the motor coefficient back emf.

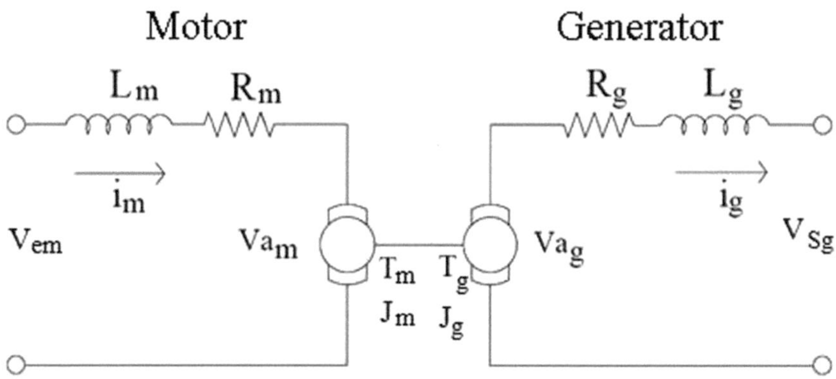

Fig. 5 Electric motor connected to the electric generator

3.4 Dynamic Model of the Electric Generator

The dynamic model of the electric generator is obtained using the voltage Kirchoff law; therefore, the dynamic of the electric generator is as follows:

$$\dot{i}_g = -\frac{R_g}{L_g} i_g + \frac{K_{1g}}{L_g} \omega_m - \frac{1}{L_g} V_{sg}, \tag{8}$$

where i_g is the generator armature current, L_g is the generator armature inductance, R_g is the generator armature resistance, V_{sg} is the output generator voltage, K_{1g} is the generator torque constant, and ω_g is the generator angular velocity. $\omega_m = \omega_g$ is considered because the electric motor and electric generator are directly connected; therefore, the generator angular velocity is given as follows:

$$\dot{\omega}_g = \frac{K_{2g}}{J_g} i_g - \frac{B_g}{J_g} \omega_g, \tag{9}$$

where J_m is the generator inertia moment, B_g is the viscous friction coefficient, K_{2g} is the generator coefficient back emf. Since $\omega_m = \omega_g$, only the equation for ω_m is considered. Considering that there is an electric energy loss between the electric motor and electric generator, the following equation is used to relate the armature currents between the motor and generator:

$$i_m = \frac{1}{C} i_g, \tag{10}$$

where $C < 1$ is a parameter selected by the designer. Obtaining the derivative of Eq. (9) gives:

$$\dot{i}_m = \frac{1}{C} \dot{i}_g, \tag{11}$$

Substituting Eqs. (5) and (8) into Eq. (11), and using Eq. (10) gives:

$$\begin{aligned} V_{sg} &= C\left(R_m \tfrac{L_g}{L_m} - R_g\right) i_m \\ &+ \left(K_{1g} + K_{1m} C \tfrac{L_g}{L_m}\right) \omega_m - C \tfrac{L_g}{L_m} V_{em}, \end{aligned} \tag{12}$$

3.5 Final Dynamic Model of the Electric Vehicle with Energy Recovery

Defining the states as $x_1 = i_m, x_2 = v, x_3 = \omega_m$, the input as $u = V_{em}$, and the output as $y = V_{sg}$, considering Eqs. (4), (5), (7), and (12) gives the following dynamic model:

$$\begin{bmatrix} \dot{x}_1 \\ \dot{x}_2 \\ \dot{x}_3 \end{bmatrix} = \begin{bmatrix} -\frac{R_m}{L_m} & 0 & -\frac{K_{1m}}{L_m} \\ 0 & -\frac{8}{m} F_n \sigma_2 & \frac{8}{m} F_n \sigma_2 r \\ \frac{K_{2m}}{J_m} & 0 & -\frac{B_m}{J_m} \end{bmatrix} \begin{bmatrix} x_1 \\ x_2 \\ x_3 \end{bmatrix} + \begin{bmatrix} \frac{1}{L_m} \\ 0 \\ 0 \end{bmatrix} u, \tag{13}$$

$$y = \left[C \left(\frac{L_g}{L_m} R_m - R_g \right) 0 \left(K_{1g} + K_{1m} C \frac{L_g}{L_m} \right) \right] \begin{bmatrix} x_1 \\ x_2 \\ x_3 \end{bmatrix} - C \frac{L_g}{L_m} u, \tag{14}$$

Equations (13) and (14) are the dynamic model of the electric vehicle with energy recovery.

Remark 3 The dynamic model of the electric motor is well known in the literature [7, 15]. However, the dynamic model of an electric generator, the wheel, and finally, the dynamic model of the combination between the electric generator, electric motor, and wheel are considered as contributions of this chapter.

Remark 4 The prototype presented in this chapter is based on the train carriages which are vehicles designed to carry much weight; therefore, they can easily carry the generators.

4 Validation of the Proposed Dynamic Model

Considering Eqs. (13) and (14), using Matlab and a real data of the dynamic measures, the proposed dynamic model of the electric vehicle with energy recovery is validated. The variables are the motor armature current x_1, electric vehicle linear velocity x_2, motor angular velocity x_3, motor input voltage u, and generator output voltage y. Table 1 shows the parameters of the electric vehicle with energy recovery.

The root mean square error (RMSE) is used and is given as follows [6, 15]:

Table 1 Parameters of the prototype

Parameter	Value	Parameter	Value
r	0.0225 m	R_m	50 Ω
σ_2	0.01 s/m	L_m	0.050 H
J_m	0.04 kgm^2	Fn	98.1 N
K_{2m}	20 kgm/A	V_{em}	24 V
K_{1m}	1.537 V/RPM	m	0.06 kg
L_g	5×10^{-6}H	R_g	1000 Ω
B_m	0.04 kgm^2/rads	C	0.001
K_{1g}	5×10^{-3} kgm^2/rads		

Fig. 6 Scope of the experiments

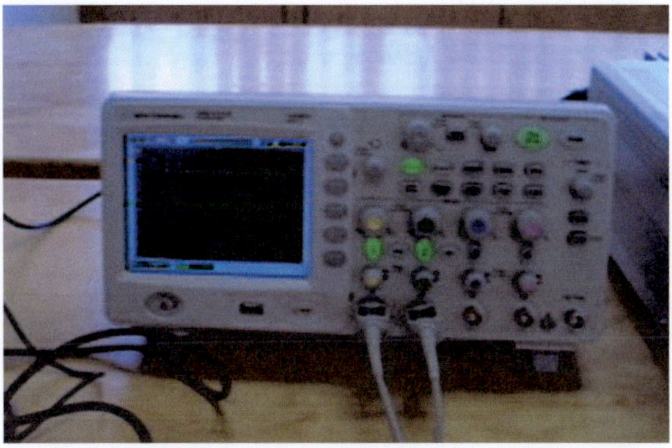

$$RMSE = \left(\frac{1}{T} \int_0^T e^2 d\tau \right)^{\frac{1}{2}}, \tag{15}$$

where $e^2 = (u_r - u)^2$, $e^2 = (x_{1r} - x_1)^2$, or $e^2 = (y_r - y)^2$, u_r, x_{1r}, and y_r are the real data of u, x_1, and y, respectively.

Figure 2 shows the electric vehicle prototype which is used for the experiments. The real measures are obtained using a scope which can provide tables with data. Figure 6 shows the scope. Figure 5 shows the circuits to obtain u (the input electric voltage) and y (the output electric voltage). Figure 7 shows the circuit to obtain the state x_1 (the electric current). The simulations are obtained using the Simulink program. Comparison results are obtained using the Matlab program.

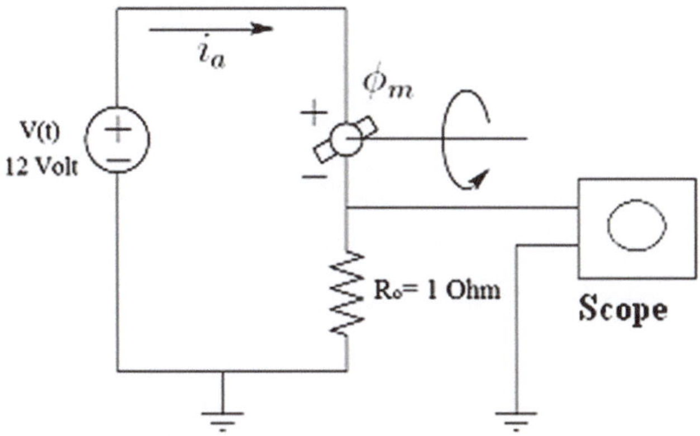

Fig. 7 Circuit to obtain the state x_1

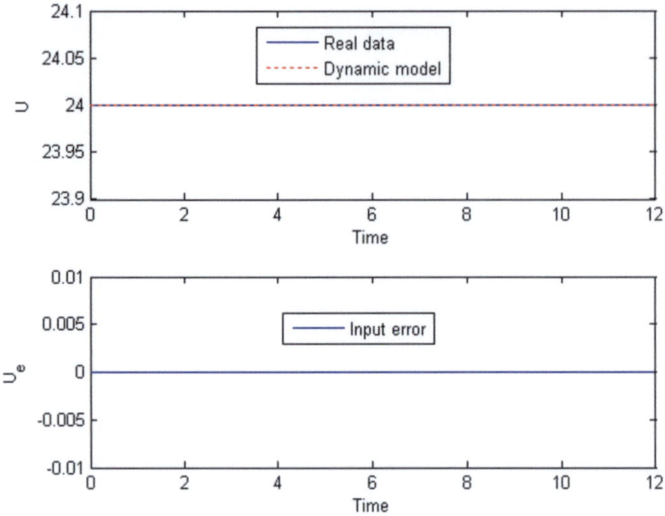

Fig. 8 Comparison results for the input u

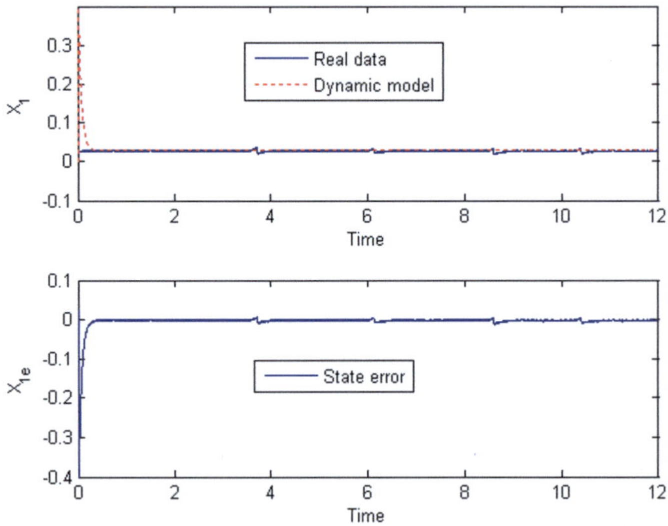

Fig. 9 Comparison results for the state x_1

Figure 8 shows the simulation, experiment, and error for the input. Figure 9 shows the simulation, experiment, and error for the state 1. Figure 10 shows the simulation, experiment, and error for the output. Table 2 shows the RMSE for the errors.

From Figs. 8, 9, and 10, it can be seen that the simulation and experiment results are almost equal, and also that the first state, input, and output reach the constant

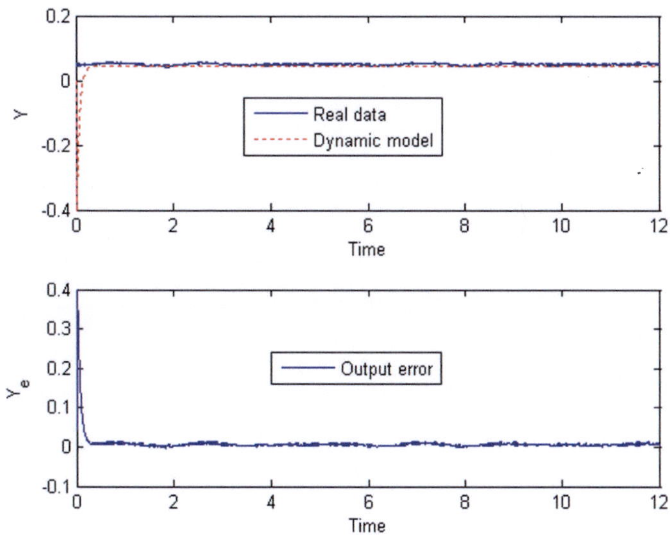

Fig. 10 Comparison results for the output y

Table 2 RMSE for the errors

	RMSE
$(u_r - u)^2$	1.4199×10^{-30}
$(x_{1r} - x_1)^2$	2.7719×10^{-4}
$(y_r - y)^2$	3.9362×10^{-4}

values in less than 0.5 s. From Table 2, it is shown that the dynamic model is a good approximation of the real process because the RMSE is near to zero.

Figure 11 shows the simulation results for the states x_2 and x_3 where state x_2 reaches 0.3299 m/s and state x_3 reaches 14.6610 rad/s in less than 0.5 s. Figure 12 shows the experiment for the angular velocity x_{3r} which gives a frequency of 2.34 Hz and is equivalent to 14.66 rad/s. Thus, the simulation values are approximated to the experiment values for the angular velocity.

5 Stability Analysis

This section presents the stability of the proposed method. System (13) is considered a linear system. Using the values of Table 1, the stability of the proposed dynamic model is obtained as follows [6, 16, 18]:

$$\det(sI - A) = 0,$$
$$\Longrightarrow s^3 + 1131.8\,s^2 + 1.473 \times 10^5 s + 2.1412 \times 10^6 = 0,$$

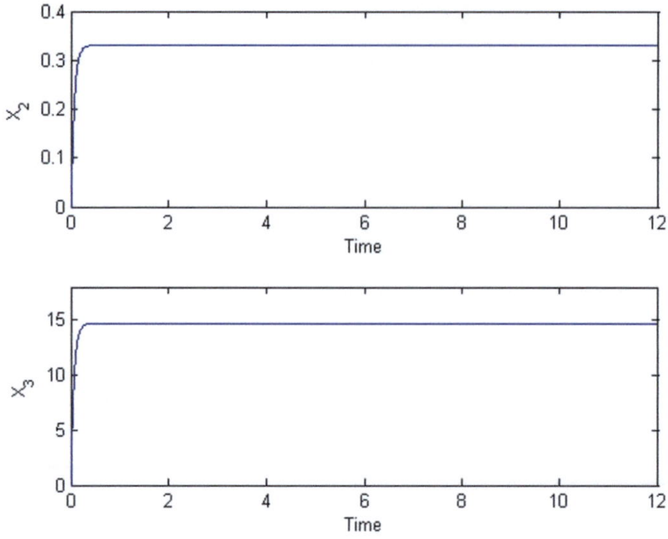

Fig. 11 Simulation for the states x_2 and x_3

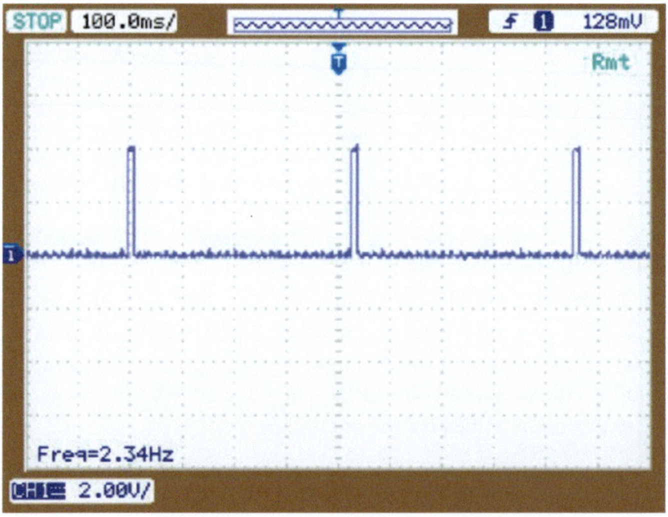

Fig. 12 Experiment for the angular velocity x_{3r}

The roots of the polynomial are $s = -16.63$, $s = -130.80$, $s = -984.37$; the above elements are known as the system eigenvalues. Since all the real parts of the eigenvalues are negative, the proposed dynamic model is guaranteed to be stable.

6 Concluding Remarks

In this chapter, the dynamic model of an electric vehicle with energy recovery was presented. The validation results showed that the proposed dynamic model gives a good approximation of the real system. The vehicle dynamic model was guaranteed to be stable given that its dynamic behavior is acceptable for present and future research. As future work, an observer or a controller for the energy recovery will be proposed to improve its performance, and an intelligent modeling will also be compared to the proposed dynamic model.

References

1. H. Alcazar, J. Martinez, L. Pantoja, C. Collazos, A. Paz, Method for incorporating awareness mechanisms in driving simulation environments. IEEE Lat. Am. Trans. **12**(1), 36–41 (2014)
2. F. Arieta, L.T. Barabasz, A. Santos, M. Nogueira, Mitigating flooding attacks on mobility in infrastructure-based vehicular networks. IEEE Lat. Am. Trans. **12**(3), 475–483 (2014)
3. F. González, J.G. Guarnizo, G. Benavides, Emulation system for a distribution center using mobile robot, controlled by artificial vision and fuzzy logic. IEEE Lat. Am. Trans. **12**(4), 557–563 (2014)
4. B. Ionescu, V. Suse, C. Gadea, B. Solomon, D. Ionescu, S. Islam, M. Cordea, Using a NIR camera for car gesture control. IEEE Lat. Am. Trans. **12**(3), 520–523 (2014)
5. R.I. Meneguette, L.A. Villas, An autonomic algorithm for data dissemination in vehicular ad hoc networks. IEEE Lat. Am. Trans. **12**(3), 430–435 (2014)
6. J.J. Rubio, Stable and optimal controls of a proton exchange membrane fuel cell. Int. J. Control. **87**(11), 2338–2347 (2014)
7. M.W. Spong, S. Hutchinson, M. Vidyasagar, *Robot Modeling and Control* (John Wiley & Sons, 2006)
8. J. Yi, L. Alvarez, X. Claeys, R. Horowitz, Emergency braking control with an observer-based dynamic tire/road friction model and wheel angular velocity measurement. Veh. Syst. Dyn. **39**, 81–90 (2003)
9. A. Buchachia, Dynamic clustering. Evol. Syst. **3**(3), 133–134 (2012)
10. E. Lughofer, Sigle pass active learning with conflict and ignorance. Evol. Syst. **3**, 251–271 (2012)
11. L. Maciel, A. Lemos, F. Gomide, R. Ballini, Evolving fuzzy systems for pricing fixed income options. Evol. Syst. **3**, 5–18 (2012)
12. J.J. Rubio, J.H. Pérez-Cruz, Z. Zamudio, A.J. Salinas, Comparison of two quadrotor dynamic models. IEEE Lat. Am. Trans. **12**(4), (2014)
13. C. Canudas de Wit, P. Tisiotras, E. Velenis, M. Basset, G. Gisinger, Dynamic frictions models for road tire longitudinal iteration, vehicle system dynamics. Int. J. Veh. Mech. Mobil. **39**(3), 189–226 (2003)
14. J.J. Rubio, C. Torres, R. Rivera, C.A. Hernandez, Comparison of four mathematical models for braking of a motorcycle. IEEE Lat. Am. Trans. **9**(5), 630–637 (2011)
15. J.J. Rubio, L. Arturo Soriano, W. Yu, Dynamic model of a wind turbine for the electric energy generation. Math. Probl. Eng. **2014**, 1–8 (2014)
16. J.B. Clempner, Mono-objective function analysis using an optimization approach. IEEE Lat. Am. Trans. **12**(2), 300–305 (2014)
17. N. Patel, C. Edwards, S.K. Spurgeon, A sliding mode observer for tire friction estimation during braking, in *American Control Conference* (2006), pp. 5867–5872
18. C.T. Chen, *Linear Systems Theory and Design* (Oxford University Press, 1999)

Modeling and Control of a Fuel Cell

Abstract In this chapter, the experimental control to obtain the maximum output voltage and the minimum input supplies in a real proton exchange membrane fuel cell is considered. The introduced technique employs a novel dynamic model that considers an outside resistor as other loss, and the experimental control which utilizes a novel law with an adaptive equation. The proposed dynamic model and control are validated by experiments and simulations.

1 Introduction

A fuel cell is an electrochemical system that converts continuously the chemical energy to electrical energy. Fuel cells have been highly employed in recent days, first because these systems have more everyday applications, and secondly due to the interest in addressing one of the most important problems such as is the environment pollution.

There are some works about control. The control of actuator systems is addressed in [1, 2]. In [3, 4], multi-objective optimization techniques for a class of nonlinear systems are proposed. A control system whose control cannot be implemented exactly but is shifted by perturbations is considered in [5]. In [7], the impact of component failures on an important control problem for an automated system is studied. The position regulation in rigid robots is addressed in [8]. In [9, 10], nonlinear controllers are designed based on a dynamic model to prolong the stack life of the fuel cells. When a parameterized controller admits a realization is investigated in [11]. In [12], the basic principles and some results of application for drives are reviewed. In [13, 14], robust intelligent controls of nonlinear systems are introduced. An adaptive scheme is proposed for robot manipulators that perform interaction tasks with uncertain parameters in [15]. In [17], a dc/dc buck power converter for the angular trajectory tracking task of a motor is presented. An optimal control of nonlinear systems is considered in [18]. In [16], a design criterion for the controller gains and setpoints in microgrids is proposed. In [20], the disturbance attenuation and robust disturbance attenuation problems for Hamiltonian systems are considered.

J. de J. Rubio et al., *Dynamic Models of Energy, Robotic, and Biological Systems*,
https://doi.org/10.1007/978-3-031-85438-5_4

The aforementioned research shows that the control is an actual and important issue; consequently, any advance in the control would be a good contribution. From the above studies, [9, 10] consider novel controllers of fuel cells; thus, the control of a fuel cell would be a great contribution.

In this chapter, a dynamic model of a fuel cell with an outside resistor is proposed to represent the behavior of the fuel cell in operation; the dynamic model validation is performed by the comparison between the experiments obtained with a fuel cell and simulations obtained with a computer. In addition, a control of the fuel cell is designed; its simulation provides the minimum amount of consumable inputs such that the maximum output voltage is obtained, experiments show the fuel cell with different fuel cell supply amount, and the case with less supply and greater output voltage matches the simulation result.

This research is organized as follows. In Sect. 2, the platform of the fuel cell for the experiments is introduced. A fuel cell dynamic model which includes an outside resistor is presented in Sect. 3. Section 4 designs the experimental control of the fuel cell. In Sect. 5, the dynamic model and the experimental control are validated by experiments and simulations. Conclusions and future research directions are detailed in Sect. 6.

2 Platform of the Fuel Cell

Figure 1 presents the prototype of the fuel cell used for the experiments and Fig. 2 shows its size. The fuel cell prototype uses a membrane electrode assembly with gas diffuser, a proton exchange membrane of Nafion 212 of active area 5.0 cm^2 with platinum (0.5 mg/cm^2) is used. Experiments were performed in the test system controlled Labview ATSM-450-NL, which is a test station for fuel cells which is composed of a unit for handling gas, a humidification system, and a device that integrates an electronic load to control the load used. The temperature of humidifiers is controlled by three temperature controllers, the test system supports up to 400 W (20 V and 20 A, or 3 V and 100 A) and can be selected to operate in modes of current and constant voltage. The data are simultaneously obtained with a system data transfer in Labview.

3 Dynamic Model of the Fuel Cell with an Outside Resistor

In this section, the fuel cell dynamic model is described. The fuel cell dynamic model is changed by including an outside resistor to know the behavior of the fuel cell in operation.

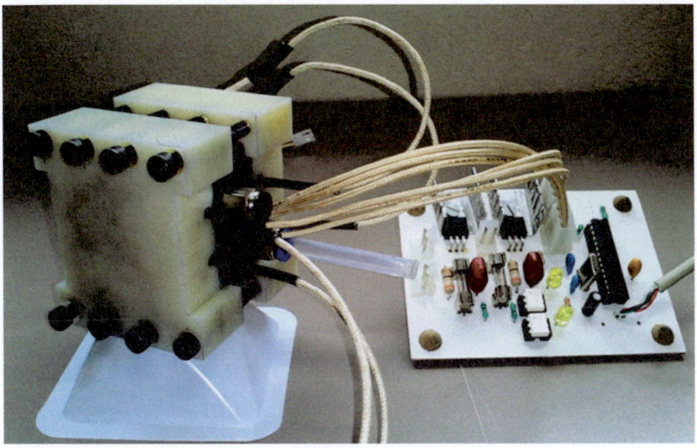

Fig. 1 Real fuel cell

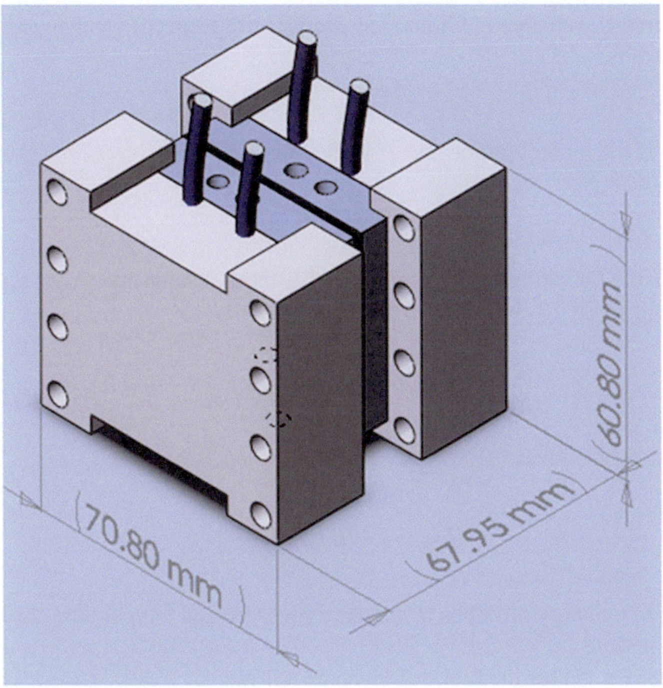

Fig. 2 Size of the designed fuel cell

3.1 Theoretical Voltage of the Fuel Cell

The theoretical voltage of the fuel cell V is as follows:

$$V = \frac{-\Delta G^o}{nF}, \tag{1}$$

where $-\Delta G^o$ is the free energy of Gibbs, n is the electrons number in a molecule of H_2, and F is the Faraday constant.

3.2 Pressure Effect in the Theoretical Voltage

In this subsection, the equations describing the behavior of the fuel cell at different pressures are shown.

In general, the change in Gibbs free energy with respect to a change in pressure is described by:

$$dG = V_m dP, \tag{2}$$

where V_m is the molar volume and P is the pressure.

For an ideal gas:

$$PV_m = RT, \tag{3}$$

where T is the operating temperature and R is the gas constant.

Substituting Eq. (3) into Eq. (2) gives:

$$dG = RT\frac{dP}{P}, \tag{4}$$

Integrating Eq. (4) gives:

$$G = G_0 + RT \ln\left(\frac{P}{P_0}\right), \tag{5}$$

where G_0 free energy of Gibbs at standard pressure and temperature, and P_0 is the standard pressure.

Consider Eq. (5) for the fuel cell given as follows:

$$\Delta G = \Delta G_0 + RT \ln\left(\frac{P_{H_2O}}{P_{H_2}\left(\frac{pO_2}{P_{std}}\right)^{1/2}}\right), \tag{6}$$

where P_{std} is a standard pressure (101325 Pa), pH_2, pO_2, and pH_2O_C are the partial pressures of hydrogen, oxygen, and water gas inside the cell, respectively.

Substituting Eq. (1) into Eq. (6) gives:

$$V = V_0 + \frac{RT}{nF} \ln \left(\frac{P_{H_2} \left(\frac{pO_2}{P_{std}} \right)^{1/2}}{P_{H_2O}} \right), \tag{7}$$

where V is the thermodynamic potential of the cell or reversible voltage based on the Nernst equation [6, 19], and V_0 is the cell-open circuit voltage.

3.3 Voltage Losses

If a fuel cell is supplied with reactive gases, but the circuit is not closed, and it is not going to generate any current, then one would expect that the potential of the fuel cell is as close to the theoretical potential of the cell. However in practice this potential, called open circuit potential, is significantly lower than the theoretical potential. These results suggest that there are voltage losses in the fuel cell even when there is no current generated.

There are different types of losses voltages during operation of a fuel cell caused by the following factors: kinetics of electrochemical reactions, electrical resistance and ionic strength, and difficulty of reagents to reach the reaction sites.

Activation Voltage Loss This voltage drop is associated with the speed of the electrochemical reactions occurring on the electrode surface, and it is presented at low voltages, in all reactions voltage exists but the product depends on the reagent and each electrode, for example the reaction hydrogen oxidation is four orders faster than the reaction of oxygen reduction magnitude. Activation polarization corresponds to the activation energy to be supplied to overcome the electronic barriers before a current flow can be established.

Let us consider the Butler-Volmer equation:

$$i = i_0 \left\{ \exp\left[\frac{-\alpha_{rd} F(L - L_r)}{RT} \right] - \exp\left[\frac{\alpha_{ox} F(L - L_r)}{RT} \right] \right\}, \tag{8}$$

where α_{rd} is a charge transfer coefficient of reduction and α_{ox} is a is a charge transfer coefficient of oxidation.

From Eq. (8) losses are obtained by activation voltage to the anode and cathode as follows:

$$L_{r,c} - L_c = \frac{RT}{\alpha F} \ln \left(\frac{i}{i_o} \right), \tag{9}$$

where L_c is the cathode voltage, α is a charge transfer coefficient, i is the output current density, and i_0 is the exchange current density related to activation losses.

$$L_a - L_{r,a} = \frac{RT}{\alpha F} \ln\left(\frac{i}{i_o}\right), \tag{10}$$

where L_a is the anode voltage.

The activation polarization of the electrode oxidation reaction is much lower than the activation polarization of the oxygen reduction reaction, so the voltage value at the anode is negligible. From Eq. (9) the activation loss which is known as the Tafel equation is as follows:

$$L_{activation} = \frac{RT}{2\alpha F} \ln\left(\frac{i + i_n}{i_0}\right), \tag{11}$$

where $L_{activation}$ is the voltage loss due to the reactions of the electrodes surface and i_n is the internal current density related to the internal current losses.

Ohmic Voltage Loss The ohmic loss occurs by the flow resistance in the electrolyte ion and electron flow resistance through the cell components; these components can be expressed by the Ohm law as follows:

$$L_{ohmic} = ri, \tag{12}$$

where L_{ohmic} is the ohmic voltage drop from the resistances of proton flow in the electrolyte, i is the output current density, and r is the area-specific resistance related to resistive losses.

Concentration Voltage Loss This voltage drop occurs when a reactant is readily consumed in the electrode by the electrochemical reaction. This voltage is given as follows:

$$L_{concentration} = me^{ni}, \tag{13}$$

where $L_{concentration}$ is the voltage loss from the reduction of concentration gases or the transport of a mass of oxygen and hydrogen, and m and n are constants in the mass transfer voltage.

Outside Resistor Voltage Loss The outside resistor voltage loss occurs by including an outside resistor to know the behavior of the fuel cell in operation. This voltage is given as follows:

$$L_{resistor} = R_r i, \tag{14}$$

where $L_{resistor}$ is the outside resistor voltage, i is the current density, and R_r is the resistor resistance.

3.4 Output Voltage Equation of the Fuel Cell with the Outside Resistor

In this research, the output stack voltage V considers the thermodynamic potential of the cell, the activation, ohmic, concentration, and outside resistor losses as can be seen in Fig. 3.

It is described as follows:

$$V_T = V - L_{activation} - L_{ohmic} - L_{concentration} - L_{resistor}, \tag{15}$$

where V, $L_{activation}$, L_{ohmic}, $L_{concentration}$, and $L_{resistor}$ are defined in Eqs. (7), (11), (12), (13), and (14), respectively.

3.5 Basic Reactions

Electrochemical reactions in a fuel cell proton exchange membrane occur on both sides of the membrane (anode and cathode) simultaneously. The basic reactions of the cell are as follows.

In the anode, the reaction is as follows:

$$H_{2,in}(g) \rightarrow 2H^+ + 2e^-, \tag{16}$$

In the cathode, the reaction is as follows:

$$\frac{1}{2}O_{2,in}(g) + 2H^+ + 2e^- \rightarrow H_2O_{c,in}(l), \tag{17}$$

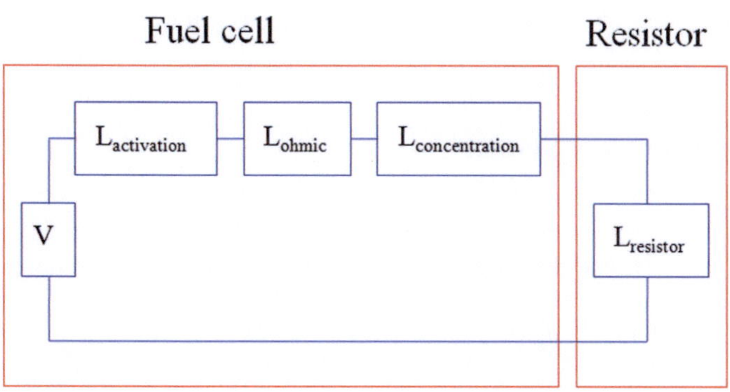

Fig. 3 Fuel cell model

The general reaction is as follows:

$$H_2(g) + \frac{1}{2}O_{2,in}(g) \rightarrow H_2O_{c,in}(l), \tag{18}$$

where g is gas and l is liquid, $H_{2,in}$, $O_{2,in}$, and $H_2O_{C,in}$ are the inlet flow rates of the hydrogen, oxygen, and water of the cathode, respectively.

3.6 State Equations

From the ideal gas law, it is known that the partial pressure of each gas is proportional to the amount of gas in the cell, to which there are three relevant contributions depending on the gas inlet flow rate, gas consumption, and gas outlet flow rate. Thus, the state equations are as follows:

$$\frac{dpH_2}{dt} = \frac{RT}{V_A}\left[H_{2,in} - 2K_rA_ci - \left(H_{2,in} - 2K_rA_ci\right)\frac{pH_2}{p_{op}}\right], \tag{19}$$

$$\frac{dpO_2}{dt} = \frac{RT}{V_C}\left[O_{2,in} - K_rA_ci - \left(O_{2,in} - K_rA_ci\right)\frac{pO_2}{p_{op}}\right], \tag{20}$$

$$\frac{dpH_2O_C}{dt} = \frac{RT}{V_C}\left[H_2O_{C,in} + 2K_rA_ci - \left(O_{2,in} + 2K_rA_ci\right)\frac{pH_2O_C}{p_{op}}\right], \tag{21}$$

where $K_r = N/4F$, A_c is the cell active area, i is defined in Eqs. (11)–(13), P_{op} is the operating pressure, $V_A$is the anode volume, V_C is the cathode volume, R and T are defined in Eq. (3), and pH_2, pO_2, and pH_2O_C are the partial pressures of hydrogen, oxygen, and water inside the cell, respectively. The water input $H_2O_{C,in}$ is not considered in the state equations because it is not an input of the process in most of the applications; thus, $H_2O_{C,in}$ will be considered as zero in this development.

3.7 The Complete System

Defining the states as $z_1 = pH_2$, $z_2 = pO_2$, $z_3 = pH_2O_C$, the inputs as $v_1 = H_{2,in}$, $v_2 = O_{2,in}$, $v_3 = i$, and the output as $y = V_T$ gives the following complete system:

$$\dot{z}_1 = \frac{RT}{V_A}\left(-\frac{v_1}{p_{op}} + 2K_rA_c\frac{v_3}{p_{op}}\right)z_1 + \frac{RT}{V_A}v_1 - \frac{RT}{V_A}2K_rA_cv_3, \tag{22}$$

$$\dot{z}_2 = \frac{RT}{V_C}\left(-\frac{v_2}{p_{op}} + K_rA_c\frac{v_3}{p_{op}}\right)z_2 + \frac{RT}{V_C}v_2 - \frac{RT}{V_C}K_rA_cv_3, \tag{23}$$

$$\dot{z}_3 = \frac{RT}{V_C}\left(-\frac{v_2}{p_{op}} - 2K_r A_c \frac{v_3}{p_{op}}\right) z_3 + \frac{RT}{V_C} 2K_r A_c v_3, \tag{24}$$

$$y = \left(V_0 + \frac{RT}{2F}\ln\left\{\frac{z_1\left(\frac{z_2}{P_{std}}\right)^{1/2}}{z_3}\right\}\right) - C\ln\left(\frac{v_3 + i_n}{i_0}\right) - r v_3 - m e^{n v_3} - R_r v_3, \tag{25}$$

The nonlinear system (22)–(25) is rewritten as follows:

$$\begin{aligned} \dot{z} &= Az + Bv = g(z, v), \\ y &= h(z, v), \end{aligned} \tag{26}$$

where $A = \begin{bmatrix} a_1 & 0 & 0 \\ 0 & a_2 & 0 \\ 0 & 0 & a_3 \end{bmatrix} \in \Re^{3\times 3}$, $a_1 = \frac{RT}{V_A}\left(-\frac{v_1}{p_{op}} + 2K_r A_c \frac{v_3}{p_{op}}\right)$, $a_2 = \frac{RT}{V_C}\left(-\frac{v_2}{p_{op}} + K_r A_c \frac{v_3}{p_{op}}\right)$, $a_3 = \frac{RT}{V_C}\left(-\frac{v_2}{p_{op}} - 2K_r A_c \frac{v_3}{p_{op}}\right)$, $B = \begin{bmatrix} b_{11} & 0 & b_{13} \\ 0 & b_{22} & b_{23} \\ 0 & 0 & b_{33} \end{bmatrix} \in \Re^{3\times 3}$, $b_{11} = \frac{RT}{V_A}$, $b_{13} = -\frac{RT}{V_A} 2K_r A_c$, $b_{22} = \frac{RT}{V_C}$, $b_{23} = -\frac{RT}{V_C} K_r A_c$, $b_{33} = \frac{RT}{V_C} 2K_r A_c$, $z = [z_1, z_2, z_3]^T$, $v = [v_1, v_2, v_3]^T$, $h(z, v) = \left(V_0 + \frac{RT}{2F}\ln\left\{\frac{z_1\left(\frac{z_2}{P_{std}}\right)^{1/2}}{z_3}\right\}\right) - \frac{RT}{2\alpha F}\ln\left(\frac{v_3 + i_n}{i_0}\right) - r v_3 - m e^{n v_3} - R_r v_3$.

4 Experimental Control of the Fuel Cell

In this section, the experimental control of the fuel cell is designed. Given any initial state $z(t_0)$, the optimal control problem is to find a vector allowable setting $v(t)$ to transfer the state to the desired region in the state space and for which a performance index is minimized.

There exists an experimental controller capable of maximizing the output voltage generated and minimizing the input supplies of the fuel cell (26), which is given as follows:

$$v = -K^{-1}\left[\left(\frac{\partial A\tilde{z}}{\partial v}\right)^T P\tilde{z} + B^T P\tilde{z}\right], \tag{27}$$

where $\tilde{z} = z - z_d$ is the tracking error, $z_d = \left[z_{d,1}, z_{d,2}, z_{d,3}\right]^T$ is the reference, A and B are defined in (26), $\frac{\partial A\tilde{z}}{\partial v} = \begin{bmatrix} \partial a_{11} & \partial a_{12} & \partial a_{13} \\ \partial a_{21} & \partial a_{22} & \partial a_{23} \\ \partial a_{31} & \partial a_{32} & \partial a_{33} \end{bmatrix} \in \Re^{3\times 3}$, $\partial a_{11} = \frac{RT}{V_A}\left(-\frac{\tilde{z}_1}{p_{op}}\right)$, $\partial a_{12} = 0$, $\partial a_{13} = \frac{RT}{V_A}\left(2K_r A_c \frac{\tilde{z}_1}{p_{op}}\right)$, $\partial a_{21} = \partial a_{31} = 0$, $\partial a_{22} = \frac{RT}{V_C}\left(-\frac{\tilde{z}_2}{p_{op}}\right)$, $\partial a_{23} =$

$\frac{RT}{V_C}\left(K_r A_c \frac{\widetilde{z}_2}{p_{op}}\right)$, $\partial a_{32} = \frac{RT}{V_C}\left(-\frac{\widetilde{z}_3}{p_{op}}\right)$, $\partial a_{33} = \frac{RT}{V_C}\left(-2K_r A_c \frac{\widetilde{z}_3}{p_{op}}\right)$, $K \in \Re^{3\times 3}$ and $P = diag\,(p_i) \in \Re^{3\times 3}$ are positive definite matrices, p_1, p_2, and p_3 are positive scalar varying with time parameters, and $\widetilde{z}$ is the system tracking error. There also exists an equation given as follows:

$$\dot{P} = -PA - A^T P - Q + PBK^{-1}B^T P + PBK^{-1}\left(\frac{\partial A\widetilde{z}}{\partial v}\right)^T P, \tag{28}$$

5 Experimental Results

In this chapter, the experimental control is validated by two experiments. The objective is that the introduced dynamic model and proposed control represent a real fuel cell process. Table 1 shows the parameters of the fuel cell.

5.1 Experiment 1

The first experiment shows the dynamic model validation. In this experiment, the proposed dynamic model is validated experimentally. The objective is that the proposed dynamic model represents the actual process of a fuel cell. The dynamic model for the fuel cell is given by Eq. (26) with $z_1 = pH_2$, $z_2 = pO_2$, and $z_3 = pH_2O_C$ as the states, $v_1 = H_{2,in}$, $v_2 = O_{2,in}$, and $v_3 = i$ as the inputs, and $y = V$ as the output, $z_{1,0} = z_{2,0} = z_{3,0} = 1$ Pa are the initial conditions. Figure 4 presents the behavior of the outside resistor R_r and output voltage V in the comparison between the simulations and experiments, obtaining that both cases give very approximate results.

Table 1 Parameters of the prototype

Parameter	Value	Parameter	Value
F	96485 C/mol	T	353 K
i_n	1×10^{-4} mA/cm^2	P_{std}	101325 Pa
m	3×10^{-6} V	A_C	136.7 cm^2
R	8.3144 J/molK	V_0	1.3 V
P_{op}	101×10^3 Pa	α	0.58
i_0	1×10^{-4} mA/cm^2	V_A	6.495 cm^2
r	3.85×10^{-4} kΩcm^2	V_C	12.96 cm^2
n	8×10^{-3} cm^2/mA	R_r	1 Ω

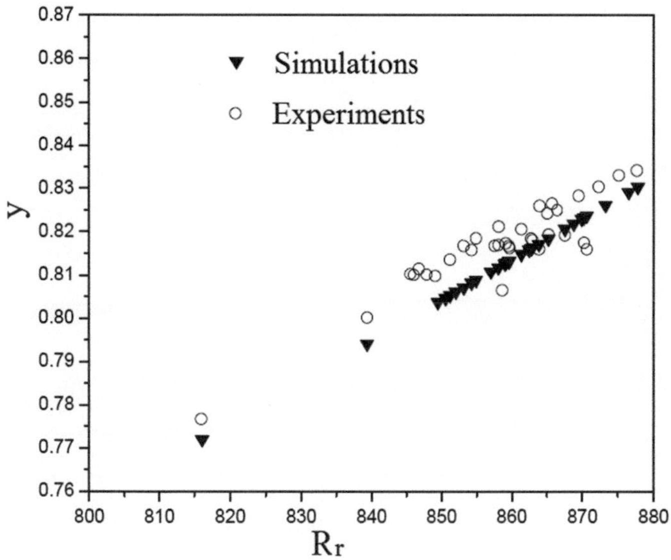

Fig. 4 Comparison between the simulation and experiment dynamic models

5.2 *Experiment 2*

The second experiment shows the control validation. In this experiment, the results of the simulation and experiments of the optimal controller applied to the fuel cell are presented. The main objective of the proposed control is to increase the voltage generated and decrease the inputs ($H_{2,in}$, $O_{2,in}$). The dynamic model for the fuel cell is given by Eq. (26) with variables z_1, z_2, z_3, v_1, v_2, v_3, y, $z_{1,0}$, $z_{2,0}$, $z_{3,0}$ are equal to the experiment 1, $z_{d,1} = z_{d,2} = z_{d,3} = 1.2$ Pa are the references. The experimental control is given by Eqs. (27) and (28) with its parameters described as $P_0 = diag(p_{,j,0}) \in \Re^{3\times3}$, $p_{1,0} = 1.2 \times 10^{-3}$, $p_{2,0} = 2.5 \times 10^{-3}$, $p_{3,0} = 2.5$, P_0 is the initial condition of P, $K = diag(1) \in \Re^{3\times3}$, $Q = diag(0.1) \in \Re^{3\times3}$.

Figures 5 and 6 present the simulation results of the lowest inputs $v_1 = H_{2,in}$, $v_2 = O_{2,in}$ which make it possible to obtain the highest output y. Note that v_1 is the double of v_2 in the input supply from H_2/O_2 0.00011 to 0.000056 mol/s and the output voltage is 0.965 V.

Three different experiments are performed in Figs. 7, 8, and 9. From the Figs. 7, 8, and 9, it can be seen that in all three cases an output voltage of 0.965 V is obtained, but with a big difference: the input supplies are H_2/O_2 from 0.00022 to 0.000012 mol/s, H_2/O_2 from 0.00019 to 0.000093 mol/s, and H_2/O_2 from 0.00011 to 0.000056 mol/s, respectively.

From Figs. 5 and 9, it can be seen that the simulation and the experiment has the same input supply in H_2/O_2 0.00011 to 0.000056 mol/s, and from Figs. 6 and 9, it can be seen that in the simulation and experiment the same output voltage of 0.965

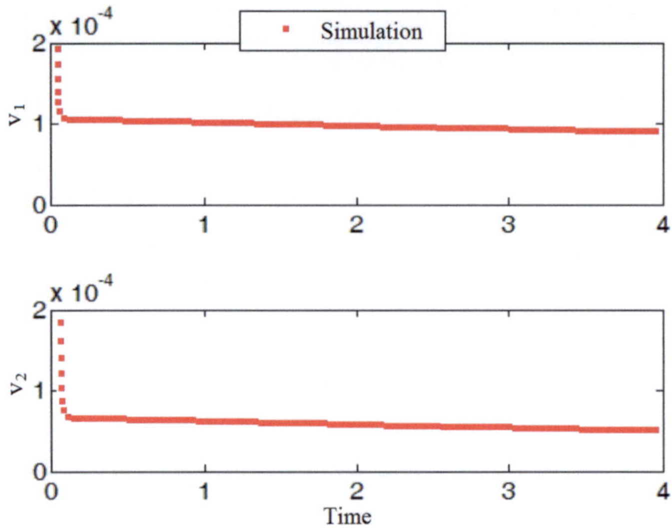

Fig. 5 Inputs for the simulation

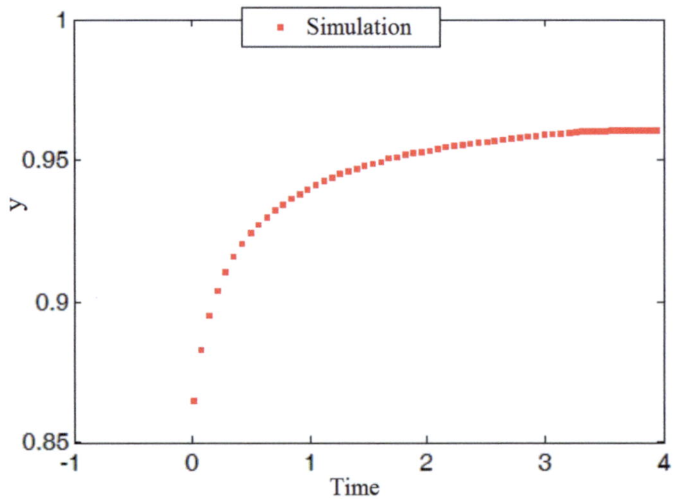

Fig. 6 Output for the simulation

V is obtained; as described above, it is concluded that the values of the simulation of Figs. 5 and 6 and the experiment of Fig. 9 are equal.

From Figs. 7, 8, and 9, it can be observed that in all three cases the same output voltage of 0.965 V is obtained, but with a big difference in the input supplies of H_2/O_2 from 0.00022 to 0.000012 mol/s, H_2/O_2 from 0.00019 to 0.000093 mol/s, and H_2/O_2 from 0.00011 to 0.000056 mol/s, respectively.

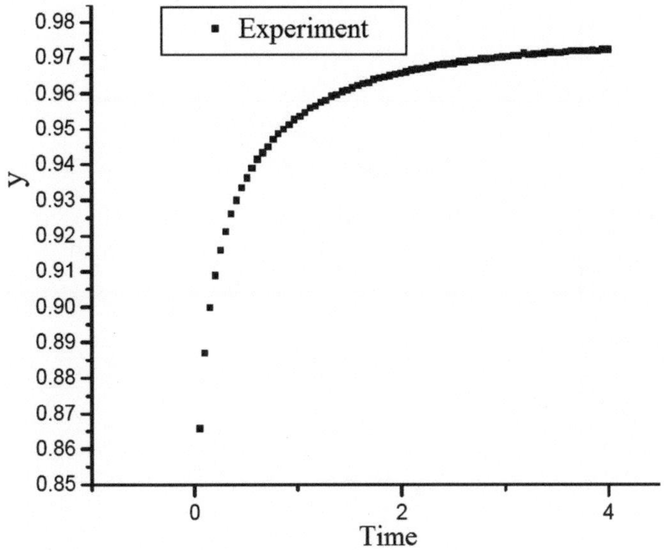

Fig. 7 Experiment 1

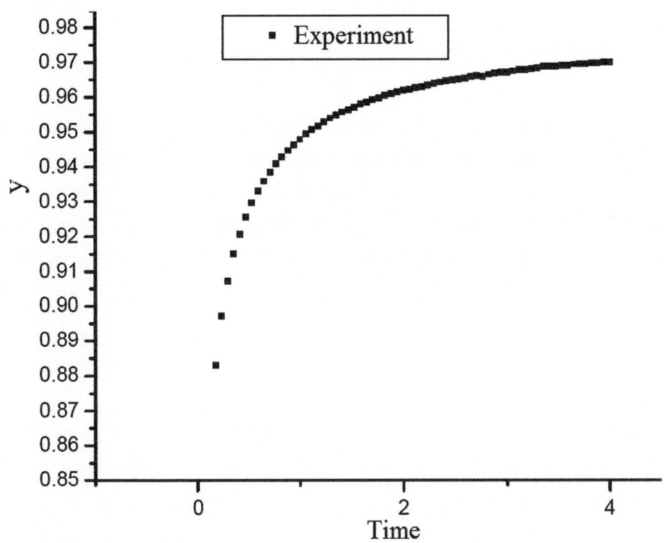

Fig. 8 Experiment 2

It can be seen that the experiment of Fig. 9 (corresponding to the simulation of Figs. 5 and 6) compared to the experiments in Figs. 7 and 8, provides the maximum output potential but the minimum input supplies. Finally, as described above, it is concluded that the simulation provides the minimum input supplies such that the maximum output voltage is obtained in the fuel cell.

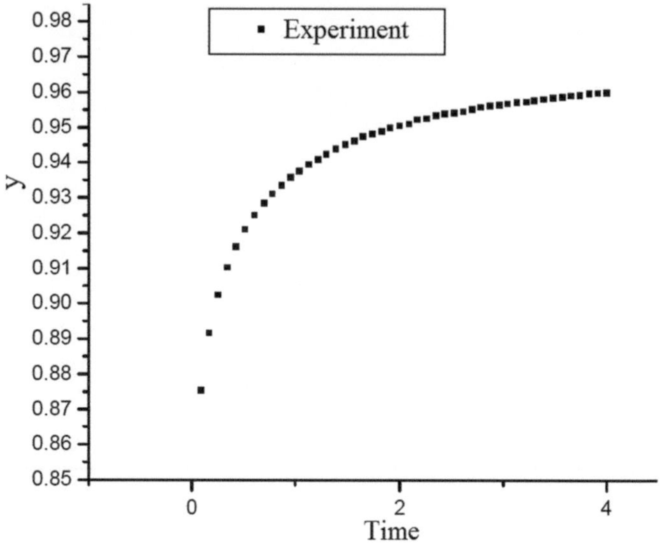

Fig. 9 Experiment 3

6 Concluding Remarks

In this chapter, the experimental controller applied to the fuel cell was presented. Several experiments showed where the maximum output voltage is obtained, but one experiment coincided with the simulation result such that the lowest amount of supply was used, while for the other experiments, even the same output voltage was obtained, but more supply was employed. As future research, the proposed method will be combined with the intelligent systems, or the proposed technology will be employed in other different systems.

References

1. C. Aguilar-Ibañez, J.A. Mendoza-Mendoza, M.S. Suarez Castanon, J. Davila, A nonlinear robust pi controller for an uncertain system. Int. J. Control. **87**(5), 1094–1102 (2014)
2. C. Aguilar-Ibañez, M.S. Suarez-Castanon, N. Cruz-Cortes, Output feedback stabilization of the inverted pendulum system: a Lyapunov approach. Nonlinear Dyn. **70**(1), 767–777 (2012)
3. V. Azhmyakov, R. Velazquez, On a variational approach to optimization of hybrid mechanical systems. Math. Probl. Eng. **2010**, 1–13 (2010)
4. V. Azhmyakov, On the set-valued approach to optimal control of sliding mode processes. J. Frankl. Inst. **349**, 1323–1336 (2012)
5. M. Belhadj, J. Salomon, G. Turinici, Ensemble controllability and discrimination of perturbed bilinear control systems on connected, simple, compact Lie groups. Eur. J. Control. **22**, 23–29 (2015)

6. D. Boda, R. Kovacs, D. Gillespie, T. Kristof, Selective transport through a model calcium channel studied by local equilibrium Monte Carlo simulations coupled to the Nernst-Planck equation. J. Mol. Liq. **189**, 100–112 (2014)
7. M. Dakil, T. Boukhobza, C. Simon, Disturbance rejection problem solvability: from structural approach to reliability/availability analysis. Eur. J. Control. **21**, 36–44 (2015)
8. V.M. Hernandez-Guzman, R.V. Carrillo-Serrano, R. Silva-Ortigoza, PD control for robot manipulators actuated by switched reluctance motors. Int. J. Control. **86**(3), 540–554 (2013)
9. W.K. Na, B. Gou, B. Diong, Nonlinear control of PME fuel cells by exact linearization. IEEE Transactions on Industrial Applications **43**(6), 1426–1433 (2007)
10. W.K. Na, B. Gou, Feedback linearization-based nonlinear control for PME fuel cells. IEEE Trans. Energy Convers. **23**(1), 179–190 (2008)
11. R. Ortega, E. Panteley, When is a parameterized controller suitable for adaptive control. Eur. J. Control. **22**, 13–16 (2015)
12. R. Ortegaa, G. Espinosa-Perez, A. Astolfi, Passivity-based control of ac drives: theory for the user and application examples. Int. J. Control. **86**(4), 625–635 (2013)
13. J.H. Perez-Cruz, J.J. Rubio, J. Pacheco, E. Soriano, State estimation in MIMO nonlinear systems subject to unknown deadzones using recurrent neural networks. Neural Comput. Appl. **25**(3–4), 693–701 (2014)
14. J.H. Pérez-Cruz, J.J. Rubio, R. Encinas, R. Balcazar, Singularity-free neural control for the exponential trajectory tracking in multiple-input uncertain systems with unknown deadzone nonlinearities. Sci. World J. **2014**, 1–10 (2014)
15. J. Pliego-Jimenez, M.A. Arteaga-Perez, Adaptive position/force control for robot manipulators in contact with a rigid surface with uncertain parameters. Eur. J. Control. **22**, 1–12 (2015)
16. J. Schiffer, R. Ortega, A. Astolfi, J. Raisch, T. Sezi, Conditions for stability of droop-controlled inverter-based microgrids. Automatica **50**, 2457–2469 (2014)
17. R. Silva-Ortigoza, V.M. Hernandez-Guzman, M. Antonio-Cruz, D. Munoz-Carrillo, Dc/dc buck power converter as a smooth starter for a dc motor based on a hierarchical control. IEEE Trans. Power Electron. **30**(2), 1076–1084 (2015)
18. C. Torres, J.J. Rubio, C. Aguilar-Ibañez, J.H. Perez-Cruz, Stable optimal control applied to a cylindrical robotic arm. Neural Comput. Appl. **24**(3), 937–944 (2014)
19. F.J. Vidal-Iglesias, J. Solla-Gullón, E. Herrero, A. Rodes, A. Aldaz, Do you really understand the electrochemical Nernst equation? Electrocatalysis **4**, 1–9 (2013)
20. Y. Yalcin, L. Goren-Sumer, A. Astolfi, Some results on disturbance attenuation for Hamiltonian systems via direct discrete-time design. Int. J. Robust Nonlinear Control. **25**(13), 1927–1940 (2015)

Dynamic Model with Sensor and Actuator for a Transelevator

Abstract In this chapter, the structural, sensor, and actuator dynamic models of a transelevator are presented; afterwards, the dynamic model with sensor and actuator of the transelevator is obtained by using the combination of the structural, sensor, and actuator dynamic models. The proposed dynamic model is validated comparing the simulation results against the experimental results. Finally, the stability analysis of the aforementioned model is studied.

1 Introduction

The structural dynamic model is used for the control applications, but when a system is controlled, a sensor and an actuator are required, so this work is interested to obtain the dynamic model with sensor and actuator for a transelevator. A transelevator is a crane similar to a Cartesian robotic arm which is moved inside a warehouse; this transelevator is used to move loads from one place to another one inside the warehouse.

The research on the robotic arms is classified into three kinds: the trajectory planning [1, 2], the position estimation [3–5], and the control [6–10].

The trajectory planning of a robotic arm has the objective to provide the best trajectory of the robotic arm from an initial point to a final point. In [1], they address the challenge of realizing full-body behaviors in scalable modular robots. The trajectories planning and a collisions detector for robotic arms are presented by [2].

The position estimation is to estimate the parameters of the position and the orientation using other parameters such as are the parameters of an image, an identifier or an observer can be used for the position estimation. In [3], spatial computing language (Proto) is applied to multi-mobile-robot systems with an actuator that turns a vector field into device motion. The identification of a golf swing robot based on four kinds of soft computing methods is investigated by [4]. In [5], an innovative neuro-evolutionary approach for mobile robot ego-motion estimation with a 3D camera is proposed.

J. de J. Rubio et al., *Dynamic Models of Energy, Robotic, and Biological Systems*,
https://doi.org/10.1007/978-3-031-85438-5_5

The control has the objective that the robotic system has to follow a desired trajectory. In [6], they study how a self-organized mobile robot flock can be steered toward a desired direction through externally guiding some of its members. An adaptive neural network sensor-less control scheme for machines is introduced by [7]. In [8], a model-free self-tuning output recurrent cerebellar model articulation controller to control an inverted pendulum is investigated. A network structure developing a biologically plausible gene regulatory networks model for robot control is adopted by [9]. In [10], a robust training algorithm of multi-input multi-output recurrent neural network and its application in the fault tolerant control of a robotic system are investigated.

For the trajectory planning, the position estimation, or the control, the dynamic models help to obtain the objective, i.e., it is necessary to obtain a dynamic model of the system or to obtain the measure of all the parameters of the system. It is less expensive to obtain a dynamic model of the system than to get the measure of all the parameters of the system.

In most of the aforementioned cases only the structural dynamic model is used, but when a system is controlled, a sensor and an actuator are required; therefore, this work is interested to obtain the dynamic model with sensor and actuator for a transelevator.

This chapter is organized as follows. In Sect. 2, the method to obtain the structural dynamic model is detailed. In Sect. 3, the structural, sensor, and actuator dynamic models are obtained. In Sect. 4, the dynamic model with sensor and actuator for a transelevator is given. In Sect. 5, the validation of the proposed dynamic model is shown. In Sect. 6, the stability analysis of the proposed model is presented. In Sect. 7, the conclusion and the future research are detailed.

2 Preliminaries

The Euler-Lagrange method is used to obtain the dynamic model of the transelevator. The first step of this method is to find the kinetic energy K_i, which is the addition of the speed of the motion and the rotation kinetic energy, and is given as follows:

$$K_i = \frac{1}{2} m_i v_i^2 + \frac{1}{2} J_i \sum_{i=1}^{n} \dot{\theta}_i^2, \tag{1}$$

where $_i = 1, \ldots, n$, n is the number of links, v_i is the speed of motion for the joint i, m_i is the center of mass of the joint i and the link i, if the joint i is rotational J_i is its inertia, θ_i is the angular position of the joint i, if the angular positions have different directions $\sum_{i=1}^{n} \dot{\theta}_i^2 = \dot{\theta}_1^2 + \dot{\theta}_2^2 + \cdots + \dot{\theta}_n^2$ or if the angular positions have the same direction $\sum_{i=1}^{n} \dot{\theta}_i^2 = \left(\dot{\theta}_1 + \dot{\theta}_2 + \cdots + \dot{\theta}_n\right)^2$, $v_i^2 = \dot{\bar{X}}_i^2 + \dot{\bar{Y}}_i^2 + \dot{\bar{Z}}_i^2$ where $\dot{\bar{X}}_i$, $\dot{\bar{Y}}_i$, and $\dot{\bar{Z}}_i$ are the derivatives of $\bar{X}_i$, $\bar{Y}_i$, and $\bar{Z}_i$, respectively, $\bar{X}_i$, $\bar{Y}_i$, and $\bar{Z}_i$ are the coordinates of the linear movement of the link i.

The second step is to find the potential energy, which is given as follows:

$$V_i = m_i g h_i, \tag{2}$$

where $_i \in 1, \ldots, n$, h_i is the height of the center of mass of the joint and the link i, and g is the gravity acceleration.

As the third step, the Lagrangian is obtained as follows:

$$L = \sum_{i=1}^{n} (K_i - V_i), \tag{3}$$

As the fourth step, the following equation is used to obtain each dynamic equation for the dynamic model:

$$\frac{d}{dt}\frac{\partial L}{\partial \dot{q}_i} - \frac{\partial L}{\partial q_i} = \overline{\tau}_i, \tag{4}$$

Remark 1 The method to obtain the dynamic model of this chapter is different from others because they use Jacobians, inertia tensors, or Christoffel symbols, while in this chapter none of these methods is used.

3 Dynamic Model of Elements of the Transelevator

3.1 Structural Dynamic Model

A transelevator is a crane similar to a Cartesian robotic arm which moves inside a warehouse. This transelevator is used to move loads from one place to another one inside the warehouse, for example, from the floor to the deposit, from the deposit to the floor, from one deposit to another one, or from a trailer to a deposit. Figure 1 shows the transelevator.

From Fig. 1 the parameters $\bar{X}_1$, $\bar{Y}_1$ and $\bar{Z}_1$ of Eq. (1) are as follows:

$$\begin{aligned} \bar{X}_1 &= x_1, \\ \bar{Y}_1 &= 0, \\ \bar{Z}_1 &= 0, \end{aligned} \tag{5}$$

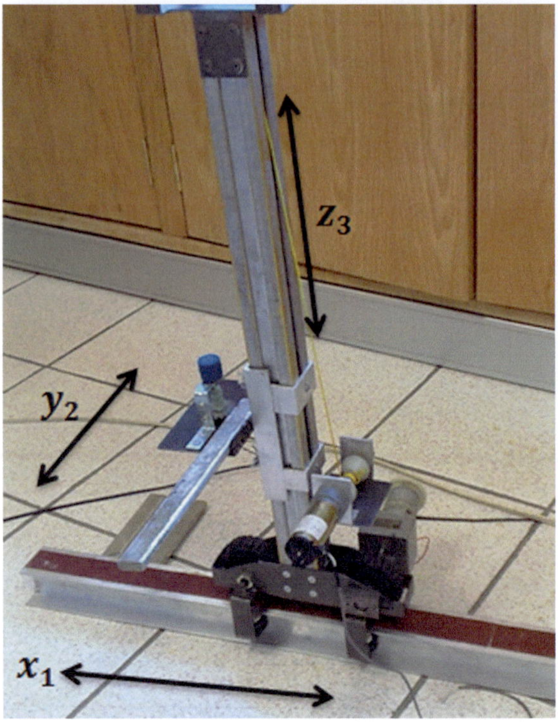

Fig. 1 The transelevator

where x_1 is the length to the mass center of the link 1. From Fig. 1, the parameter x_1 is bounded as follows $0 \leq x_1 \leq x_{\max}$. Using (1) and (5), the kinetic energy for joint 1 is as follows:

$$K_1 = \frac{1}{2} m_1 \dot{x}_1^2, \tag{6}$$

From Fig. 1 the parameters x_2, y_2, and z_2 of Eq. (1) are as follows:

$$\begin{aligned} \overline{X}_2 &= x_1, \\ \overline{Y}_2 &= 0, \\ \overline{Z}_2 &= z_2, \end{aligned} \tag{7}$$

where z_2 is the length to the mass center of the link 2. From Fig. 1, the parameter z_2 is bounded as follows $0 \leq z_2 \leq z_{\max}$. Using Eqs. (1) and (7), the kinetic energy for joint 2 is as follows:

$$K_2 = \frac{1}{2} m_2 \dot{x}_1^2 + \frac{1}{2} m_2 \dot{z}_2^2, \tag{8}$$

From Fig. 1 the parameters $\overline{X}_3$, $\overline{Y}_3$ and $\overline{Z}_3$ of Eq. (1) are as follows:

$$\begin{aligned}\overline{X}_3 &= x_1,\\ \overline{Y}_3 &= y_3,\\ \overline{Z}_3 &= z_2,\end{aligned} \tag{9}$$

where y_3 is the length to the mass center of the link 3. From Fig. 1, the parameter y_3 is bounded as follows $0 \leq y_3 \leq y_{\max}$. Using Eqs. (1) and (9), the kinetic energy for joint 3 is as follows:

$$K_3 = \frac{1}{2} m_3 \dot{x}_1^2 + \frac{1}{2} m_3 \dot{z}_2^2 + \frac{1}{2} m_3 \dot{y}_3^2, \tag{10}$$

From Fig. 1, the potential energy for the three links is as follows:

$$\begin{aligned}V_1 &= 0,\\ V_2 &= m_2 g z_2,\\ V_3 &= m_3 g z_2,\end{aligned} \tag{11}$$

Substituting Eqs. (6), (8), (10), and (11) into Eq. (3) gives the Lagrangian as follows:

$$L = \frac{1}{2} m_{13} \dot{x}_1^2 + \frac{1}{2} m_{23} \dot{z}_2^2 + \frac{1}{2} m_3 \dot{y}_3^2 - m_{23} g z_2, \tag{12}$$

where $m_{13} = m_1 + m_2 + m_3$ and $m_{23} = m_2 + m_3$.

Using the Euler-Lagrange method of Eqs. (4) in Eq. (12) for joint 1 gives:

$$m_{13} \ddot{x}_1 = \tau_1, \tag{13}$$

where τ_1 is the force needed to move the link 1.

Using the Euler-Lagrange method of Eqs. (4) in Eq. (12) for joint 2 gives:

$$m_{23} \ddot{z}_2 + m_{23} g = \tau_2, \tag{14}$$

where τ_2 is the force needed to move link 2.

Using the Euler-Lagrange method of Eqs. (4) in Eq. (12) for joint 3 gives:

$$m_3 \ddot{y}_3 = \tau_3, \tag{15}$$

where τ_3 is the force needed to move link 3 from the home position to another one.

The structural dynamic model of the transelevator crane is given by Eqs. (13), (14), and (15).

Remark 2 The method of this chaoter is similar to the method used by [11], but [11] assumes that the link masses are concentrated at the end of the links and the inertia is not considered, while in this chapter the link masses are concentrated at the half of the link and the inertia is considered. In addition, [11] does not present the dynamic models of the transelevator.

3.2 Actuator Dynamic Model

It is necessary to monitor and to act over some variables to control a transelevator; therefore, an actuator and a sensor are required.

Figure 2 is used to obtain the following dynamic model of a motor of each link.

$$L\frac{di_a}{dt} + R_{mi}i_{ai} = V_i - V_{bi}, \tag{16}$$

where:

$$V_{bi} = K_{bi}\dot{\theta}_m, \tag{17}$$

where $i = 1, 2, 3$, i_{ai} is the current in the motor link i, L_i is the inductance of the motor for the link i, R_{mi} is the resistance of the motor for link i, V_i is the input voltage of the motor for link i, k_{bi} is the constant back emf of the motor for link i, and $\dot{\theta}_i$ is the speed of the angle of the motor of link i.

Figure 3 shows the actuator circuit; this circuit is used to obtain the current applied for the motors in each link i_{ai} as function of the voltage of the motor V_i of Eq. (16).

From Fig. 3, the following is obtained:

$$V_{fi} = V_{Rc_i} + V_{mi}, \tag{18}$$

where V_{f_i} is the input voltage for link i for the actuator circuit, V_{Rc_i} is the voltage in the resistance for link i for the actuator circuit, $V_{mi} = V_i$ is the input voltage of the motor for link i in the actuator circuit, it is known that:

$$V_{Rc_i} = Ro_i i_{ci}, \tag{19}$$

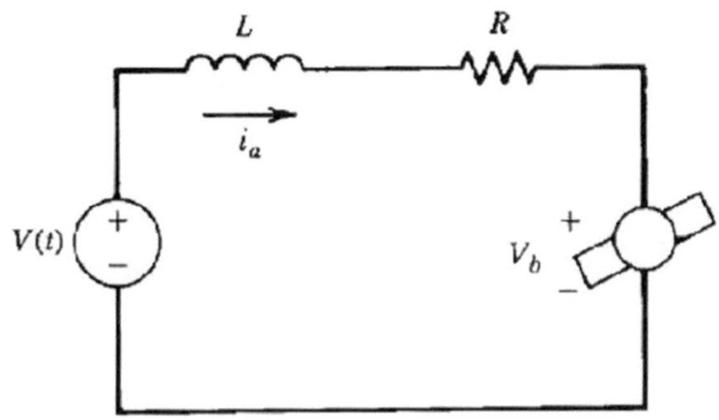

Fig. 2 Circuit of a motor controlled by DC

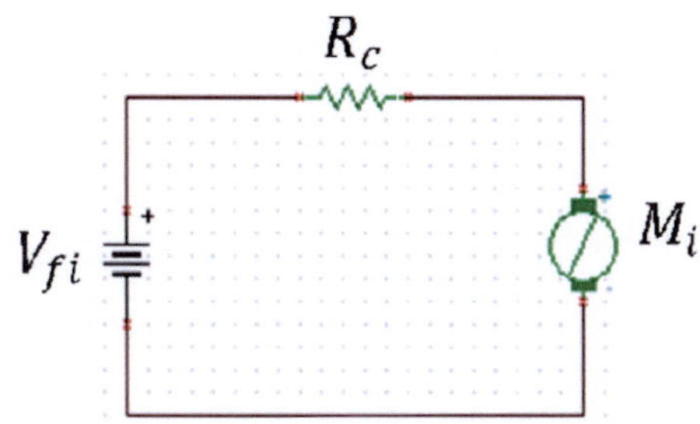

Fig. 3 Actuators circuit

where $i = 1, 2, 3$, $R_{ci} = R_{oi}$ is the resistance for the actuator circuit, i_{ci} is the current in the resistance R_{ci}.

Substituting Eq. (19) into Eq. (18) gives:

$$V_{f_i} = Rc_i ic_i + V_{m_1}, \tag{20}$$

and as the circuit of Fig. 3 is a series circuit, which is known that:

$$i_{ci} = i_{mi} = i_{vfi}, \tag{21}$$

where i_{ci} is the current in the resistance R_{c_i} for link i, $i_{ai} = i_{mi}$ is the current in the motor for link i, and i_{vfi} is the source current for link i.

Substituting Eq. (21) in Eq. (20) and solving V_{m_i} gives:

$$\begin{aligned} V_{f_i} &= Rc_i i_{mi} + V_{m_i}, \\ V_{m_i} &= V_{f_i} - Rc_i i_{ci}, \end{aligned} \tag{22}$$

From [12], it is known that:

$$\tau_{m_i} = k_{mi} i_{m_i}, \tag{23}$$

where k_{mi} is the constant torque for link i, i_{mi} is the current in the motor for link i, $\tau_{m_i} = \tau_i$ is the torque in the motor, and $V_{mi} = V_i$.

3.3 Sensor Dynamic Model

Figure 4 shows the sensor circuit, it is known as a voltage divider where the output voltage is time-varying depending of the measured position in each link; i.e., this circuit is used to obtain the displacements of each link in function its the motor angle $\dot{\theta}_i$, $i = 1, 2, 3$. It is important to know that:

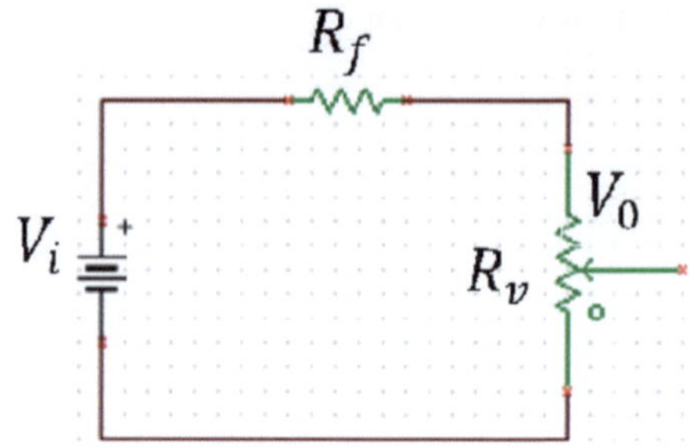

Fig. 4 Voltage divider sensor circuit

$$\begin{aligned}\theta_1 &= \frac{\theta_{1\,\max}}{x_{\max}} x_1, \\ \theta_2 &= \frac{\theta_{2\,\max}}{z_{2\,\max}} z_2, \\ \theta_3 &= \frac{\theta_{3\,\max}}{y_{3\,\max}} y_3,\end{aligned} \tag{24}$$

where the derivative of Eq. (24) gives:

$$\begin{aligned}\dot{\theta}_1 &= \frac{\theta_{1\,\max}}{x_{\max}} \dot{x}_1, \\ \dot{\theta}_2 &= \frac{\theta_{2\,\max}}{z_{2\,\max}} \dot{z}_2, \\ \dot{\theta}_3 &= \frac{\theta_{3\,\max}}{y_{3\,\max}} \dot{y}_3,\end{aligned} \tag{25}$$

where $\theta_{i\,\max}$ is the maximum angle of the potentiometer (radians), $x_{1\,\max}$, $y_{3\,\max}$, and $z_{2\,\max}$ are the distance in each link (m), and x_1, z_2, and y_3 are the displacements of each link.

From Fig. 4, the following is obtained:

$$\frac{V_{oi}}{V_{oi\,\max}} = \frac{\theta_i}{\theta_{i\,\max}}, \tag{26}$$

where θ_i is the angle of the motor of each link, $\theta_{i\,\max}$ is the maximum angle for the potentiometer of each link, V_{oi} is the measured voltage in the potentiometer, and $V_{oi\,\max}$ is the maximum measured voltage in the potentiometer.

4 Dynamic Model with Sensor and Actuator for a Transelevator

Substituting Eq. (23) into Eq. (13) for the structural dynamic model for the first link x gives:

$$m_{13}\ddot{x}_1 = k_{m1} i_{m1}, \tag{27}$$

Substituting Eqs. (17) and (22) into Eq. (16) for $i = 1$ gives:

$$L_1 \frac{d}{dt} i_{m1} + R_{m1} i_{m1} = V_{f1} - Rc_1 i_{m1} - k_{b1} \dot{\theta}_1, \tag{28}$$

Substituting Eq. (25) into Eq. (28) gives:

$$L_1 \frac{d}{dt} i_{m1} + (R_{m1} + R_{c1}) i_{m1} + k_{b1} \frac{\theta_{1\max}}{x_{\max}} \dot{x}_1 = V_{f1}, \tag{29}$$

From Eq. (26), the output for $i = 1$ is obtained as follows:

$$V_{o1} = \frac{V_{o1\max}}{\theta_{1\max}} \theta_1, \tag{30}$$

Equations (27), (29), and (30) describe the dynamic behavior of the first link. Substituting Eq. (23) into Eq. (14) for the second link z gives:

$$m_{23} \ddot{z}_2 + m_{23} g = k_{m2} i_{m2}, \tag{31}$$

Substituting Eqs. (17) and (22) into Eq. (16) for $i = 2$ gives:

$$L_2 \frac{d}{dt} i_{m2} + R_{m2} i_{m2} = V_{f2} - Rc_2 i_{m2} - k_{b2} \dot{\theta}_2, \tag{32}$$

Substituting Eq. (25) into Eq. (32) gives:

$$L_2 \frac{d}{dt} i_{m2} + (R_{m2} + R_{c2}) i_{m2} + k_{b2} \frac{\theta_{2\max}}{z_{\max}} \dot{z}_2 = V_{f2}, \tag{33}$$

From Eq. (26), the output for $i = 2$ is obtained as follows:

$$V_{o2} = \frac{V_{o2\max}}{\theta_{2\max}} \theta_2, \tag{34}$$

Equations (31), (33), and (34) describe the dynamic behavior of the second link z.

Substituting Eq. (23) into Eq. (15) and analyzing the model dynamic for the third link gives:

$$m_3 \ddot{y}_3 = k_{m3} i_{m3}, \tag{35}$$

Substituting Eqs. (17) and (22) into Eq. (16) for $i = 3$ gives:

$$L_3 \frac{d}{dt} i_{m3} + R_{m3} i_{m3} = V_{f3} - Rc_3 i_{m3} - k_{b3} \dot{\theta}_3, \tag{36}$$

Substituting Eq. (25) into Eq. (36) gives:

$$L_3\frac{d}{dt}i_{m3} + (R_{m3} + R_{c3})i_{m3} + k_{b3}\frac{\theta_{3\max}}{y_{\max}}\dot{y}_3 = V_{f3}, \tag{37}$$

From Eq. (26), the output for $i = 3$ is obtained as follows:

$$V_{o3} = \frac{V_{o3\max}}{\theta_{3\max}}\theta_3, \tag{38}$$

Equations (35), (37), and (38) describe the dynamic behavior of the third link y.

Let us define the parameters $V_{oi\max} = \text{constant}$, $R_{ci} = \text{constant}$, $R_{mi} = \text{constant}$, $\theta_{i\max} = \text{constant}$, $x_{\max} = \text{constant}$, $z_{\max} = \text{constant}$, $y_{\max} = \text{constant}$, the inputs U_i, the states X_j and the outputs Y_i as follows:

$$\begin{aligned}
&U_1 = V_{f_1}, U_2 = V_{f_2}, U_3 = V_{f_3},\\
&X_1 = x_1, X_2 = \dot{x}_1, X_3 = i_{m1},\\
&X_4 = z_2, X_5 = \dot{z}_2, X_6 = i_{m2},\\
&X_7 = y_3, X_8 = \dot{y}_3, X_9 = i_{m3},\\
&Y_1 = V_{o1}, Y_2 = V_{o2}, Y_3 = V_{o3},
\end{aligned} \tag{39}$$

where $i = 1, 2, 3$, $j = \overline{1, 9}$.

Substituting the inputs, the states, and the outputs of Eq. (39) into Eqs. (27), (29) (30), (31), (33), (34), (35), (37), and (38) yields:

$$\dot{X}_1 = X_2, \tag{40}$$

$$\dot{X}_2 = \frac{k_{m1}}{m_{13}}X_3, \tag{41}$$

$$\dot{X}_3 = -\frac{k_{b1}\theta_{1\max}}{L_1 x_{\max}}X_2 - \frac{(R_{m1} + R_{c1})}{L_1}X_3 + \frac{1}{L_1}u_1, \tag{42}$$

$$\dot{X}_4 = X_5, \tag{43}$$

$$\dot{X}_5 = \frac{k_{m2}}{m_{23}}X_6 - g, \tag{44}$$

$$\dot{X}_6 = -\frac{k_{b2}\theta_{2\max}}{L_2 z_{\max}}X_5 - \frac{(R_{m2} + R_{c2})}{L_2}X_6 + \frac{1}{L_2}u_2, \tag{45}$$

$$\dot{X}_7 = X_8, \tag{46}$$

$$\dot{X}_8 = \frac{k_{m3}}{m_3} X_9, \tag{47}$$

$$\dot{X}_9 = -\frac{k_{b3}\theta_{3\max}}{L_2 y_{\max}} X_8 - \frac{(R_{m3} + R_{c3})}{L_3} X_9 + \frac{1}{L_3} u_3, \tag{48}$$

$$Y_1 = \frac{V_{o1\max}}{\theta_{1\max}} X_1, \tag{49}$$

$$Y_2 = \frac{V_{o2\max}}{\theta_{2\max}} X_4, \tag{50}$$

$$Y_3 = \frac{V_{o3\max}}{\theta_{3\max}} X_7, \tag{51}$$

Equations (40)–(51) describe the combined dynamic behavior of the transelevator.

5 Validation of the Dynamic Model

To validate the dynamic model, the simulation results will be compared with the experimental results. The simulations are obtained using Matlab, while the experimental results are obtained using the prototype of Fig. 1. Figure 5 shows the sensor and actuator which are connected to the prototype of Fig. 1 to obtain the experimental results.

The dynamic model of the transelevator with sensor and actuator is described by Eqs. (40)–(51). Table 1 shows the parameters used in the simulation results and the experimental results.

Where V_1, V_2, and V_3 are the voltages of the circuit of Fig. 2, R_{m1}, R_{m2}, and R_{m3} are the values of motor resistance, L_1, L_2, and L_3 are the values of motor inductance, R_{c1}, R_{c2}, and R_{c3} are the values of resistance for the circuit of Fig. 3, k_{b1}, k_{b2}, and k_{b1} are the constants back emf of the motor, V_{f1}, V_{f2}, and V_{f3} are the motor supply voltages, k_{m1}, k_{m2}, and k_{m3} are the nominal torques of the motors, $\theta_{1\max}$, $\theta_{2\max}$, and $\theta_{3\max}$ are the maximum angles found by the potentiometer, $x_{\max}$, $z_{\max}$, and $y_{\max}$ are the maximum distances that run through the links, $m_{13} = m_1 + m_2 + m_3$, and $m_{23} = m_2 + m_3$, and m_3 are the link masses.

In this section, the root mean square error (RMSE) for the inputs and outputs is used to find the effectiveness of the proposed dynamic model, and is given as follows:

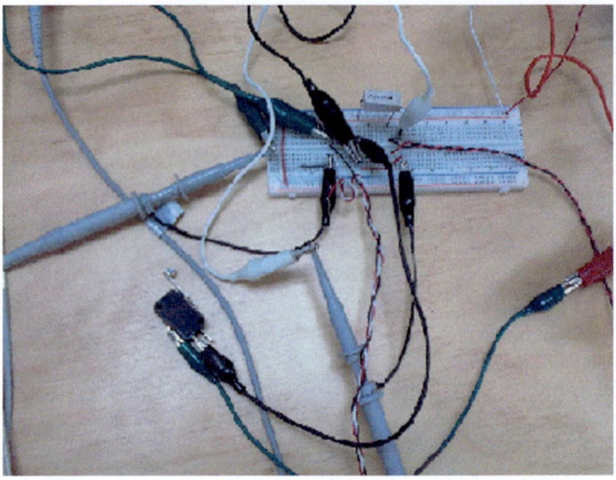

Fig. 5 Circuit of the sensor and the actuator

Table 1 Parameters of links 1, 2, and 3

Parameter	Parameter	Parameter
$V_1 = 5\,\text{V}$	$V_2 = 5\,\text{V}$	$V_3 = 5\,\text{V}$
$R_{m1} = 22.8\,\Omega$	$R_{m2} = 125.5\,\Omega$	$R_{m3} = 17\,\Omega$
$R_{c1} = 1\,\Omega$	$R_{c2} = 1\,\Omega$	$R_{c3} = 1\,\Omega$
$L_1 = 42.5\,\text{mH}$	$L_2 = 96.1\,\text{mH}$	$L_3 = 29.9\,\text{mH}$
$k_{m1} = 10\,\text{Nm/A}$	$k_{m2} = 1 \times 10^3\,\text{Nm/A}$	$k_{m3} = 1\,\text{Nm/A}$
$k_{b1} = 27.50\,\text{Vs/rad}$	$k_{b2} = 0.014\,\text{Vs/rad}$	$k_{b3} = 0.26\,\text{Vs/rad}$
$V_{f1} = 14\,\text{V}$	$V_{f2} = 10\,\text{V}$	$V_{f3} = 4\,\text{V}$
$V_{o1\,\max} = 2.36\,\text{V}$	$V_{o2\,\max} = 2.3\,\text{V}$	$V_{o3\,\max} = 2\,\text{V}$
$m_{13} = 2.9020\,\text{kg}$	$m_{23} = 0.5480\,\text{kg}$	$m_3 = 0.150\,\text{kg}$
$\theta_{1\,\max} = 12.56\,\text{rad}$	$\theta_{2\,\max} = 42.4115\,\text{rad}$	$\theta_{3\,\max} = 10.9956\,\text{rad}$
$x_{\max} = 0.45\,\text{m}$	$z_{\max} = 0.29\,\text{m}$	$y_{\max} = 0.23\,\text{m}$

$$RMSE = \left(\frac{1}{T} \int_0^T e^2 d\tau \right)^{\frac{1}{2}}, \tag{52}$$

where $e^2 = e_u^2 = (U_{1r} - U_1)^2 + (U_{2r} - U_2)^2 + (U_{3r} - U_3)^2$, or $e^2 = e_y^2 = (Y_{1r} - Y_1)^2 + (Y_{2r} - Y_2)^2 + (Y_{3r} - Y_3)^2$, U_{ir} and Y_{ir} are the real data of U_i and Y_i, respectively.

Figure 6 shows the simulation and the experiment of the input voltage and the output voltage, denoted as dynamic model and real data, respectively.

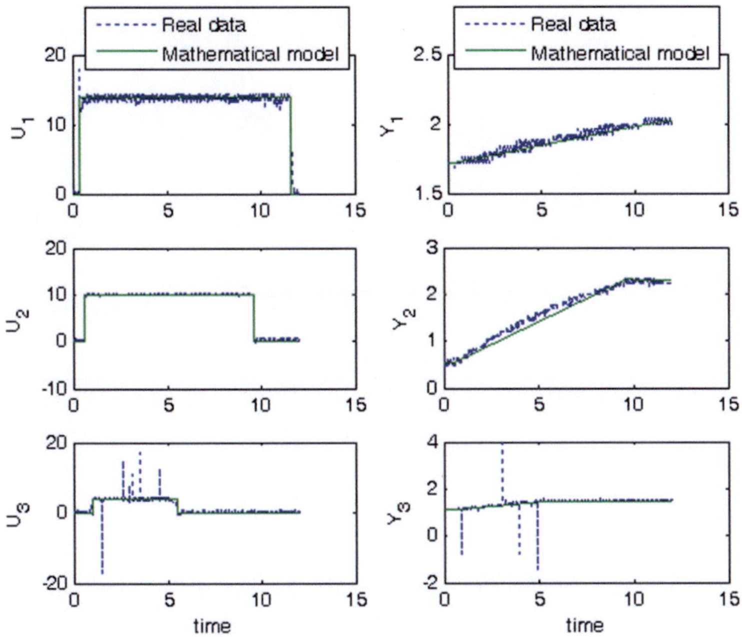

Fig. 6 Comparison results from simulation and experiment

From Fig. 6, it can be seen that both results are almost equal, for the inputs are 14 V for U_1 and U_{1r}, 10 V for U_2 and U_{2r}, and 4 V for U_3 and U_{3r}, respectively, and for the output are 2.0216 V for Y_1 and Y_{1r}, 2.2796 V for Y_2 and Y_{2r}, and 1.4921 V for Y_3 and Y_{3r}, respectively.

The error of the input $U_{ir} - U_i$ and the output $Y_{ir} - Y_i$ denoted as U_{ei} and Y_{ei}, respectively, are shown in Fig. 7.

From Fig. 7, it can be observed that both results are almost equal.

The simulation results for the states X_j are shown in Fig. 8.

Figure 8 shows the states X_1, X_4, and X_7 as the displacements x_1, z_2, and y_3, the states X_2, X_5, and X_8 as the velocities of the displacements $\dot{x}_1$, $\dot{z}_2$, and $\dot{y}_3$, and the states X_3, X_5, and X_9 as the armature current in the motors i_1, i_2, and i_3.

Table 2 shows the RMSE using Eq. (52) for the errors $e^2 = e_u^2$, or $e^2 = e_y^2$, using the dynamic model described by Eqs. (40)–(51).

In Table 2, it is shown that the dynamic model is a good approximation of the real process because the RMSEs are near to zero.

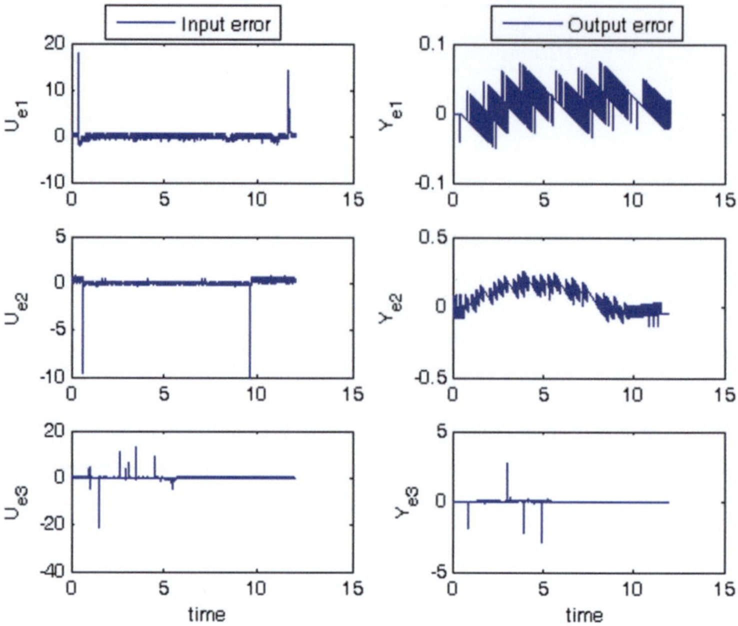

Fig. 7 Error results from simulation and experiment

6 Stability Analysis

This section presents the stability of the proposed dynamic model.

The dynamic model of Eqs. (40)–(51) can be rewritten as follows:

$$\begin{aligned} \dot{X} &= AX + BU + F, \\ Y &= CX, \end{aligned} \tag{53}$$

where:

$$A = \begin{bmatrix} 0 & 1 & 0 & 0 & 0 & 0 & 0 & 0 & 0 \\ 0 & 0 & \frac{k_{m1}}{m_{13}} & 0 & 0 & 0 & 0 & 0 & 0 \\ 0 & -\frac{k_{b1}\theta_{1\max}}{L_1 x_{\max}} & -\frac{(R_{m1}+R_{c1})}{L_1} & 0 & 0 & 0 & 0 & 0 & 0 \\ 0 & 0 & 0 & 0 & 1 & 0 & 0 & 0 & 0 \\ 0 & 0 & 0 & 0 & 0 & \frac{k_{m2}}{m_{23}} & 0 & 0 & 0 \\ 0 & 0 & 0 & 0 & -\frac{k_{b2}\theta_{2\max}}{L_2 z_{\max}} & -\frac{(R_{m2}+R_{c2})}{L_2} & 0 & 0 & 0 \\ 0 & 0 & 0 & 0 & 0 & 0 & 0 & 1 & 0 \\ 0 & 0 & 0 & 0 & 0 & 0 & 0 & 0 & \frac{k_{m3}}{m_3} \\ 0 & 0 & 0 & 0 & 0 & 0 & 0 & -\frac{k_{b3}\theta_{3\max}}{L_2 y_{\max}} & -\frac{(R_{m3}+R_{c3})}{L_3} \end{bmatrix},$$

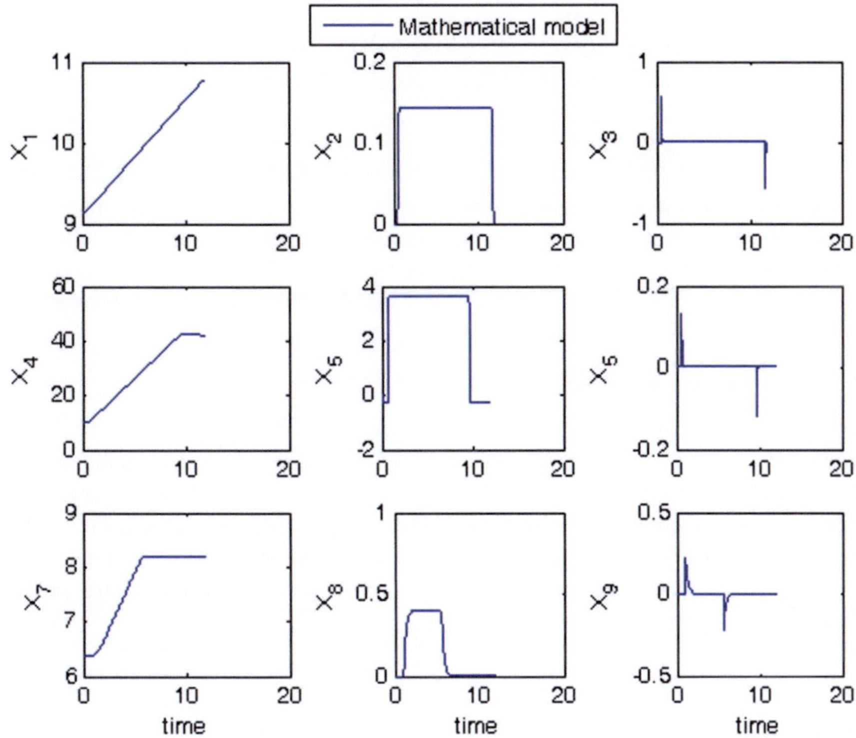

Fig. 8 Simulation results for the states

Table 2 RMSE for the errors

	RMSE
e_u^2	0.6553
e_y^2	0.0080

$$
\begin{aligned}
B &= \begin{bmatrix} 0\,0\,\frac{1}{L_1}\,0\,0\,\frac{1}{L_{21}}\,0\,0\,\frac{1}{L_3} \end{bmatrix}^T, \\
F &= \begin{bmatrix} 0\,0\,0\,0\,-g\,0\,0\,0\,0 \end{bmatrix}^T, \\
C &= \begin{bmatrix} \frac{V_{o1\max}}{\theta_{1\max}} & 0\,0 & 0 & 0\,0 & 0 & 0\,0 \\ 0 & 0\,0 & \frac{V_{o2\max}}{\theta_{2\max}} & 0\,0 & 0 & 0\,0 \\ 0 & 0\,0 & 0 & 0\,0 & \frac{V_{o3\max}}{\theta_{3\max}} & 0\,0 \end{bmatrix},
\end{aligned} \tag{54}
$$

Since F is only a constant element, the system (53) is considered as a linear system. Using the values in Table 1, the stability of the proposed dynamic model is obtained as follows:

$$\det(sI - A) = 0,$$
$$\Longrightarrow 7056 \times 10^{12}s^3 + 1.7440 \times 10^{12}s^4 + 6.7166 \times 10^{10}s^5 \quad (55)$$
$$+6.1353 \times 10^8 s^6 + 1.9706 \times 10^6 s^7 + 2478.3\, s^8 + s^9 = 0,$$

The roots of the polynomial are $s = -337.37 + 285.77i, s = -337.37 - 285.77i$, $s = 103.34 + 167.10i$, $s = 103.34 - 167.10i$, $s = -1279.4$, $s = -730.88$, $s = 0$, $s = 0$, and $s = 0$; the above elements are the system eigenvalues. Since not all the real parts of the eigenvalues are negative, the proposed dynamic model is not guaranteed to be stable.

7 Concluding Remarks

In this chapter, the combined dynamic model for a transelevator was obtained. The proposed dynamic model was validated with real measures where the proposed approach gave a good approximation of the real process. In addition, the stability analysis was presented where the aforementioned model was not guaranteed to be stable. As a future research, an observer, a control, or an identifier will be applied for the proposed dynamic model.

References

1. D.J. Christensen, J. Campbell, K. Stoy, Anatomy-based organization of morphology and control in self-reconfigurable modular robots. Neural Comput. Appl. **19**, 787–805 (2010)
2. J.J. Rubio, E. Garcia, J. Pacheco, Trajectory planning and collisions detector for robotic arms. Neural Comput. Appl. **21**, 2105–2114 (2012)
3. J. Bachrach, J. Beal, J. McLurkin, Composable continuous-space programs for robotic swarms. Neural Comput. Appl. **19**, 825–847 (2010)
4. C. Chen, Y. Inoue, K. Shibata, Identification of a golf swing robot using soft computing approach. Neural Comput. Appl. **20**, 729–740 (2011)
5. I. Villaverde, M. Graña, Neuro-evolutionary mobile robot egomotion estimation with a 3D ToF camera. Neural Comput. Appl. **20**, 345–354 (2011)
6. H. Celikkanat, E. Sahin, Steering self-organized robot flocks through externally guided individuals. Neural Comput. Appl. **19**, 849–865 (2010)
7. H. Chaoui, P. Sicard, Adaptive Lyapunov-based neural network sensorless control of permanent magnet synchronous machines. Neural Comput. Appl. **20**, 717–727 (2011)
8. C.-H. Chiu, Self-tuning output recurrent cerebellar model articulation controller for a wheeled inverted pendulum control. Neural Comput. Appl. **19**, 1153–1164 (2010)
9. W.-P. Lee, T.-H. Yang, Combining GRN modeling and demonstration-based programming for robot control. Neural Comput. Appl. **20**, 909–921 (2011)
10. Y. Wu, F. Sun, J. Zheng, Q. Song, A robust training algorithm of discrete-time MIMO RNN and application in fault tolerant control of robotic system. Neural Comput. Appl. **19**, 1013–1027 (2010)
11. F.L. Lewis, D.M. Dawson, C.T. Abdallah, *Control of Robot Manipulators, Theory and Practice* (2004). ISBN: 0-8247-4072-6
12. M.W. Spong, S. Hutchinson, M. Vidyasagar, *Robot Modeling and Control* (John Wiley & Sons, 2006). ISBN-13: 978-0-471-64990-8

Dynamic Model with Sensor and Actuator for an Articulated Robotic Arm

Abstract In this chapter, the dynamic model with sensor and actuator for the articulated robotic arm is obtained by using the combination of the structural, the sensor and the actuator dynamic models. The proposed approach is validated comparing the simulation results against the experimental results.

1 Introduction

The structural dynamic model is used for the control applications; however, when a system is controlled, a sensor and an actuator are required. The research on the robotic arms is classified into three kinds: the trajectory planning [1, 2], the position estimation [3–5], and the control [6–10].

The trajectory planning of a robotic arm has the objective to provide the best trajectory of the robotic arm from an initial point to a final point. In [1], they address the challenge of realizing full-body behaviors in scalable modular robots. In [2], the trajectories planning and a collisions detector for robotic arms are presented.

The position estimation is to estimate the parameters of the position and the orientation using other parameters such as are the parameters of an image, an identifier or an observer can be used for the position estimation. In [3], they show that spatial computing language (proto) can be applied to multi-mobile-robot systems with an actuator that turns a vector field into device motion. In [4], the identification of a golf swing robot based on four kinds of soft computing methods is investigated. An innovative neuro-evolutionary approach for mobile robot ego-motion estimation with a 3D camera is proposed in [5].

The control has the objective that the robotic system has to follow a desired trajectory. In [6], they study how a self-organized mobile robot flock can be steered toward a desired direction through externally guiding some of its members. An adaptive neural network sensor-less control scheme for machines is introduced in [7]. In [8], a model-free self-tuning output recurrent cerebellar model articulation controller to control an inverted pendulum is investigated. A network structure develop a biologically plausible gene regulatory networks model for robot control is adopted by [9]. In

J. de J. Rubio et al., *Dynamic Models of Energy, Robotic, and Biological Systems*,
https://doi.org/10.1007/978-3-031-85438-5_6

[10], a robust training algorithm of multi-input multi-output recurrent neural network and its application in the fault tolerant control of a robotic system are investigated.

For the trajectory planning, the position estimation, or the control, the dynamic models help to obtain the objective, e.g., it is necessary to obtain a system dynamic model or to obtain the measure of all the system parameters. It is less expensive to obtain a system dynamic model than to get the measure of all the system parameters.

In most of the aforementioned cases only the structural dynamic model is used, but when a system is controlled, a sensor and an actuator are required; therefore, this work aims to obtain the combined dynamic model for an articulated robotic arm.

This chapter is organized as follows. In Sect. 2, the method to obtain the structural dynamic model is detailed. In Sect. 3, the structural, sensor, and actuator dynamic models are obtained. In Sect. 4, the dynamic model with sensor and actuator for an articulated robotic arm is obtained. In Sect. 5, the validation of the proposed method is detailed. In Sect. 6, the conclusion and the future research are detailed.

2 Preliminaries

The Euler Lagragian method is used to obtain the structural dynamic model of the robotic arms. The first step of this method is to find the kinetic energy K_i, which is the addition of the speed of the motion and the rotation kinetic energy, and is given as follows:

$$K_i = \frac{1}{2} m_i v_i^2 + \frac{1}{2} J_i \sum_{i=1}^{n} \dot{\theta}_i^2, \tag{1}$$

where $_i = 1, \ldots, n$, n is the number of links, v_i is the speed of motion for the joint i, m_i is the center of mass of the joint i and the link i, if the joint i is rotational J_i is its inertia, θ_i is the angular position of the joint i, if the angular positions have different directions $\sum_{i=1}^{n} \dot{\theta}_i^2 = \dot{\theta}_1^2 + \dot{\theta}_2^2 + \cdots + \dot{\theta}_n^2$ or if the angular positions have the same direction $\sum_{i=1}^{n} \dot{\theta}_i^2 = \left(\dot{\theta}_1 + \dot{\theta}_2 + \cdots + \dot{\theta}_n\right)^2$, $v_i^2 = \dot{\overline{X}}_i^2 + \dot{\overline{Y}}_i^2 + \dot{\overline{Z}}_i^2$ where $\dot{\overline{X}}_i$, $\dot{\overline{Y}}_i$, and $\dot{\overline{Z}}_i$ are the derivatives of $\overline{X}_i$, $\overline{Y}_i$, and $\overline{Z}_i$, respectively, $\overline{X}_i$, $\overline{Y}_i$, and $\overline{Z}_i$ are the coordinates of the linear movement of the link i.

The second step is to find the potential energy, which is given as follows:

$$V_i = m_i g h_i, \tag{2}$$

where $_i \in 1, \ldots, n$, h_i is the height of the center of mass of the joint and the link i, and g is the gravity acceleration.

As the third step, the Lagrangian is obtained as follows:

$$L = \sum_{i=1}^{n} (K_i - V_i), \tag{3}$$

As the fourth step, the following equation is used to obtain each dynamic equation:

$$\frac{d}{dt}\frac{\partial L}{\partial \dot{q}_i} - \frac{\partial L}{\partial q_i} = \tau_i, \tag{4}$$

where $_i \in 1, \ldots, n, q_i = \theta_i$ for a rotation joint and $q_i = l_{ci}$ for a prismatic joint, and τ_i is the torque for a rotation joint or is the force for a prismatic joint.

Remark 1 The method to obtain the structural dynamic model of this chapter is different from others because they use the Jacobians, the inertia tensors, or the Christoffel symbols while in this chapter none of these methods is used. The above approach is similar with the introduced by [11, 12], with the difference that the first is for a cylindrical robotic arm and the second is for a transelevator, while this study considers the articulated robotic arm.

3 Dynamic Model of the Articulated Robotic Arm

3.1 Structural Dynamic Model

Figure 1 shows the prototype of the articulated robotic arm.

For the articulated robotic arm, Fig. 2 is considered.

From Fig. 2, the upper sight is given in Fig. 3.

From Fig. 2, the lateral sight is given in Fig. 4.

From the upper sight of Fig. 3, the first link produces a rotation around the $\overline{Z}_1$ axis, and the kinetic energy for joint 1 is as follows:

$$K_1 = \frac{1}{2} J_1 \dot{\theta}_1^2, \tag{5}$$

From the sight of Figs. 3 and 4, the parameters $\overline{X}_2$, $\overline{Y}_2$, and $\overline{Z}_2$ of Eq. (1) are as follows:

$$\begin{aligned} \overline{X}_2 &= l_{c2} C_2 C_1, \\ \overline{Y}_2 &= l_{c2} C_2 S_1, \\ \overline{Z}_2 &= l_{c2} S_2, \end{aligned} \tag{6}$$

Fig. 1 Articulated robotic arm

where $C_1 = \cos(\theta_1)$, $S_1 = \sin(\theta_1)$, $S_2 = \sin(\theta_2)$, $C_2 = \cos(\theta_2)$, and $l_{c2} = \frac{l_2}{2}$ is the length to the center of mass of the link and joint 2. Using Eqs. (2) and (6), the kinetic energy for joint 2 is as follows:

$$K_2 = \frac{1}{2} m_2 l_{c2}^2 C_2^2 \dot{\theta}_1^2 + \frac{1}{2} m_2 l_{c2}^2 \dot{\theta}_2^2 + \frac{1}{2} J_2 \left(\dot{\theta}_1^2 + \dot{\theta}_2^2 \right), \tag{7}$$

From the sight of Figs. 3 and 4, the parameters $\overline{X}_3$, $\overline{Y}_3$, and $\overline{Z}_3$ of Eq. (1) are as follows:

$$\begin{gathered} \overline{X}_3 = l_2 C_2 C_1 + l_{c3} C_{23} C_1, \\ \overline{Y}_3 = l_2 C_2 S_1 + l_{c3} C_{23} S_1, \\ \overline{Z}_3 = l_2 S_2 + l_{c3} S_{23}, \end{gathered} \tag{8}$$

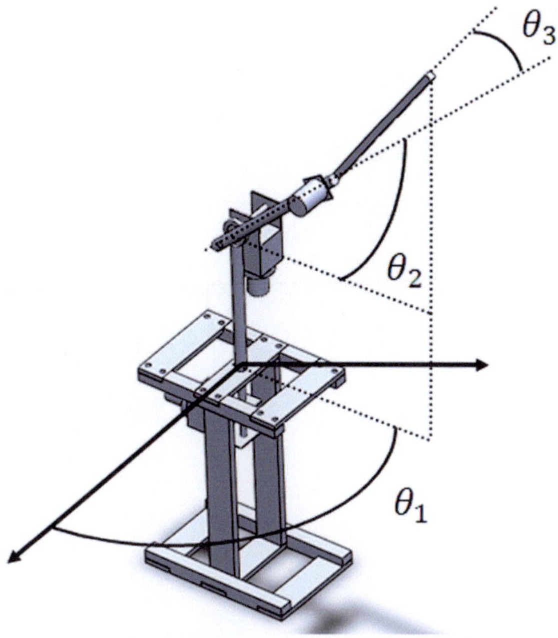

Fig. 2 Articulated robotic arm in SolidWorks

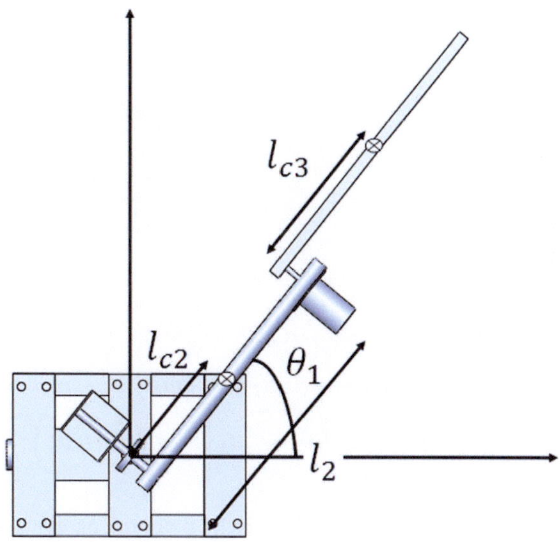

Fig. 3 Upper sight of the robot

where $C_{23} = \cos(\theta_2 + \theta_3)$, $S_{23} = \sin(\theta_2 + \theta_3)$, l_2 is the length to link 2, and $l_{c3} = \frac{l_3}{2}$ is the length to the center of mass of the link and joint 3. Using Eqs. (1) and (8), the kinetic energy for joint 3 is as follows:

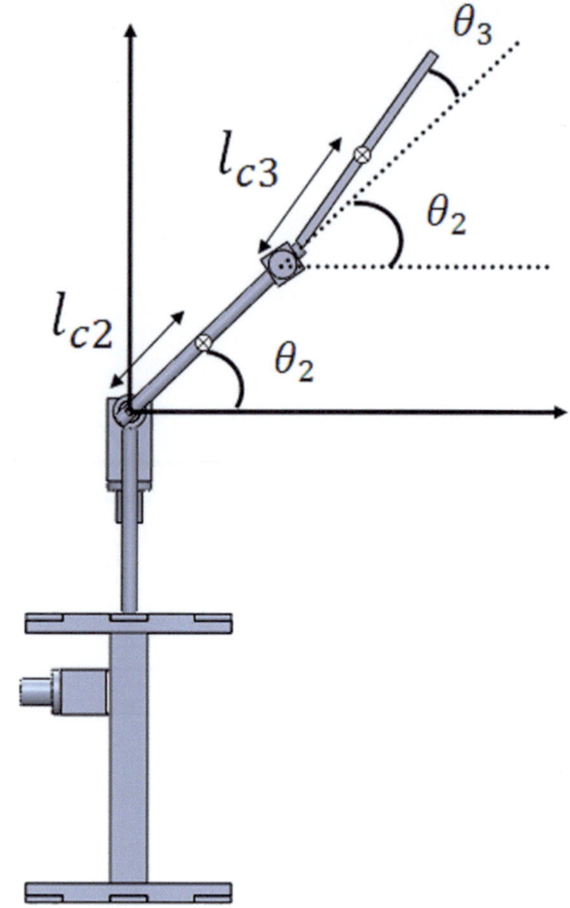

Fig. 4 Lateral sight of the robot

$$
\begin{aligned}
K_3 = {} & m_3 l_2 l_{c3} C_2 C_{23} \dot{\theta}_1^2 + \tfrac{1}{2} m_3 l_2^2 C_2^2 \dot{\theta}_1^2 + \tfrac{1}{2} m_3 l_{c3}^2 C_{23}^2 \dot{\theta}_1^2 + \tfrac{1}{2} m_3 l_2^2 \dot{\theta}_2^2 \\
& \tfrac{1}{2} m_3 l_{c3}^2 \dot{\theta}_2^2 + m_3 l_{c3}^2 \dot{\theta}_2 \dot{\theta}_3 + \tfrac{1}{2} m_3 l_{c3}^2 \dot{\theta}_3^2 + m_3 l_2 l_{c3} C_3 \dot{\theta}_2^2 \\
& + m_3 l_2 l_{c3} C_3 \dot{\theta}_2 \dot{\theta}_3 + \tfrac{1}{2} J_3 \left[\dot{\theta}_1^2 + \left(\dot{\theta}_2 + \dot{\theta}_3 \right)^2 \right],
\end{aligned}
\tag{9}
$$

From the lateral sight of Fig. 4, the potential energy for the three links is as follows:

$$
\begin{aligned}
V_1 &= m_1 g l_{c1}, \\
V_2 &= m_2 g \left(l_1 + l_{c2} S_2 \right), \\
V_3 &= m_3 g (l_1 + l_2 S_2 + l_{c3} S_{23}),
\end{aligned}
\tag{10}
$$

where l_{c1} is the length to the center of mass of the link and joint 1 and l_2 is the length to link 2. Substituting Eqs. (5)–(10) into Eq. (3) gives the Lagrangian as follows:

$$\begin{aligned}
L &= \tfrac{1}{2}J_{13}\dot{\theta}_1^2 + \tfrac{1}{2}\left[m_2 l_{c2}^2 C_2^2 + 2m_3 l_2 l_{c3} C_2 C_{23} + m_3 l_2^2 C_2^2 + m_3 l_{c3}^2 C_{23}^2\right]\dot{\theta}_1^2 \\
&+ \tfrac{1}{2}\left[J_{23} + m_3 l_2^2 + m_3 l_{c3}^2 + m_2 l_{c2}^2 + 2m_3 l_2 l_{c3} C_3\right]\dot{\theta}_2^2 \\
&+ \left[J_3 + m_3 l_{c3}^2 + m_3 l_2 l_{c3} C_3\right]\dot{\theta}_2\dot{\theta}_3 + \tfrac{1}{2}\left[m_3 l_{c3}^2 + J_3\right]\dot{\theta}_3^2 - m_1 g l_{c1} \\
&- m_2 g\left(l_1 + l_{c2} S_2\right) - m_3 g(l_1 + l_2 S_2 + l_{c3} S_{23}),
\end{aligned} \tag{11}$$

where $J_{13} = J_1 + J_2 + J_3$, $J_{23} = J_2 + J_3$. Using the Euler-Lagrange method of Eq. (4) in Eq. (11) for joint 1 gives:

$$\begin{aligned}
&\left[J_{13} + \left(m_2 l_{c2}^2 + m_3 l_2^2\right) C_2^2 + 2m_3 l_2 l_{c3} C_2 C_{23} + m_3 l_{c3}^2 C_{23}^2\right]\ddot{\theta}_1 \\
&+ \left[-2\left(m_2 l_{c2}^2 + m_3 l_2^2\right) S_2 C_2 - 2m_3 l_2 l_{c3} S_2 C_{23} - 2m_3 l_2 l_{c3} C_2 S_{23} - 2m_3 l_{c3}^2 S_{23} C_{23}\right]\dot{\theta}_1\dot{\theta}_2 \\
&+ \left[-2m_3 l_2 l_{c3} C_2 S_{23} - 2m_3 l_{c3}^2 S_{23} C_{23}\right]\dot{\theta}_1\dot{\theta}_3 = \tau_1,
\end{aligned} \tag{12}$$

where τ_1 is the torque needed to move link 1. Using the Euler-Lagrange method of Eq. (4) in Eq. (11) for joint 2 gives:

$$\begin{aligned}
&\left[J_{23} + m_3 l_2^2 + m_3 l_{c3}^2 C_2^2 + m_2 l_{c2}^2 + 2m_3 l_2 l_{c3} C_3\right]\ddot{\theta}_2 + \left[J_3 + m_3 l_{c3}^2 + m_3 l_2 l_{c3} C_3\right]\ddot{\theta}_3 \\
&- 2m_3 l_2 l_{c3} S_3 \dot{\theta}_2\dot{\theta}_3 - m_3 l_2 l_{c3} S_3 \dot{\theta}_3^2 + \left[m_2 l_{c2} + m_3 l_2\right] g C_2 + m_3 g l_{c3} C_{23} = \tau_2,
\end{aligned} \tag{13}$$

where τ_2 is the torque needed to move link 2. Using the Euler-Lagrange method of Eq. (4) in Eq. (11) for joint 3 gives:

$$\left[J_3 + m_3 l_{c3}^2 + m_3 l_2 l_{c3} C_3\right]\ddot{\theta}_2 + \left[J_3 + m_3 l_{c3}^2\right]\ddot{\theta}_3 - m_3 l_2 l_{c3} S_3 \dot{\theta}_2\dot{\theta}_3 + m_3 g l_{c3} C_{23} = \tau_3, \tag{14}$$

where τ_3 is the torque needed to move link 3.

The obtained structural dynamic model is given by Eqs. (12), (13), and (14).

Remark 2 The structural dynamic model of the articulated robotic arm of this chapter is different with the dynamic models presented by [13, 14] because [13, 14] do not consider the motion of the first link.

4 Actuator Dynamic Model

It is necessary to monitor and to perform over some variables to control an articulated robotic arm, so an actuator and a sensor are required.

Figure 5 is used to obtain the motor dynamic model of each link:

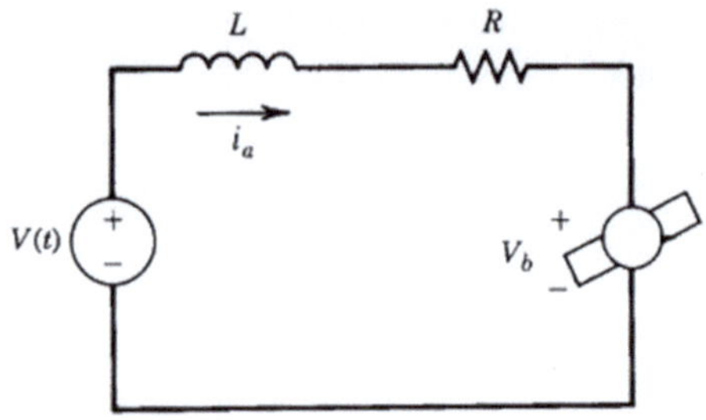

Fig. 5 Circuit of a motor controlled by DC

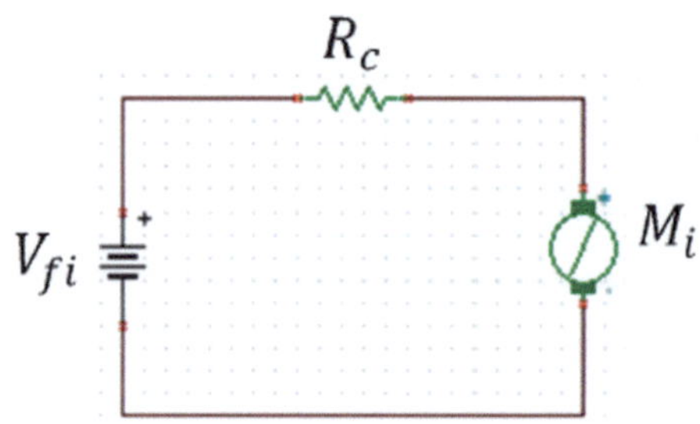

Fig. 6 Actuators circuit

$$L_i \frac{di_{ai}}{dt} + R_{mi} i_{ai} = V_i - V_{bi}, \tag{15}$$

where:

$$V_{bi} = K_{bi} \dot{\theta}_n \tag{16}$$

where $i = 1, 2, 3$, i_{ai} is the current in the motor for link i, L_i is the inductance of the motor for the link i, R_{mi} is the resistance of the motor for link i, V_i is the input voltage of the motor for link i, k_{bi} is the constant back emf of the motor for link i, and $\dot{\theta}_i$ is the speed of the angle of the motor of link i.

Figure 6 shows the actuators circuit; this circuit is used to obtain the current applied for the motors in each link i_{ai} as a function of the voltage of the motor V_i of Eq. (15).

From Fig. 6, the following is obtained:

$$V_{fi} = V_{Rci} + V_{mi}, \tag{17}$$

where V_{fi} is the input voltage for link i for the actuator circuit, V_{Rci} is the voltage in the resistance for link i for the actuator circuit, $V_{mi} = V_i$ is the input voltage of the motor for link i for the actuator circuit, it is known that:

$$V_{Rci} = Ro_i i_{ci}, \tag{18}$$

where $i = 1, 2, 3$, $Rc_i = Ro_i$ is the resistance for the actuator circuit, and i_{ci} is the current in the resistance Rc_i.

Substituting Eq. (18) into Eq. (17) gives:

$$V_{fi} = Rc_i i_{ci} + V_{mi}, \tag{19}$$

and as the circuit of Fig. 6 is a series circuit, it is known that:

$$i_{ci} = i_{mi} = i_{vfi}, \tag{20}$$

where i_{ci} is the current in the resistance Rc_i for link i, $i_{ai} = i_{mi}$ is the current in the motor for link i, and i_{vfi} is the source current for link i.

Substituting Eq. (20) into Eq. (19) and solving for V_{mi} gives:

$$\begin{aligned} V_{fi} &= Rc_i i_{mi} + V_{mi}, \\ V_{mi} &= V_{fi} - Rc_i i_{mi}, \end{aligned} \tag{21}$$

From [15], it is known that:

$$\tau_{mi} = k_{mi} i_{mi} - b_{mi}\dot{\theta}_i, \tag{22}$$

where k_{mi} is the torque constant for link i, i_{mi} is the current in the motor for link i, b_{mi} is a shock absorber, and $\tau_{mi} = \tau_i$ is the torque in the motor.

4.1 Sensor Dynamic Model

Figure 7 shows the sensors circuit; it is known as a voltage divider where the output voltage is time-varying depending of the measured position in each link. In other words, this circuit is used to obtain the displacements of each link in function its the motor its the motor angle $\dot{\theta}_i$, where $i = 1, 2, 3$, $V_{oi\,\max}$ is the maximum voltage for the sensors circuit for link i, V_{oi} is the output variable voltage for the sensors circuit for link i, R_{fi} is a constant resistance, and R_{vi} is a variable resistance.

Fig. 7 Sensors circuit

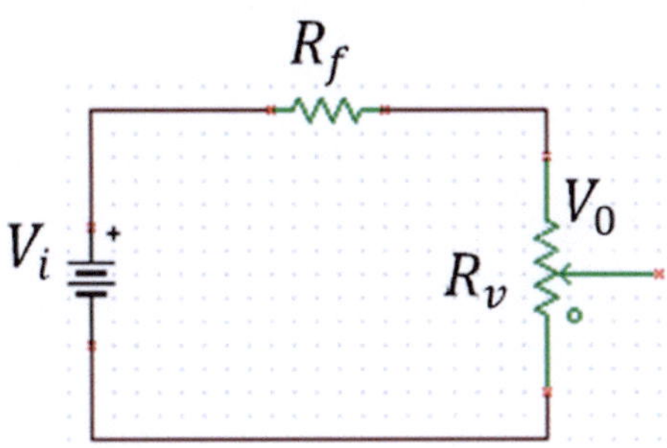

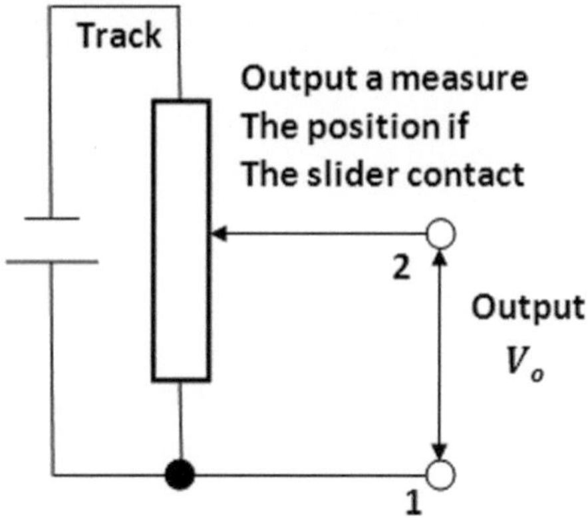

Fig. 8 Potentiometer as a sensor of position

A potentiometer consists of a resistance element with a sliding contact which can be moved over the length of the element [16] and connected as shown in Fig. 8, where $V_{oi\,\max}$ is a constant supply voltage, V_{oi} is the output voltage between terminals 1 and 2 and is a part of the input voltage, the part is depending on the ratio of the resistance R_{vi} between terminals 1 and 2 compared with the total resistance R of the entire length of the track across which the supply voltage.

From Fig. 7, the following is obtained:

$$\frac{V_{oi}}{V_{oi\,\max}} = \frac{\theta_i}{\theta_{i\,\max}}, \tag{23}$$

From Eq. (23), θ_i is the angle of the motor of each link, $\theta_{i\,\max}$ is the maximum angle of each link.

5 Dynamic Model with Sensor and Actuator for the Articulated Robotic Arm

Substituting Eq. (22) into Eq. (12) for the structural dynamic model for the first link θ_1 gives:

$$\begin{aligned}&\left[J_{13} + \left(m_2 l_{c2}^2 + m_3 l_2^2\right) C_2^2 + 2m_3 l_2 l_{c3} C_2 C_{23} + m_3 l_{c3}^2 C_{23}^2\right] \ddot{\theta}_1 \\ &+ \left[-2\left(m_2 l_{c2}^2 + m_3 l_2^2\right) S_2 C_2 - 2m_3 l_2 l_{c3} S_2 C_{23} - 2m_3 l_2 l_{c3} C_2 S_{23} - 2m_3 l_{c3}^2 S_{23} C_{23}\right] \dot{\theta}_1 \dot{\theta}_2 \\ &+ \left[-2m_3 l_2 l_{c3} C_2 S_{23} - 2m_3 l_{c3}^2 S_{23} C_{23}\right] \dot{\theta}_1 \dot{\theta}_3 = k_{m1} i_{m1} - b_{m1} \dot{\theta}_1,\end{aligned} \tag{24}$$

Substituting Eq. (16) into Eq. (15) for $i = 1$ gives:

$$L_1 \frac{d}{dt} i_{m1} + R_{m1} i_{m1} = V_{m1} - k_{b1} \dot{\theta}_1, \tag{25}$$

Substituting Eq. (21) into Eq. (25) for $i = 1$ gives:

$$L_1 \frac{d}{dt} i_{m1} + (R_{m1} + R_{c1}) i_{m1} + k_{b1} \dot{\theta}_1 = V_{f1}, \tag{26}$$

From Eq. (23), the output for $i = 1$ is obtained as follows:

$$V_{o1} = \frac{V_{o1\max}}{\theta_{1\max}} \theta_1, \tag{27}$$

Equations (24), (26), and (27) describe the dynamic behavior of the first link θ_1. Substituting Eq. (22) into Eq. (13) for the second link θ_2 gives:

$$\left[J_{23} + m_3 l_2^2 + m_3 l_{c3}^2 C_2^2 + m_2 l_{c2}^2 + 2 m_3 l_2 l_{c3} C_3\right] \ddot{\theta}_2 + \left[J_3 + m_3 l_{c3}^2 + m_3 l_2 l_{c3} C_3\right] \ddot{\theta}_3$$
$$- 2 m_3 l_2 l_{c3} S_3 \dot{\theta}_2 \dot{\theta}_3 - m_3 l_2 l_{c3} S_3 \dot{\theta}_3^2 + [m_2 l_{c2} + m_3 l_2] g C_2 + m_3 g l_{c3} C_{23} = k_{m2} i_{m2} - b_{m2} \dot{\theta}_2, \tag{28}$$

Substituting Eq. (16) into Eq. (15) for $i = 2$ gives:

$$L_2 \frac{d}{dt} i_{m2} + R_{m2} i_{m2} = V_{m2} - k_{b2} \dot{\theta}_2, \tag{29}$$

Substituting Eq. (21) into Eq. (25) for $i = 2$ gives:

$$L_2 \frac{d}{dt} i_{m2} + (R_{m2} + R_{c2}) i_{m2} + k_{b2} \dot{\theta}_2 = V_{f2}, \tag{30}$$

From Eq. (23), the output for $i = 2$ is obtained as follows:

$$V_{o2} = \frac{V_{o2\max}}{\theta_{2\max}} \theta_2, \tag{31}$$

Equations (28), (30), and (31) describe the dynamic behavior of the second link θ_2.

Substituting Eq. (22) into Eq. (14) for the third link θ_3 gives:

$$\left[J_3 + m_3 l_{c3}^2 + m_3 l_2 l_{c3} C_3\right] \ddot{\theta}_2 + \left[J_3 + m_3 l_{c3}^2\right] \ddot{\theta}_3 - m_3 l_2 l_{c3} S_3 \dot{\theta}_2 \dot{\theta}_3 + m_3 g l_{c3} C_{23} = k_{m3} i_{m3} - b_{m3} \dot{\theta}_3, \tag{32}$$

Substituting Eq. (16) into Eq. (15) for $i = 3$ gives:

$$L_3 \frac{d}{dt} i_{m3} + R_{m3} i_{m3} = V_{m3} - k_{b3} \dot{\theta}_3, \tag{33}$$

Substituting Eq. (21) into Eq. (25) for $i = 3$ gives:

$$L_3 \frac{d}{dt} i_{m3} + (R_{m3} + R_{c3}) i_{m3} + k_{b3} \dot{\theta}_3 = V_{f3}, \tag{34}$$

From Eq. (23), it is obtained the output for $i = 3$ as follows:

$$V_{o3} = \frac{V_{o3\max}}{\theta_{3\max}} \theta_3, \tag{35}$$

Equations (32), (34), and (35) describe the dynamic behavior of the third link θ_3.

Let us define the parameters $V_{oi\max} =$ constant, $R_{ci} =$ constant, $R_{mi} =$ constant, $\theta_{i\max} =$ constant, the inputs U_i, the states X_j and the outputs Y_i as follows:

$$\begin{aligned}
&U_1 = V_{f1}, U_2 = V_{f2}, U_3 = V_{f3},\\
&X_1 = \theta_1, X_2 = \dot{\theta}_1, X_3 = i_{m1},\\
&X_4 = \theta_2, X_5 = \dot{\theta}_2, X_6 = i_{m2},\\
&X_7 = \theta_3, X_8 = \dot{\theta}_3, X_9 = i_{m3},\\
&Y_1 = V_{o1}, Y_2 = V_{o2}, Y_3 = V_{o3},
\end{aligned} \tag{36}$$

where $i = 1, 2, 3$, and $j = \overline{1, 9}$.

Substituting the inputs, the states, and the outputs of Eq. (36) into Eqs. (24), (26), (27), (28), (30), (31), (32), (34), and (35) yields:

$$\dot{X}_1 = X_2, \tag{37}$$

$$\begin{aligned}
\dot{X}_2 = &\frac{k_{m1} X_3 - b_{m1} X_2 - \left[2 m_3 l_2 l_{c3} C_2 S_{23} + 2 m_3 l_{c3}^2 S_{23} C_{23}\right] X_2 X_8}{\left[J_{13} + \left(m_2 l_{c2}^2 + m_3 l_2^2\right) C_2^2 + 2 m_3 l_2 l_{c3} C_2 C_{23} + m_3 l_{c3}^2 C_{23}^2\right]}\\
&\frac{+\left[2\left(m_2 l_{c2}^2 + m_3 l_2^2\right) S_2 C_2 + 2 m_3 l_2 l_{c3} S_2 C_{23} + 2 m_3 l_2 l_{c3} C_2 S_{23} + 2 m_3 l_{c3}^2 S_{23} C_{23}\right] X_2 X_5}{\left[J_{13} + \left(m_2 l_{c2}^2 + m_3 l_2^2\right) C_2^2 + 2 m_3 l_2 l_{c3} C_2 C_{23} + m_3 l_{c3}^2 C_{23}^2\right]},
\end{aligned} \tag{38}$$

$$\dot{X}_3 = -\frac{k_{b1}}{L_1} X_2 - \frac{(R_{m1} + R_{c1})}{L_1} X_3 + \frac{1}{L_1} U_1, \tag{39}$$

$$\dot{X}_4 = X_5, \tag{40}$$

$$\dot{X}_5 = \frac{k_{m2}X_6 - b_{m2}X_5 - \left[J_3 + m_3 l_{c3}^2 + m_3 l_2 l_{c3} C_3\right] \dot{X}_8}{\left[J_{23} + m_3 l_2^2 + m_3 l_{c3}^2 C_2^2 + m_2 l_{c2}^2 + 2m_3 l_2 l_{c3} C_3\right]} \frac{+2m_3 l_2 l_{c3} S_3 X_5 X_8 + m_3 l_2 l_{c3} S_3 X_8^2 - [m_2 l_{c2} + m_3 l_2] g C_2 - m_3 g l_{c3} C_{23}}{\left[J_{23} + m_3 l_2^2 + m_3 l_{c3}^2 C_2^2 + m_2 l_{c2}^2 + 2m_3 l_2 l_{c3} C_3\right]}, \tag{41}$$

$$\dot{X}_6 = -\frac{k_{b2}}{L_2} X_5 - \frac{(R_{m2} + R_{c2})}{L_2} X_6 + \frac{1}{L_2} U_2, \tag{42}$$

$$\dot{X}_7 = X_8, \tag{43}$$

$$\dot{X}_8 = \frac{k_{m3}X_9 - b_{m3}X_8 - \left[J_3 + m_3 l_{c3}^2 + m_3 l_2 l_{c3} C_3\right] \dot{X}_5 + m_3 l_2 l_{c3} S_3 X_5 X_8 - m_3 g l_{c3} C_{23}}{\left[J_3 + m_3 l_{c3}^2\right]}, \tag{44}$$

$$\dot{X}_9 = -\frac{k_{b3}}{L_3} X_8 - \frac{(R_{m3} + R_{c3})}{L3} X_9 + \frac{1}{L_3} U_3, \tag{45}$$

$$Y_1 = \frac{V_{o1\,\max}}{\theta_{1\,\max}} X_1, \tag{46}$$

$$Y_2 = \frac{V_{o2\,\max}}{\theta_{2\,\max}} X_4, \tag{47}$$

$$Y_3 = \frac{V_{o3\,\max}}{\theta_{3\,\max}} X_7, \tag{48}$$

where $S_4 = \sin(X_4)$, $C_4 = \cos(X_4)$, $S_{47} = \sin(X_4 + X_7)$, $C_{47} = \cos(X_4 + X_7)$. Equations (37)–(48) describe the dynamic behavior of the articulated robotic arm with sensor and actuator.

6 Validation of the Proposed Dynamic Model

To validate the dynamic model, the simulation results will be compared with the experimental results. The simulations are obtained using Matlab, while the experimental results are obtained using the prototype of Fig. 1. Figure 9 shows the sensor and actuator which are connected to the prototype of Fig. 1 to obtain the experimental results.

Fig. 9 Circuit of the sensor and the actuator

Table 1 Parameters of links 1, 2, and 3

Parameter	Parameter	Parameter
$V_1 = 5\,\text{V}$	$V_2 = 5\,\text{V}$	$V_3 = 5\,\text{V}$
$R_{m1} = 22.8\,\Omega$	$R_{m2} = 17\,\Omega$	$R_{m3} = 17\,\Omega$
$R_{c1} = 1\,\Omega$	$R_{c2} = 1\,\Omega$	$R_{c3} = 1\,\Omega$
$L_1 = 98\,\text{mH}$	$L_2 = 98\,\text{mH}$	$L_3 = 30\,\text{mH}$
$k_{m1} = 8.1\,\text{Nm/A}$	$k_{m2} = 150\,\text{Nm/A}$	$k_{m3} = 10\,\text{Nm/A}$
$k_{b1} = 8\,\text{Vs/rad}$	$k_{b2} = 9\text{Vs/rad}$	$k_{b3} = 24\,\text{Vs/rad}$
$b_{m1} = 1\,\text{Kgm}^2\,\text{rad/s}$	$b_{m2} = 15\,\text{Kgm}^2\,\text{rad/s}$	$b_{m3} = 18\,\text{Kgm}^2\,\text{rad/s}$
$V_{f1} = 12\,\text{V}$	$V_{f2} = 12\,\text{V}$	$V_{f3} = 15\,\text{V}$
$V_{o1\,\max} = 2.5\,\text{V}$	$V_{o2\,\max} = 2.5\,\text{V}$	$V_{o3\,\max} = 2.5\,\text{V}$
$\theta_{1\,\max} = 2\pi\,\text{rad}$	$\theta_{2\,\max} = \pi\,\text{rad}$	$\theta_{3\,\max} = \frac{\pi}{2}\,\text{rad}$
$J_{13} = 0.04624\,\text{kgm}^2$	$J_{23} = 0.02545\,\text{kgm}^2$	$J_3 = 0.01273\,\text{kgm}^2$
	$m_2 = 0.34\,\text{kg}$	$m_3 = 0.24\,\text{kg}$
	$l_2 = 0.293\,\text{m}$	$l_3 = 0.28\,\text{m}$

The dynamic model of the articulated robotic arm with sensor and actuator is described by Eqs. (37)–(48). Table 1 shows the parameters used in the simulation results and the experimental results.

Where V_1, V_2, and V_3 are the voltages of the circuit of Fig. 7, R_{m1}, R_{m2}, and R_{m3} are the values of motor resistance, L_{m1}, L_{m2}, and L_{m3} are the values of motor inductance, R_{c1}, R_{c2}, and R_{c3} are the values of resistance for the circuit of Fig. 6, k_{b1}, k_{b2}, and

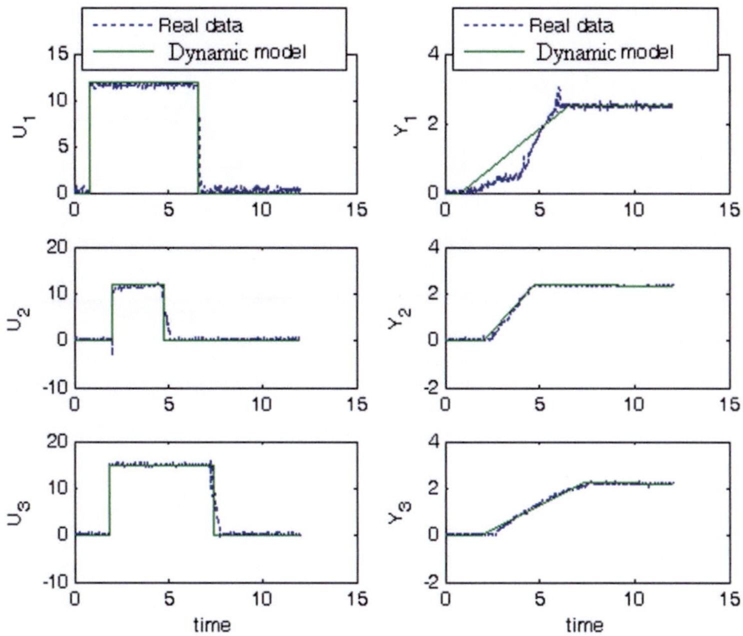

Fig. 10 Comparison results from simulation and experiment

k_{b1} are the constants back emf of the motor, V_{f1}, V_{f2}, and V_{f3} are the motor supply voltages, k_{m1}, k_{m2}, and k_{m3} are the torque constants of the motors, $\theta_{1\max}$, $\theta_{2\max}$, and $\theta_{3\max}$ are the maximum angles found by the potentiometer, $m_{13} = m_1 + m_2 + m_3$, $m_{23} = m_2 + m_3$, and m_3 are the link masses, $J_{13} = J_1 + J_2 + J_3$, $J_{23} = J_2 + J_3$, J_3 are the inertia, l_2 and l_3 are the length of the links, and $l_{c2} = \frac{l_2}{2}$ and $l_{c3} = \frac{l_3}{2}$ are the length to the center of mass of the links.

In this section, the root mean square error (RMSE) for the inputs and outputs is used to find the effectiveness of the proposed dynamic model, and is given as follows:

$$RMSE = \left(\frac{1}{T} \int_{0}^{T} e^2 d\tau \right)^{\frac{1}{2}}, \tag{49}$$

where $e^2 = e_u^2 = (U_{1r} - U_1)^2 + (U_{2r} - U_2)^2 + (U_{3r} - U_3)^2$, or $e^2 = e_y^2 = (Y_{1r} - Y_1)^2 + (Y_{2r} - Y_2)^2 + (Y_{3r} - Y_3)^2$, and U_{ir} and Y_{ir} are the real data of U_i and Y_i, respectively.

Figure 10 shows the simulation and the experiment of the input voltage and the output voltage denoted as dynamic model and real data, respectively.

In Fig. 10 it can be seen that both results are almost equal, for the inputs are 12 V for U_1 and U_{1r}, 12 V for U_2 and U_{2r}, and 15 V for U_3 and U_{3r}, respectively, and for

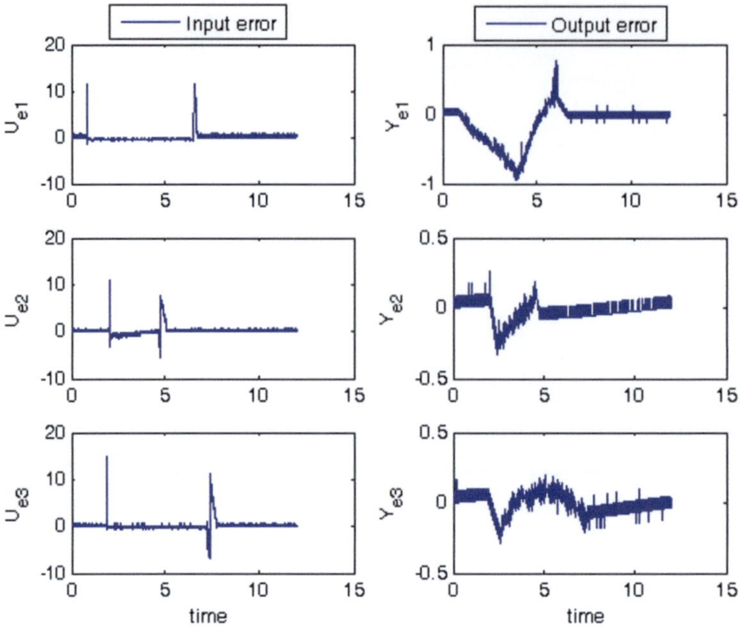

Fig. 11 Error results from simulation and experiment

Table 2 RMSE for the errors

	RMSE
e_u^2	1.7801
e_y^2	0.0505

the output are 2.5258 V for Y_1 and Y_{1r}, 2.3149 V for Y_2 and Y_{2r}, and 2.1917 V for Y_3 and Y_{3r}, respectively.

Figure 11 presents the error of the input $U_{ir} - U_i$ and the output $Y_{ir} - Y_i$ denoted as U_{ei} and Y_{ei}, respectively.

From Fig. 11 it is shown that both results are almost equal.

Figure 12 introduces the simulation results for the states X_j.

Figure 12 shows the states X_1, X_4, and X_7 as the displacements θ_1, θ_2, and θ_3, the states X_2, X_5, and X_8 as the velocities of the displacements $\dot{\theta}_1$, $\dot{\theta}_2$, and $\dot{\theta}_3$, and the states X_3, X_5, and X_9 as the armature current in the motors i_1, i_2, and i_3.

Table 2 presents the RMSE using Eq. (49) for the errors $e^2 = e_u^2$, or $e^2 = e_y^2$, using the dynamic model described by Eqs. (37)–(48).

From Table 2, it can be seen that the dynamic model is a good approximation of the real process because the RMSEs are near to zero.

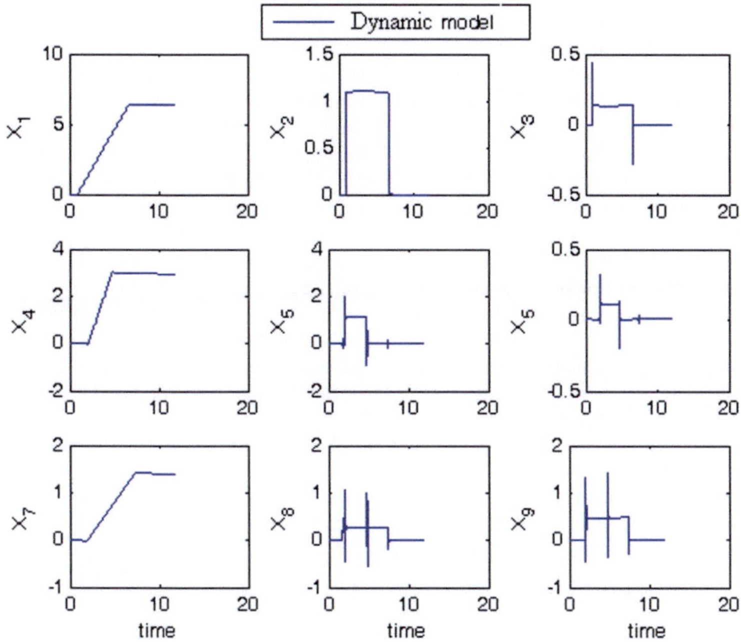

Fig. 12 Simulation results for the states

7 Concluding Remarks

In this chapter, the dynamic model with sensor and actuator for an articulated robotic arm was obtained. The proposed method was validated with real measures where the proposed approach gave a good approximation of the real process. As future research, an observer, a control or an identifier will be applied for the proposed dynamic model.

References

1. D.J. Christensen, J. Campbell, K. Stoy, Anatomy-based organization of morphology and control in self-reconfigurable modular robots. Neural Comput. Appl. **19**, 787–805 (2010)
2. J.J. Rubio, E. Garcia, J. Pacheco, Trajectory planning and collisions detector for robotic arms. Neural Comput. Appl. **21**, 2105–2114 (2012)
3. J. Bachrach, J. Beal, J. McLurkin, Composable continuous-space programs for robotic swarms. Neural Comput. Appl. **19**, 825–847 (2010)
4. C. Chen, Y. Inoue, K. Shibata, Identification of a golf swing robot using soft computing approach. Neural Comput. Appl. **20**, 729–740 (2011)
5. I. Villaverde, M. Graña, Neuro-evolutionary mobile robot egomotion estimation with a 3D ToF camera. Neural Comput. Appl. **20**, 345–354 (2011)
6. H. Celikkanat, E. Sahin, Steering self-organized robot flocks through externally guided individuals. Neural Comput. Appl. **19**, 849–865 (2010)

7. H. Chaoui, P. Sicard, Adaptive Lyapunov-based neural network sensorless control of permanent magnet synchronous machines. Neural Comput. Appl. **20**, 717–727 (2011)
8. C.-H. Chiu, Self-tuning output recurrent cerebellar model articulation controller for a wheeled inverted pendulum control. Neural Comput. Appl. **19**, 1153–1164 (2010)
9. W.-P. Lee, T.-H. Yang, Combining GRN modeling and demonstration-based programming for robot control. Neural Comput. Appl. **20**, 909–921 (2011)
10. Y. Wu, F. Sun, J. Zheng, Q. Song, A robust training algorithm of discrete-time MIMO RNN and application in fault tolerant control of robotic system. Neural Comput. Appl. **19**, 1013–1027 (2010)
11. J.J. Rubio, C. Torres, C. Aguilar, Optimal control based in a mathematical model applied to robotic arms. Int. J. Innov. Comput. Inf. Control. **7**(8), 5045–5062 (2011)
12. J.J. Rubio, J. Pacheco, J.H. Perez-Cruz, F. Torres, Mathematical model with sensor and actuator for a transelevator. Neural Comput. Appl. **24**, 277–285 (2014)
13. B. Armstrong, O. Khatib, J. Burdick, The explicit dynamic model and inertial parameters of the PUMA 560 arm, in *Proceedings. 1986 IEEE Conference on Robotics and Automation, San Francisco* (1986), pp. 510–518
14. F.L. Lewis, D.M. Dawson, C.T. Abdallah, *Control of Robot Manipulators, Theory and Practice* (2004). ISBN: 0-8247-4072-6
15. M.W. Spong, S. Hutchinson, M. Vidyasagar, *Robot Modeling and Control* (John Wiley & Sons, 2006). ISBN-13: 978-0-471-64990-8
16. W. Bolton, *Control Systems* (Newnes, 2002)

Inverse Dynamics Model of a Delta-Type Parallel Robot

Abstract In this chapter, the inverse dynamics model of a delta-type parallel robot is introduced with the goal of relating the dynamic behavior of the torque with the dynamic behavior of the position, velocity, and acceleration. Results obtained from the programming of this inverse dynamics model of the delta-type parallel robot are compared for two kinds of simulation software (Simulink and Working Model) with the goal to reach its validation.

1 Introduction

Now, most of the robots present an anthropomorphic configuration which is inspired in the human arm. They are commonly conformed by a succession of rigid bodies, each one jointed to the previous and to the next by a rotation joint; this architecture is called a serial robot. Nevertheless, they present problems relating to a low precision in the velocity of their movements. Then, other kind of configuration must be designed to increase the velocities of movements in robots.

The delta-type parallel robots are closed kinematics chain mechanisms in which the end-effector is united to the base by two kinematics chains. The delta-type parallel robots present an acceptable performance in function of the precision, stiffness, and their availability to move the loads in a high velocity [1–3].

Since the original design of a delta-type parallel robot was presented [1], many investigations have been presented to make the delta-type parallel robots more flexible. Solutions for the kinematics and dynamics models of delta-type parallel robots are studied in [4–8]. A device of four degrees of freedom is designed for medicine which is based on a delta-type parallel robot [9].

In general, the modeling and control of a delta-type parallel robot of closed kinematics chain is complex, especially when conventional methods are employed. In [10, 11], the authors utilize the method of virtual work to determine the dynamics model of delta-type parallel robots, and they compare the simulations obtained with this model and its real behavior. There exist other investigations in which the dynamics model is determined by the Euler-Lagrange method [12, 13]. In all the cases, the

J. de J. Rubio et al., *Dynamic Models of Energy, Robotic, and Biological Systems*,
https://doi.org/10.1007/978-3-031-85438-5_7

methods should reach the equations of the dynamics model which represent the system behavior.

The dynamics model of the delta-type parallel robot can be described by the inverse dynamics analysis, which is defined as follows: for the inverse dynamics problem, the relevant goal is to determine the forces of actuators and/or torques, which must be exerted by the actuators to produce a given trajectory of the end-effector [14–17]. In general, the inverse dynamics model of a delta-type parallel robot is complex, that is way the methods of Euler-Lagrange and virtual work are used as the same as in [18–22], in all the cases the direct kinematics model is necessary.

The problem is that the approaches described in [18–22], to get the inverse dynamics model of a delta-type parallel robot require of the rotation matrix or the Jacobian, this fact produces a very complex inverse dynamics model. In this work, a more simple approach to get the inverse dynamics model of a delta-type parallel robot is advised with the novelty that it does not require of the rotation matrix or the Jacobian.

In this work, the approach to get the inverse dynamics model of a delta-type parallel robot is detailed, where it takes into account the behavior of the pick and place configuration, i.e., the movement is restricted to one direction. The pick and place machines are robots utilized for the positioning of objects. Since they have high velocity they are particularly utilized in home-works of components setting, in electric circuits mounting, and in product packaging.

The organization of this work is as follows. Section 2 discuses the direct kinematics of the delta-type parallel robot. The inverse dynamics model of the delta-type parallel robot are addressed in Sect. 3. Section 4 compares the results of the inverse dynamics model in Simulink and Working Model. Conclusions and forthcoming work are detailed in Sect. 5.

2 Direct Kinematics

To make the kinematics, analysis is necessary to replace the links by vectors, as is shown in Figs. 1 and 2, where the schematic diagram of the pick and place is shown. We can write the equations which are as follows:

$$R_O + R_A + R_B + R_E = h, \tag{1}$$

Rewriting Eq. (1) in terms of its components gives

$$h_j = (L_O + L_A C\theta + L_B C\phi - L_E)\,\widehat{i} + (L_A S\theta + L_B S\phi)\,\widehat{j}, \tag{2}$$

where C is the cosine and S is the sine of the angle. Dividing the components of Eq. (2) yields the following equations:

$$L_O + L_A C\theta + L_B C\phi - L_E = 0, \tag{3}$$

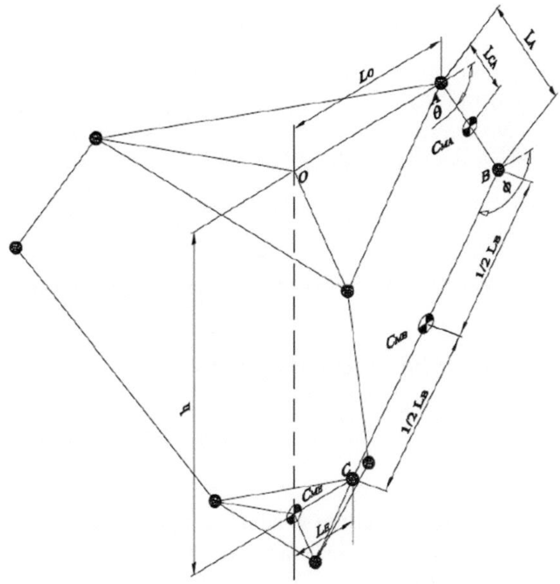

Fig. 1 Schematic diagram of a delta-type parallel robot in the pick and place configuration

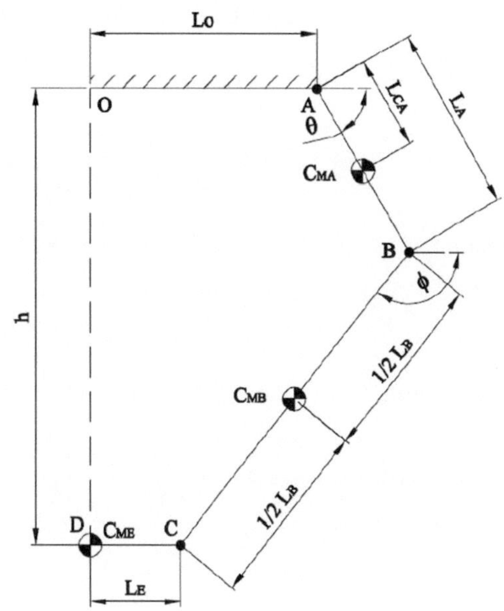

Fig. 2 Vectorial representation of the delta-type parallel robot

$$h = L_A S\theta + L_B S\phi, \tag{4}$$

It is important to note that in Eq. (3), the input θ corresponds to the link position, while the output ϕ is necessary to be represented in terms of θ, as given in the next equation:

$$C\theta = \frac{L_E - L_O - L_A C\theta}{L_B}, \tag{5}$$

Substituting ϕ into Eq. (4), the position of the end-effector can be determined. To find the angular velocity of ϕ and the linear velocity of h, Eqs. (3) and (4) are derived with respect to the time t:

$$\dot{\phi} = -\frac{L_A S\theta}{L_B S\phi}\dot{\theta}, \tag{6}$$

$$\dot{h} = L_A \dot{\theta} C\theta + L_B \dot{\phi} C\phi, \tag{7}$$

Substituting Eq. (6) into Eq. (7) gives:

$$\dot{h} = L_A \left(\frac{S(\theta + \phi)}{S\phi} \right) \dot{\phi}, \tag{8}$$

The previous procedure is developed to obtain the acceleration of the coupling link and of the end-effector, via the derivation of the Eqs. (6) and (7) with respect to the time.

$$- L_A \dot{\theta}^2 C\theta - L_A \ddot{\theta} S\theta - L_B \dot{\phi}^2 C\phi - L_B \ddot{\phi} S\phi = 0, \tag{9}$$

Substituting Eq. (6) into Eq. (9), gives the following:

$$\ddot{\phi} = \frac{L_A}{L_B} \left(\frac{C\theta}{S\phi} + \frac{L_A S^2\theta}{L_B S^3\phi} C\phi \right) \dot{\theta}^2 + \frac{L_A S\theta}{L_B S\phi} \ddot{\theta}, \tag{10}$$

Getting the derivative of Eq. (7) with respect to the time gives:

$$\ddot{h} = -L_A \dot{\theta}^2 S\theta - L_A \ddot{\theta} C\theta + L_B \dot{\phi}^2 S\phi - L_B \ddot{\phi} S\phi, \tag{11}$$

Substituting Eqs. (6) and (10) into Eq. (11) gives the following:

$$\ddot{h} = L_A \left(\frac{L_A S^2\theta C^2\phi}{L_B S^3\phi} + \frac{L_A S^2\theta}{L_B S\phi} + \frac{C\theta C\phi}{S\phi} - S\theta \right) \dot{\theta}^2 + L_A \left(\frac{S\theta C\phi}{S\phi} + C\theta \right) \ddot{\theta}, \tag{12}$$

3 Inverse Dynamics

For the inverse dynamics problem, the time history of a desired trajectory is given and the problem is to determine the forces of actuators and/or torques required to produce that motion. In this part, the Euler-Lagrange method is used to get the inverse dynamics model. Figure 3 will be utilized in this procedure.

A position vector for the link mass is as follows:

$$r_{CA} = (L_O + L_{CA} C\theta)\widehat{i} + L_{CA} S\theta \widehat{j}, \tag{13}$$

Obtaining the derivative of the Eq. (13), we get the velocity vector of the mass center in the link:

$$v_{CA} = -L_{CA}\dot{\theta} S\theta \widehat{i} + L_{CA}\dot{\theta} C\theta \widehat{j}, \tag{14}$$

The square norm of the before vector can be expressed as follows:

$$v_{CA}^2 = L_{CA}^2 \dot{\theta}^2 S^2\theta + L_{CA}^2 \dot{\theta}^2 C^2\theta, \tag{15}$$

The position vector for the mass center in the coupling link is defined as follows:

$$r_{CB} = \left(L_O + L_A C\theta + \frac{L_B}{2} C\phi\right)\widehat{i} + \left(L_A S\theta - \frac{L_B}{2} S_\phi\right)\widehat{j}, \tag{16}$$

Getting the derivative of Eq. (16), we obtain the velocity vector of the mass center in the coupler:

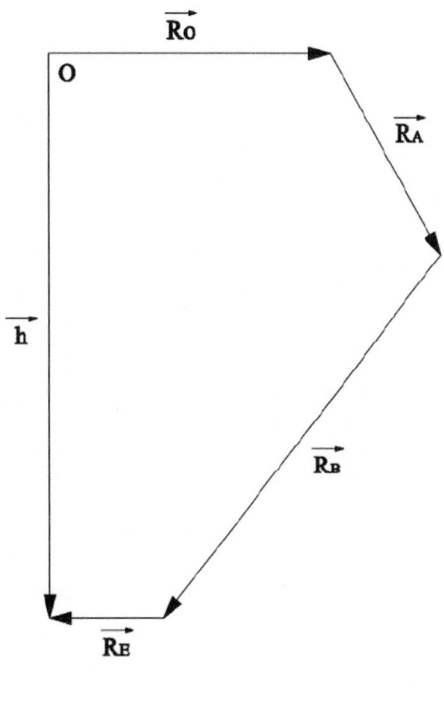

Fig. 3 Simplified scheme of the delta-type parallel robot in the pick and place configuration

$$v_{CB} = \left(-L_A\dot{\theta}S\theta - \frac{L_B}{2}\dot{\phi}S\phi\right)\hat{i} + \left(L_A\dot{\theta}C\theta - \frac{L_B}{2}\dot{\phi}C\phi\right)\hat{j}, \tag{17}$$

The square norm on the velocity vector can be rewritten as follows:

$$v_{CB}^2 = L_A^2\dot{\theta}^2 + \frac{L_B^2}{4}\dot{\phi}^2 - L_A L_B C(\theta + \phi)\dot{\theta}\dot{\phi}, \tag{18}$$

Finally, the position vector of the mass center in the end-effector is as follows:

$$r_{CE} = \left(L_A S\theta - L_B S_\phi\right)\hat{j}, \tag{19}$$

Nevertheless, by considering a kinematics analysis in Fig. 3, it is known that the square norm of the velocity vector in the end-effector is as follows:

$$v_{CE}^2 = L_A^2 \frac{S^2(\theta + \phi)}{S^2\phi}\dot{\theta}^2, \tag{20}$$

With Eqs. (15), (18), and (20), the kinetic energy of the mechanism is calculated by:

$$T = \frac{1}{2}\left(M_A v_{CA}^2 + I_A\dot{\theta}^2\right) + \frac{1}{2}\left(M_B v_{CB}^2 + I_B^2\dot{\phi}^2\right) + \frac{1}{2}M_E v_{CE}^2, \tag{21}$$

Using Eqs. (4), (13), and (16), the potential energy of the mechanism is as follows:

$$V = g\left(M_A L_{CA} + M_B L_A + M_E L_A\right)S\theta - gL_B\left(\frac{1}{2}M_B + M_E\right)S\phi, \tag{22}$$

The Lagrangian of the machine is:

$$\begin{aligned} L = \tfrac{1}{2}&\left(M_A v_{CA}^2 + I_A\dot{\theta}^2 + M_B v_{CB}^2 + I_B^2\dot{\phi}^2 + M_E v_{CE}^2\right) \\ &-g\left(M_A L_{CA} + M_B L_A + M_E L_A\right)S\theta + gL_B\left(\tfrac{1}{2}M_B + M_E\right)S\phi, \end{aligned} \tag{23}$$

Substituting Eqs. (6), (15), and (18) into Eq. (23) gives:

$$\begin{aligned} L = &\tfrac{1}{2}\left(M_A L_{CA}^2 + M_B L_A^2 + I_A\right) + \tfrac{1}{2}L_A^2\left(\tfrac{I_B}{L_B^2} + \tfrac{M_B}{4}\right)\tfrac{S^2\theta}{S^2\phi}\dot{\theta}^2 + \tfrac{1}{2}M_B L_A^2\tfrac{S\theta C(\theta+\phi)}{S\phi}\dot{\theta}^2 \\ &+\tfrac{1}{2}M_E L_A^2\tfrac{S^2(\theta+\phi)}{S^2\phi}\dot{\theta}^2 - g\left(M_A L_{CA} + M_B L_A + M_E L_A\right)S\theta + gL_B\left(\tfrac{1}{2}M_B + M_E\right)S\phi, \end{aligned} \tag{24}$$

To make the writing of the Euler-Lagrange equations easier, the following variables are defined:

$$\begin{aligned}
K_1 &= M_A L_{CA}^2 + M_B L_A^2 + I_A, \\
K_2 &= L_A^2 \left(\tfrac{I_B}{L_B^2} + \tfrac{M_B}{4} \right), \\
K_3 &= M_B L_A^2, \\
K_4 &= M_E L_A^2, \\
K_5 &= g \left(M_A L_{CA} + M_B L_A + M_E L_A \right), \\
K_6 &= g L_B \left(\tfrac{1}{2} M_B + M_E \right),
\end{aligned} \tag{25}$$

$$\begin{aligned}
F_1 &= \tfrac{S^2\theta}{S^2\phi}, \\
F_2 &= \tfrac{S\theta C(\theta+\phi)}{S\phi}, \\
F_3 &= \tfrac{S^2(\theta+\phi)}{S^2\phi}, \\
F_4 &= S\theta, \\
F_5 &= S\phi,
\end{aligned} \tag{26}$$

Substituting the variables of Eqs. (25) and (26) into Eq. (24), the Lagrangian can be rewritten as follows:

$$L = \frac{1}{2} \left(K_1 + K_2 F_1 + K_3 F_2 + K_4 F_3 \right) \dot{\theta}^2 - K_5 F_4 + K_6 F_5, \tag{27}$$

Taking into account that the main variable is the angle θ, the Euler-Lagrange method is written as follows:

$$\frac{d}{dt} \left(\frac{\partial L}{\partial \dot{\theta}} \right) - \frac{\partial L}{\partial \theta} = \tau_{EXT}, \tag{28}$$

where τ_{EXT} is the torque applied to the link. Getting the partial derivative in the Lagrangian with respect to the derivative of θ gives:

$$\frac{\partial L}{\partial \dot{\theta}} = \left(K_1 + K_2 F_1 + K_3 F_2 + K_4 F_3 \right) \dot{\theta}, \tag{29}$$

Getting the derivative of Eq. (29) with respect to time gives:

$$\frac{d}{dt} \left(\frac{\partial L}{\partial \dot{\theta}} \right) = \left(K_1 + K_2 F_1 + K_3 F_2 + K_4 F_3 \right) \ddot{\theta} + \left(K_1 + K_2 \frac{dF_1}{dt} + K_3 \frac{dF_2}{dt} + K_4 \frac{dF_3}{dt} \right) \dot{\theta}, \tag{30}$$

where:

$$\begin{aligned}
\frac{dF_1}{dt} &= 2 \frac{C\theta S\theta}{S^2\phi} \dot{\theta} - 2 \frac{S\theta C\theta}{S^3\phi} \dot{\phi}, \\
\frac{dF_2}{dt} &= \frac{S\theta C(\theta+\phi)}{S\phi} \dot{\theta} - \frac{S\theta C\phi C(\theta+\phi)}{S^2\phi} \dot{\phi} - 2 \frac{S\theta S(\theta+\phi)}{S^2\phi} (\dot{\theta} + \dot{\phi}), \\
\frac{dF_3}{dt} &= 2 \frac{C(\theta+\phi) S(\theta+\phi)}{S^2\phi} (\dot{\theta} + \dot{\phi}) - 2 \frac{S^2(\theta+\phi) C\phi}{S\phi} \dot{\phi},
\end{aligned} \tag{31}$$

Getting the partial derivative of the Lagrangian with respect to θ gives:

$$\frac{\partial L}{\partial \theta} = \frac{1}{2}\left(K_2\frac{dF_1}{\partial \theta} + K_3\frac{dF_2}{\partial \theta} + K_4\frac{dF_3}{\partial \theta}\right)\dot{\theta}^2 - K_5\frac{dF_4}{\partial \theta} + K_6\frac{dF_5}{\partial \theta}, \tag{32}$$

where:

$$\begin{aligned}
\frac{dF_1}{\partial \theta} &= 2\frac{C\theta S\theta}{S^2\phi} - 2\frac{L_A C\phi S^3\theta}{L_B S^4\phi},\\
\frac{dF_2}{\partial \theta} &= \frac{S\theta C(\theta+\phi)}{S\phi} - \frac{L_A C\phi S^2\theta C(\theta+\phi)}{L_B S^3\phi} - \frac{S\theta S(\theta-\phi)\left(1-\frac{L_A S\theta}{L_B S\phi}\right)}{S\phi},\\
\frac{dF_3}{\partial \theta} &= 2\frac{L_A C\phi S\theta S^2(\theta+\phi)}{L_B S^4\phi} + 2\frac{C(\theta+\phi)S(\theta+\phi)\left(1+\frac{L_A S\theta}{L_B S^2\phi}\right)}{S\phi},\\
\frac{dF_4}{\partial \theta} &= C\theta,\\
\frac{dF_5}{\partial \theta} &= \frac{L_A C\phi S\theta}{L_B S^2\phi},
\end{aligned} \tag{33}$$

To make the writing of the inverse dynamics model easier, the following variables are chosen:

$$\begin{aligned}
F_6 &= K_1 + K_2F_1 + K_3F_2 + K_4F_3,\\
F_7 &= K_2\frac{dF_1}{\partial \theta} + K_3\frac{dF_2}{\partial \theta} + K_4\frac{dF_3}{\partial \theta},\\
F_8 &= \frac{1}{2}\left(K_2\frac{dF_1}{\partial \theta} + K_3\frac{dF_2}{\partial \theta} + K_4\frac{dF_3}{\partial \theta}\right),\\
F_9 &= -K_5\frac{dF_4}{\partial \theta} + K_6\frac{dF_5}{\partial \theta},
\end{aligned} \tag{34}$$

Finally, the equation of the inverse dynamics model is:

$$F_6\ddot{\theta} + F_7\dot{\theta} - F_8\dot{\theta}^2 - F_9 = \tau_{EXT}, \tag{35}$$

Equations (25), (26), (34), and (35) describe the inverse dynamics model of the delta-type parallel robot.

4 Simulations

Equations (25), (26), (34), and (35) of the inverse dynamics model for the delta-type parallel robot are programmed in two software known as Simulink and Working Model. The target is to find that the results programmed in both software Simulink and Working Model are similar via the obtaining of a small error between both to say that the inverse dynamics model of the delta-type parallel robot is validated. A tridimensional model in SolidWorks is shown in Fig. 4, where the mass and inertial properties of the mechanism are considered. The dimensions of the mass and momentums are presented in Table 1.

By considering the properties of the machine, an interval of the angle θ between $[-70^\circ \le \theta \le 70^\circ]$ is considered with the goal of avoiding collisions of elements in the mechanism. Figure 4 shows the superior and inferior values of θ in the end-effector.

The simulation results are validated with a model computed in Working Model, which is shown in Fig. 5. In Working Model, rectangles represent the rigid bodies of

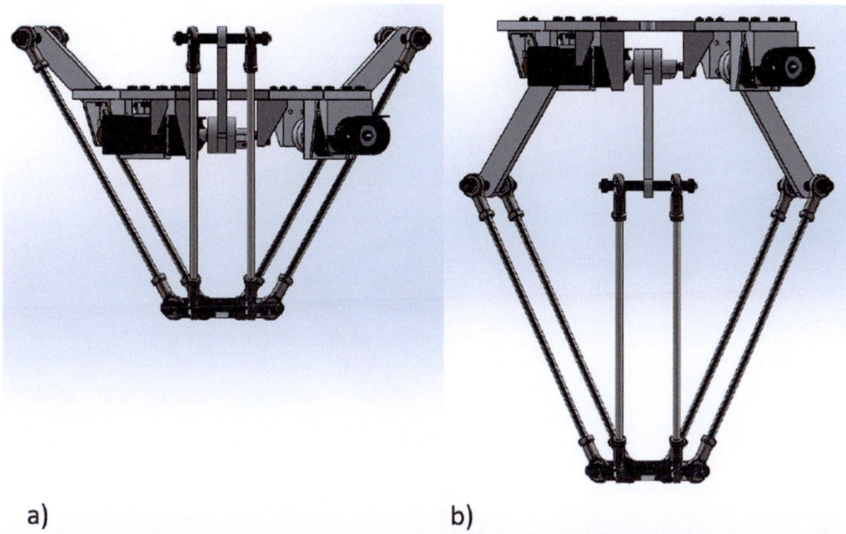

Fig. 4 **a** Position corresponding to the angle $\theta = 70°$, **b** position corresponding to the angle $\theta = -70°$

Table 1 Properties to the links in the mechanism

Link	Mass	Length	Inertia moment
Fixed	–	$L_O = 0.09\,\text{m}$	$V_3 = 5\,\text{V}$
Crank	$M_A = 0.0265\,\text{Kg}$	$L_A = 0.12\,\text{m}$	$R_{m3} = 17\,\Omega$
Coupler	$M_B = 0.2686\,\text{Kg}$	$L_B = 0.27\,\text{m}$	$R_{c3} = 1\,\Omega$
End-effector	$M_E = 0.05\,\text{Kg}$	$L_E = 0.035\,\text{m}$	$L_3 = 30\,\text{mH}$

the mechanism and it employs the same mass and inertial properties of the inverse dynamics model.

For simulation 1, the position of the motor link described by the angle changes from $\theta = -35°$ (-0.61 rad) to $\theta = 50°$ (0.87 rad) with a constant torque of 0.5 Nm^2. Figure 6 shows the torque and Figs. 7, 8, 9, 10, 11, and 12 show the angle, velocity, and acceleration.

Figures 7, 8, 9, 10, 11, and 12 show that Simulink and Working Model give similar results. Thus, the inverse dynamics model is validated for this example.

For simulation 2, the position of the motor link described by the angle changes from $\theta = -35°$ (-0.61 rad) to $\theta = 50°$ (0.87 rad) with a constant torque of 1 Nm^2. Figure 13 shows the torque and Figs. 14, 15, 16, 17, 18, and 19 show the angle, velocity, and acceleration.

Figures 14, 15, 16, 17, 18, and 19 show that the Simulink and Working Model results are similar. Thus, the inverse dynamics model is validated for this example.

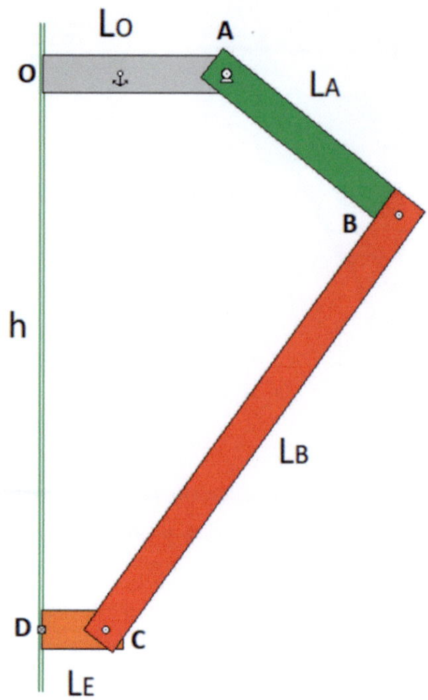

Fig. 5 The Working Model mechanism

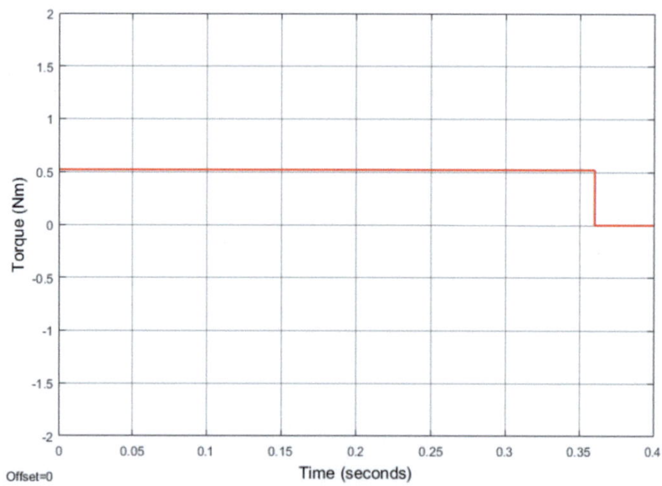

Fig. 6 Torque of 0.5 Nm

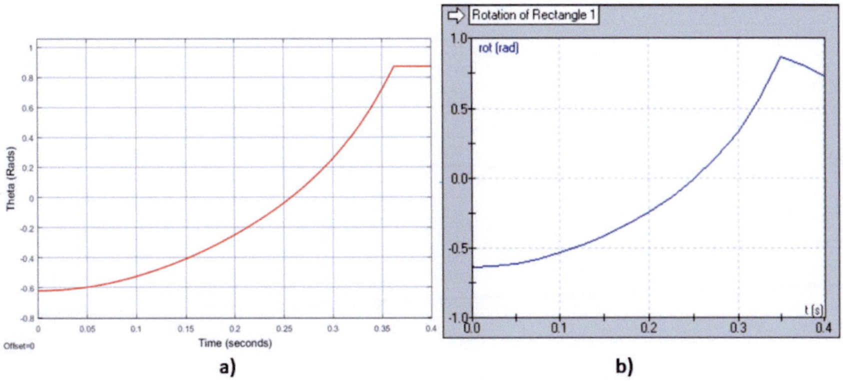

Fig. 7 Output $\theta - t$ with an torque of 0.5 Nm. **a** Simulink result. **b** Working Model result

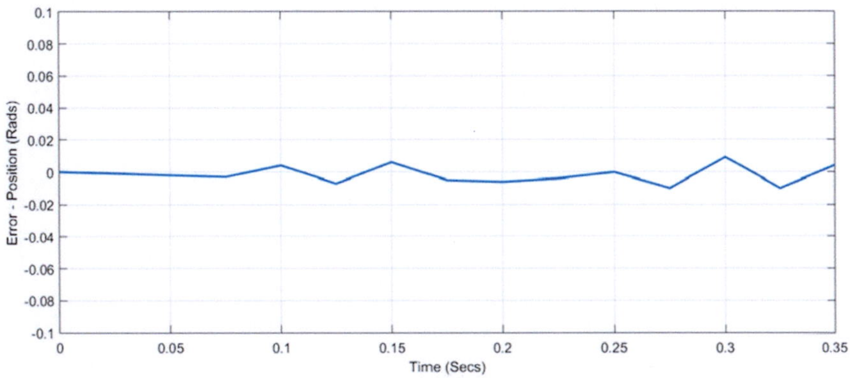

Fig. 8 θ error between the Simulink and Working Model results with a torque of 0.5 Nm

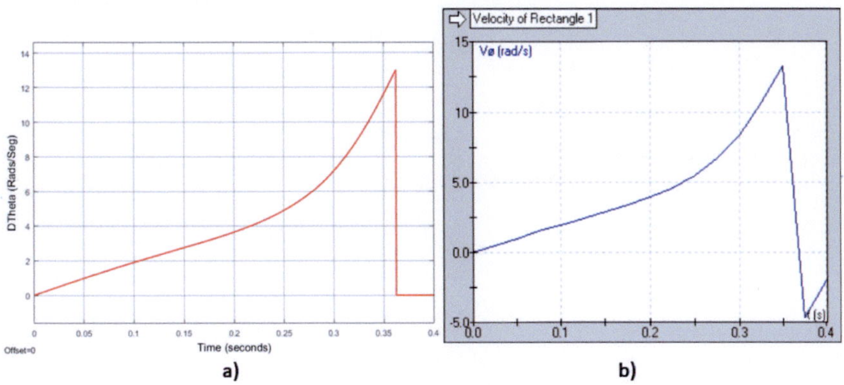

Fig. 9 Output $\dot{\theta} - t$ with a torque of 0.5 Nm. **a** Simulink result. **b** Working Model result

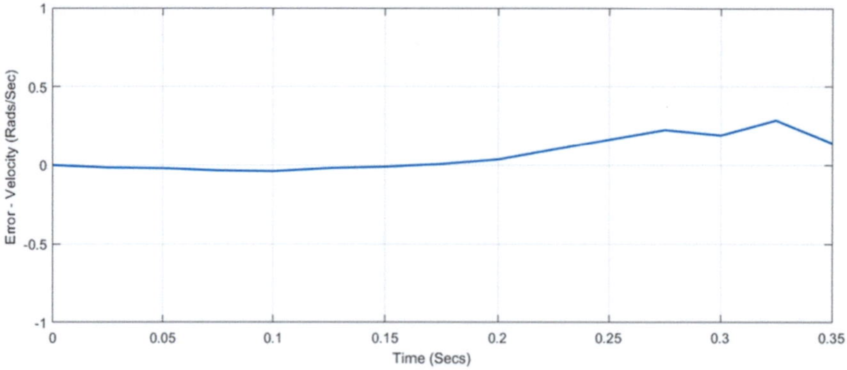

Fig. 10 $\dot{\theta}$ error between the Simulink and Working Model results with a torque of 0.5 Nm

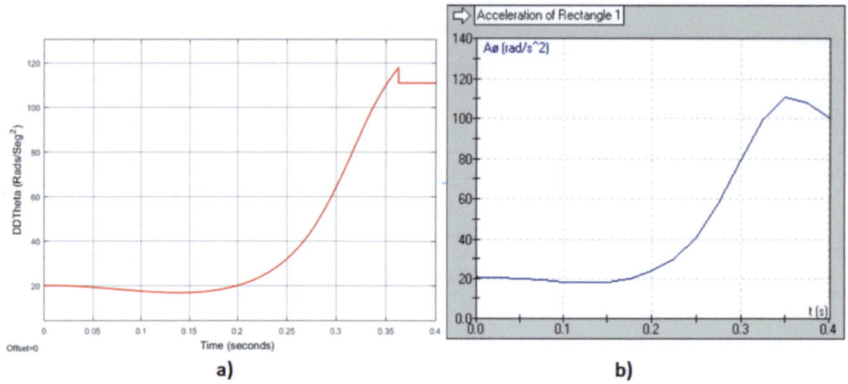

Fig. 11 Output $\ddot{\theta} - t$ with a torque of 0.5 Nm. **a** Simulink result. **b** Working Model result

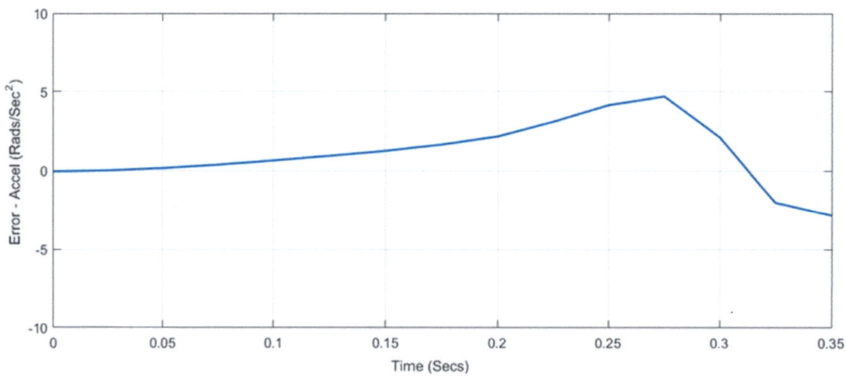

Fig. 12 $\ddot{\theta}$ error between the Simulink and Working Model results with a torque of 0.5 Nm

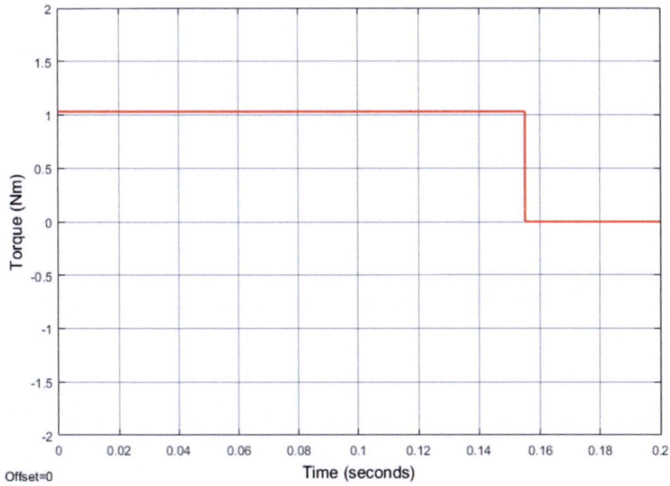

Fig. 13 Torque of 1 Nm

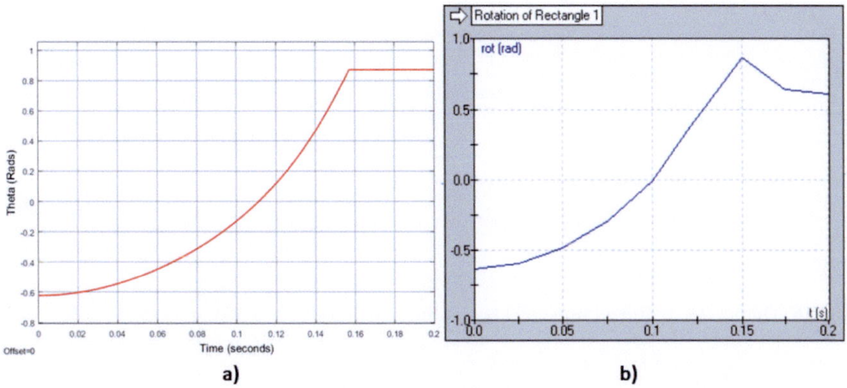

Fig. 14 Output $\theta - t$ with a torque of 1 Nm. **a** Simulink results. **b** Working Model results

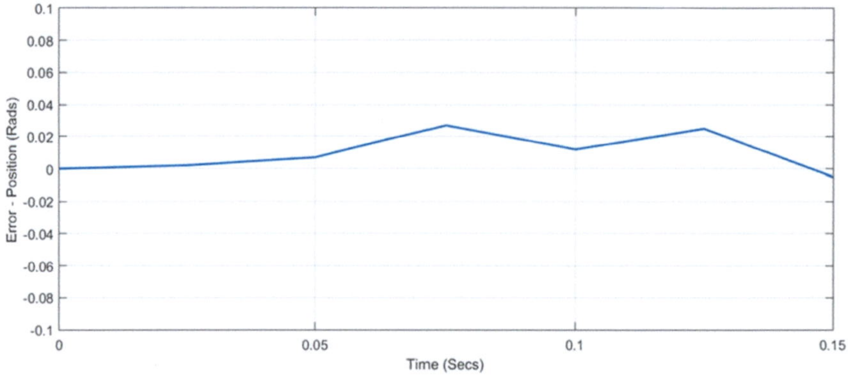

Fig. 15 θ error between the Simulink and Working Model results with a torque of 1 Nm

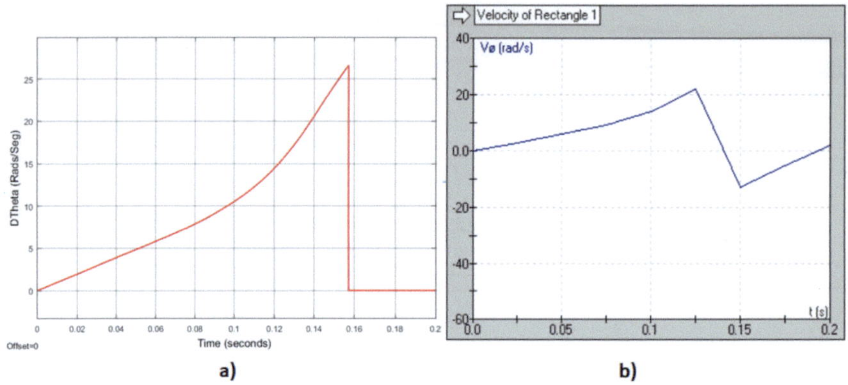

Fig. 16 Output $\dot{\theta} - t$ with a torque of 1 Nm. **a** Simulink results. **b** Working Model results

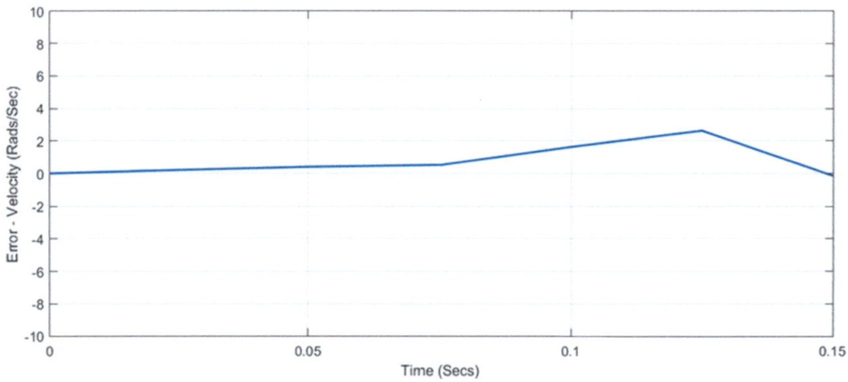

Fig. 17 $\dot{\theta}$ error between the Simulink and Working Model results with a torque of 1 Nm

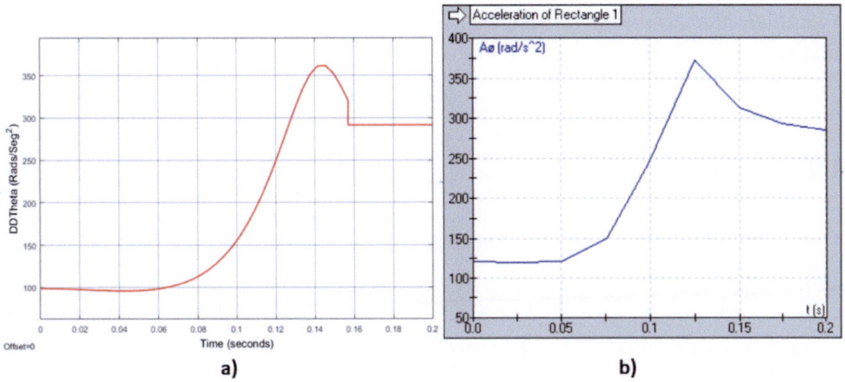

Fig. 18 Output $\ddot{\theta} - t$ with a torque of 1 Nm. **a** Simulink results. **b** Working Model results

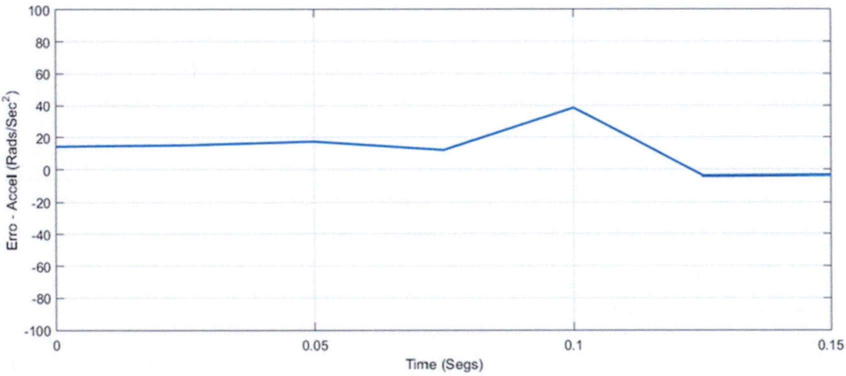

Fig. 19 $\ddot{\theta}$ error between the Simulink and Working Model results with a torque of 1 Nm

5 Concluding Remarks

In this chapter, the inverse dynamics model of a delta-type parallel robot was proposed for the pick and place application. The inverse dynamics model was designed based on the Euler-Lagrange method, which relates the dynamic behavior of the torque with the dynamic behavior of the position, velocity, and acceleration in the robot. From the inverse dynamics model of the delta-type parallel robot, two kinds of software, Simulink and Working Model, were computed and compared, yielding very similar results via the obtaining of a small error between both, which validates the proposed inverse dynamics model. In the forthcoming work, the artificial intelligence will be utilized to learn the behavior of the inverse dynamics model or the inverse dynamics model which considers the movement of the delta-type parallel robot in other directions will be studied, other software as is the MSC Adams will be employed to simulate the proposed inverse dynamic model, or the control of the delta-type parallel robot will be designed.

References

1. R. Clavel, A fast robot with parallel geometry, in *18th International Symposium on Industrial Robot* (1988), pp. 91–100
2. J.P. Merlet, *Parallel Robots*, 2nd edn. (Springer, Dordrecht, The Netherlands, 2006)
3. R. Aracil, J. Saltaren, M. Sabater, O. Reinoso, Robots paralelos: maquinas con un pasado para una robótica del futuro. Revista Iberoamericana de Automática e Informática Industrial **3**(1), 16–28 (2006)
4. C.A. Avizzano, A. Filippeschi, J.M. Villegas, E. Ruffaldi, An optimal geometric model for clavels delta robot, in *2015 IEEE European Modelling Symposium* (2015), pp. 232–237
5. M. Maya, E. Castillo, A. Lomeli, E. Gonzalez, A. Cardenas, Workspace and payload-capacity of a new reconfigurable delta parallel robot. Int. J. Adv. Robot. Syst. **10**(56), 1–11 (2013)
6. M. Vulliez, S. Zeghloul, O. Khatib, Kinematic analysis of the delthaptic, in *Advances in Robot Kinematics* (2017), pp. 181–189
7. J. Gallardo-Alvarado, R. Rodriguez-Castro, L. Perez-Gonzales, C.R. Aguilar Najera, Kinematics of the 3(RPSP)-s fully spherical parallel manipulator by means of screw theory. Robotics **7**, 1–12 (2018)
8. A. Al-Ibadi, S. Nefti-Meziani, S. Davis, Design, kinematics and controlling a novel soft robot arm with parallel motion. Robotics **7**, 1–14 (2018)
9. H. Saafi, C. Preault, M. Laribi, A novel kinematic of a 4 dofs haptic device based on the delta robot architecture, in *Advances in Service and Industrial Robotics* (2017), pp. 699–706
10. Y. Li, Q. Xu, Dynamic modeling and robust control of a 3-PRC translational parallel kinematic machine. Robot. Comput. Integr. Manuf. **35**(3), 630–640 (2015)
11. P. Xu, B. Li, C. Cheung, Dynamic analysis of a linear delta robot in hybrid polishing machine based on the principle of virtual work, in *18th International Conference on Advanced Robotics (ICAR)* (2017)
12. L. Angel, J. Viola, Parametric identification of a delta type parallel robot, in *IEEE Colombian Conference on Robotics and Automation (CCRA)* (2017)
13. Y. Kuo, Mathematical modeling and analysis of the delta robot with flexible links. Comput. & Math. Appl. **71**(10), 1973–1989 (2016)
14. R.L. Norton, *Diseño de Maquinaria* (Cuarta Edición, McGraw Hill, México, 2009)
15. J.M. Rico, J. Duffy, Forward and inverse acceleration analyses of in-parallel manipulators. J. Mech. Des. **122**(3), 299–303 (2000)
16. Y. Li, Q. Xu, Kinematics and inverse dynamics analysis for a general 3-PRS spatial parallel mechanism. Robotica **23**, 219–229 (2005)
17. J. Gallardo, J.M. Rico, A. Frisoli, Dynamics of parallel manipulators by means of screw theory. Mech. Mach. Theory **38**(11), 1113–1131 (2003)
18. J.J. Craig, *Robótica* (Tercera Edición, Pearson Education, México, 2006)
19. S. Staicu, Inverse dynamics of the 3-PRR planar parallel robot. Robot. Auton. Syst. **57**, 556–563 (2009)
20. S. Staicu, Recursive modelling in dynamics of delta parallel robot. Robotica **27**, 199–207 (2009)
21. W. Khalil, O. Ibrahim, General solution for the dynamic modeling of parallel robots. J. Intell. & Robot. Syst. **49**, 19–37 (2007)
22. Q. Zhe, L. Xia-chu, Z. Zhuan, Application value of slider-crank mechanism in pick and place operation of delta robot, in *MATEC Web of Conferences*, vol. 153 (2018)

Acquisition System and Approximation of Brain Signals

Abstract In this chapter, the acquisition system of one channel is introduced to obtain the biological brain signals. Such system consists of a low pass filter, an amplifier, a high pass filter, and a data acquisition board. A novel slopes algorithm with bounded output is proposed for approximation of the brain signals. The proposed method is compared with both the least squares and nearest neighbor algorithms.

1 Introduction

There are two kind of signal approximation: one is the estimation of parameters [1–6], and the other is the interpolation [7–12].

The estimation of parameters is the estimation of some parameters or functions with the objective of approximating a general nonlinear behavior. In [1], a biologically plausible thalamocortical neural population model is extended. In [2], the distributed signal estimation in sensor networks is considered. The work of [3] is focused on the efficient solution for three-dimensional time-harmonic eddy current problems with the conjugate gradient method. In [4], a real-time approach for identification of second-order of complex valued signals is introduced. In [5], a dynamic reconstruction model, which integrates the measurement information and physical evolution information of objects of interest, is presented. In [6], a gas chamber and four defect models are designed. The above works present good results for the estimation of parameters. However, this chapter is not focused on this issue, and the aforementioned works do not present a medical instrumentation application.

The interpolation is the consideration of some points of the input-output data with the objective of approximating a general nonlinear behavior. The studies of [9, 10] use the least squares for design of some kind of evolving systems. In [11], the authors use the least squares for training of a support vector machine algorithm. In [12], the authors use the least squares algorithm for non-negative tensor factorizations. The work of [7] uses the nearest neighbor method for codification of a fractal image. In [8], the authors apply the nearest neighbor approach for pattern recognition problem of one electromyographic signal. From the above studies, two interesting interpolation methods are highly considered such as are the least squares of [9–12], and the nearest

J. de J. Rubio et al., *Dynamic Models of Energy, Robotic, and Biological Systems*,
https://doi.org/10.1007/978-3-031-85438-5_8

neighbor of [7, 8]. Since this chapter is focused on this issue, it would be interesting to design a novel interpolation method for the approximation of nonlinear behaviors.

In this chapter, a second kind of approximation of a signal is used, i.e., a new kind of data interpolation is proposed which is called the slopes algorithm. The proposed method is better than other interpolation algorithms because in the other approaches, a straight line from the initial point to final point, or the initial point or final point are taken as the approximation of the signal, while in the proposed method, a function from the initial point to final point is used to approximate the signal.

The chapter is structured as follows. In Sect. 2, the proposed acquisition system is introduced. In Sect. 3, the slopes algorithm for approximation of brain signals is presented, its output is guaranteed to be bounded, and its steps are explained. In Sect. 4, the proposed method is compared with other two interpolation techniques. Finally in Sect. 5, the conclusion and the future research are detailed.

2 Acquisition of the EEG Signals

A biological signal acquisition system is required to obtain the electroencephalography signal (EEG). The biological signal acquisition system is described in Fig. 1.

The following subsection describes the EEG signals.

2.1 EEG Signals

The difference of the potential in one membrane is obtained by the exchange between the ions (Na+, Cl–, K+). The neurons have a potential difference between inside and outside of the brain which is called rest potential; this potential represents constant changes because of the impulses given by the neighbor neurons [13, 14]. This potential's difference can be measured in the brain cortex using electrodes which convert the ion flow in electric flow. The characteristic of the EEG is of $5-300\,\mu$V in amplitude and of $0-150$ Hz in frequency [15].

The EEG signals are similar to the periodic waves but they can change from one time to other, and they have some characteristics which let their approximation [16, 17], such as are the amplitude, frequency, morphology, band, rhythm, and duration [13].

Fig. 1 Biological signal adquisition system

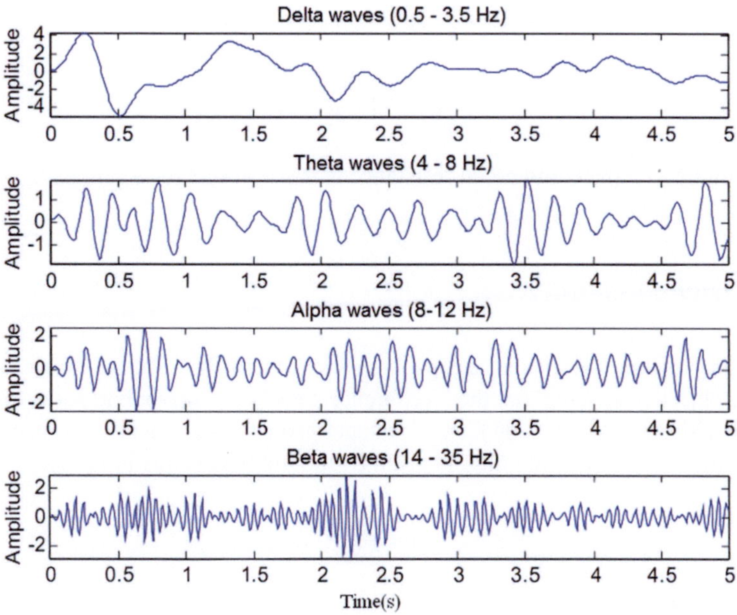

Fig. 2 The EEG signals

The following paragraphs show the characteristics which are considered for an adult in vigilance [13]. Please see Fig. 2.

Alpha rhythm signal. This is the normal rhythm signal of the bottom, and is the most stable and typical in the human. This is found in the frequencies of 8−12 Hz ± 1 Hz. The amplitude is between 20 and 60 μV. It can be seen generally in posterior regions with more amplitude in the occipital lobes.

Beta rhythm signal. It is found in the frequencies >13 Hz, in general between 14−35 Hz. The amplitude is usually low, from $5to10$ μV and is symmetric [13, 18].

Theta rhythm signal. This has a frequency of 4−8 Hz is of half of low voltage, and is found in the temporal regions [13, 18].

Delta rhythm signal. This is found in the second and third stages of the dream. It has a frequency of 0.5−3.5 Hz and the amplitude is generally higher than 75 μV [13, 18].

The rhythm obtained in this chapter is the alpha waves.

The following subsections describe the elements used in the acquisition system.

2.2 *Instrumentation Amplifier*

The AD620 integrated circuit is selected because it is highly recommended for biological signals; all the components are found inside of the electronic circuit, except one resistance which is used to determine the desired gain [19–21].

The desired gain is found using the following equation:

$$G = 1 + \left[\frac{49.4K}{R_G}\right], \tag{1}$$

Using Eq. (1), the commercial resistance is $R_G = 100\Omega$ for a gain of $G = 200$.

2.3 High Pass Filter

The high pass filter is a resistance capacitor passive filter (RC). The RC high pass filter has the objective of removing the interference signals (noise) such as is the touch of the electrode and the skin, and the DC voltages given by the patient movements [22].

The cut frequency of the filter is given by the following equation [23]:

$$f_c = \frac{1}{2\pi RC}, \tag{2}$$

where $R = 1\ \mathrm{M}\Omega$ and $C = 1\ \mu\mathrm{F}$.

2.4 Amplification

The objective of the amplification stage is to avoid the amplitude saturation of the EEG acquisition. The amplifier and not the inverter circuit with constant gain of the operational amplifier of [23] is used. In this stage, a OP07C integrated circuit is used because it requires low power [24].

The gain of the amplification is given by:

$$G = \frac{V_s}{V_1} = 1 + \frac{R_2}{R_1}, \tag{3}$$

In this stage, the selected gain is $G = 20$, and using Eq. (3), the resistances R_1 and R_2 are obtained as $R_1 = 2.7\ \mathrm{K}\Omega$ and $R_2 = 47\ \mathrm{K}\Omega$.

2.5 Low Pass Filter

In [25], it can be seen that if the order of the low pass filter increases, then the slope and the filter behavior also increases; the MAX7401 integrated circuit is used because it is an eighth-order filter which is recommended for low frequencies [26].

The cut frequency of the MAX7401 is given as follows:

$$f_{osc}(KHz) = \frac{k \cdot 10^3}{C_{osc}}, \tag{4}$$

where $k = 38$, $f_{osc} = 100 f_c$, and f_c is the cut frequency.

Using Eq. (4), C_{osc} is obtained as $C_{osc} = 47$ nF for a frequency of $f_c = 15$ Hz.

2.6 Final Electronic Circuit

Figure 3 shows the final electronic circuit of the acquisition system.

2.7 Data Acquisition

The acquisition board of National Instruments of the Fig. 4 is used to digitalize and to send the obtained signal to a personal computer it is called NI myDAQ and it is a device of easy application. Figure 5 shows one program designed to save the real data in one .xml file using the Labview software.

The board only is used to connect the proposed acquisition system and the personal computer.

Remark 1 The acquisition board of Fig. 4 with the Labview program of Fig. 5, the final electronic circuit of Fig. 3, and one special electrode are used to obtain the real data of a brain signal. The real signal will be used for approximation.

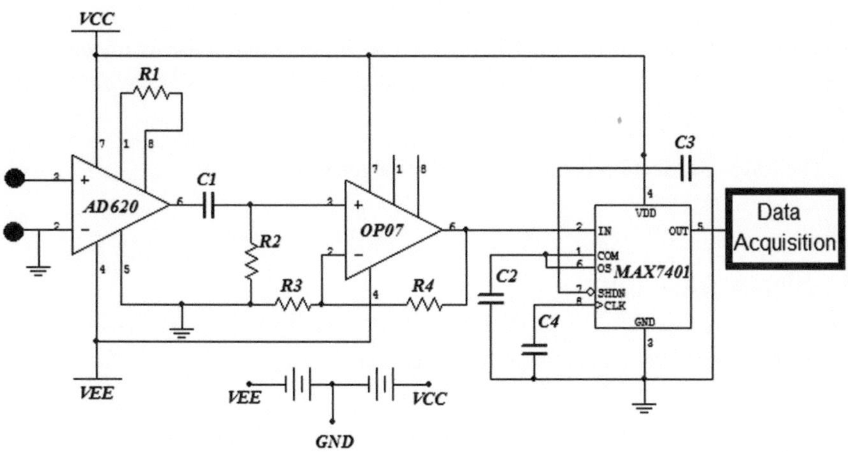

Fig. 3 Electronic circuit of the acquisition system

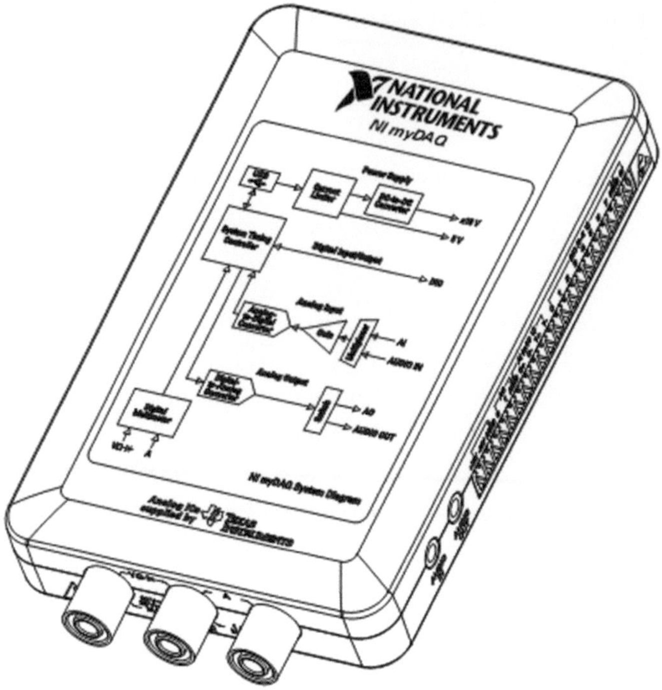

Fig. 4 NI myDAQ data acquisition board

Remark 2 Only 1 signal is obtained and not 10 because there exists one epileptic focus where an epileptic seizure starts; there are many cases where only in this point remains the signal. It is assumed that the obtained signal is the epileptic focus of an epileptic seizure [27].

Remark 3 The real EEG signal is polluted with noise; the noise is rejected with the filters constructed with the AD620 integrated circuit of Fig. 3, and with a special electrode.

The following section presents the slopes algorithm.

3 Slopes Algorithm

The slopes algorithm is described in this section.

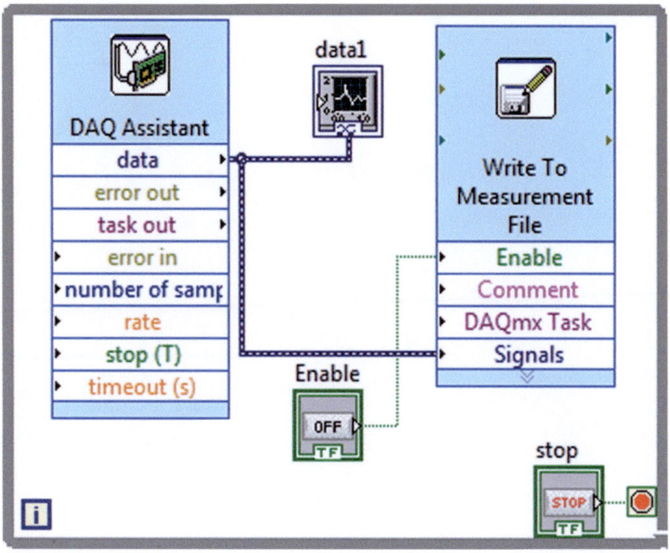

Fig. 5 Labview program

3.1 Detailed Description of the Algorithm

Consider the function $y_k = f(x_k) \in \Re$ with $x_k \in \Re$, for $k = 1, 2, \ldots, T$, where T is the iterations number. The approximation consists of finding $\widehat{y}_k$ such that it approximates y_k.

The slope of y_k denoted as m_k using the x_k and y_k data of the real brain signal is obtained as follows:

$$m_k = \frac{y_k - y_{k-1}}{x_k - x_{k-1}}, \tag{5}$$

The real brain signal is divided into N intervals; each interval considers a slope sign change in y_k, and the signal taken from x_k for each interval is denoted by j.

Figure 6 shows the approximation of a signal using the slopes algorithm.

Equation (6) describes the approximation of a signal using the proposed slopes algorithm:

$$\widehat{y}_k = (1 - \lambda_k) \cdot y_{i,j,k} + \lambda_k \cdot y_{f,j,k}, \tag{6}$$

where $y_{i,j,k}$ is the initial value of y_k in the interval j, $y_{f,j,k}$ is the final value of y_k in the interval j, k is the variant iteration inside of interval j, λ_k is a variant-in-time parameter of the interval j, λ_k is given as follows:

$$\lambda_k = \frac{k - k_{i,j}}{k_{f,j} - k_{i,j}}, \tag{7}$$

Fig. 6 Slopes algorithm

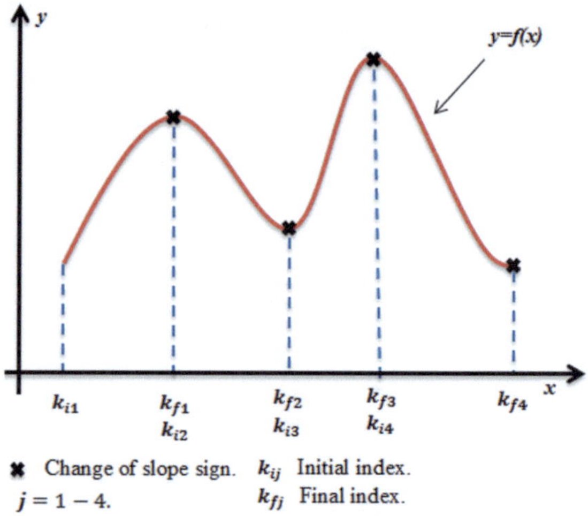

where $k_{i,j}$ is the initial value of λ_k in the interval j, and $k_{f,j}$ is the final value of λ_k in the interval j.

It is known that $k_{i,j} \leq k \leq k_{f,j}$ for each interval j; consequently, $0 \leq \lambda_k \leq 1$, and λ_k always increases.

The variant parameter λ_k is important in the proposed slopes algorithm because it allows $\widehat{y}_k$ to approximate y_k from the initial point to the final point for each interval j.

3.2 *Boundedness of the Slopes Algorithm Output*

In this section the slopes algorithm output will be bounded.

Substituting Eq. (7) into Eq. (6) of the slopes algorithm gives:

$$\widehat{y}_k = \left(1 - \frac{k - k_{i,j}}{k_{f,j} - k_{i,j}}\right) \cdot y_{i,j,k} + \frac{k - k_{i,j}}{k_{f,j} - k_{i,j}} \cdot y_{f,j,k}, \tag{8}$$

Equation (8) can be rewritten as follows:

$$\widehat{y}_k = y_{i,j,k} + \frac{k - k_{i,j}}{k_{f,j} - k_{i,j}} \left(y_{f,j,k} - y_{i,j,k}\right), \tag{9}$$

3.3 The Proposed Algorithm

Finally, the slopes algorithm for approximation of brain signals is as follows:

1. Obtain the slope of y_k denoted as m_k using the x_k and y_k data of the brain signal and using Eq. (5).
2. For each slope sign change of y_k, obtain one interval denoted by j; the maximum number of intervals is N.
3. For each interval j, obtain λ_k with Eq. (7).
4. For each interval j, obtain $\widehat{y}_k$ as the approximation of y_k using Eq. (6).

4 Results and Discussions

An acquisition system is used to obtain real data of two brain signals. The acquisition system has an amplification of 4000 and a cut frequency of 15 Hz. The acquisition system is applied with a 28-year-old healthy man with closed eyes, the electrode is localized in F3 because of the international system 10–20. See Fig. 7, and references [28, 29]. Figure 8 shows the real acquisition system.

The brain signals are obtained with the NI myDAQ which is configured to obtain 1000 iterations per second. The first brain signal is obtained in one second from 5.5s to 6.5s for example 1, and the second brain signal is obtained in one second from 150s to 151s for example 2.

The slopes algorithm is compared with the least squares algorithm of [9–12], and with the nearest neighbor of [7, 8] for approximation of two brain signals.

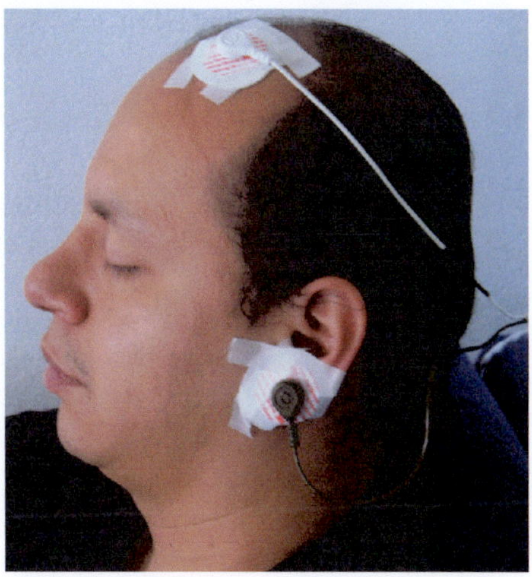

Fig. 7 The electrodes on the man

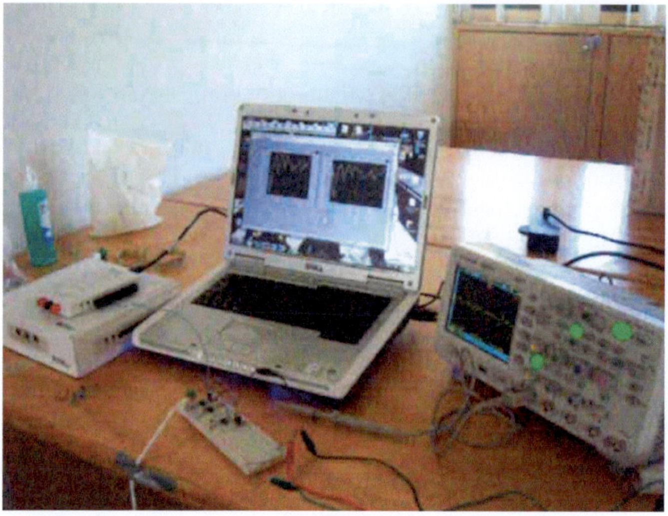

Fig. 8 The acquisition system

To find the best algorithm, the root mean square error (RMSE) is used, which is described as follows:

$$\text{RMSE} = \left(\frac{1}{T} \sum_{k=1}^{T} e_i^2(k) \right)^{\frac{1}{2}} \tag{10}$$

where T is the iterations number, and $e_i(k) = y_k - \hat{y}_k$ is the approximation error for each iteration.

4.1 Example 1: The First Brain Behavior

Figure 9 shows the approximation of the brain signal using the slopes, least squares, and nearest neighbor algorithms for example 1.

From the first view of Fig. 9, it can be seen that the approximation with the three algorithms is good; however, for each slope change on the real signal, the least squares considers a straight line to join the points, nearest neighbor considers the start or final point, and slopes considers a curve to join the points such that the last algorithm is the most approximated to the brain behavior.

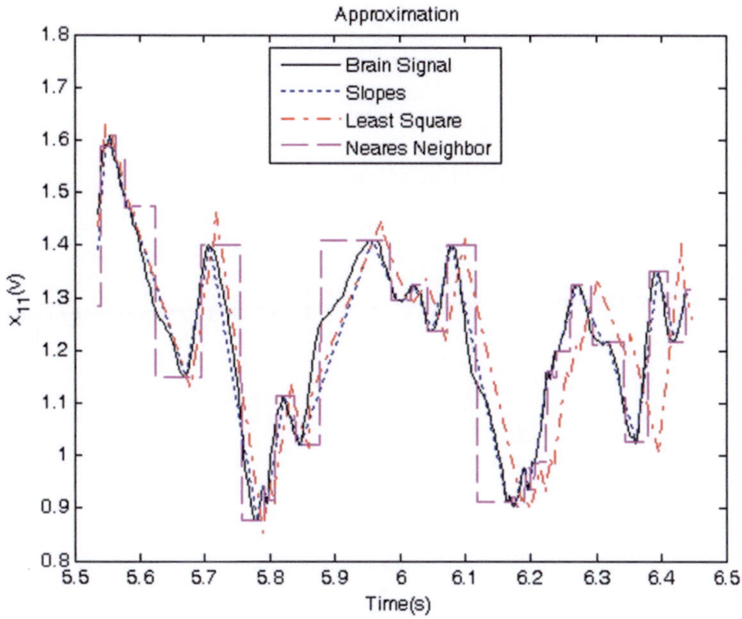

Fig. 9 Approximation results for example 1

4.2 Example 2: The Second Brain Behavior

Figure 10 shows the approximation of the brain signal using the slopes, least squares, and nearest neighbor algorithms.

From the first view of Fig. 10, it can be seen that the approximation with the three algorithms is good; however, for each slope change on the real signal, the least squares considers a straight line to join the points, nearest neighbor considers the start or final point, and slopes considers a curve to join the points such that the last algorithm is the most approximated to the brain behavior.

4.3 Comparison of the Algorithms

The comparison results of the least squares, nearest neighbor, and slopes algorithms using the RMSE of Eq. (10) are shown in Table 1 and in Fig. 11 for example 1, and in Table 1 and Fig. 12 for example 2.

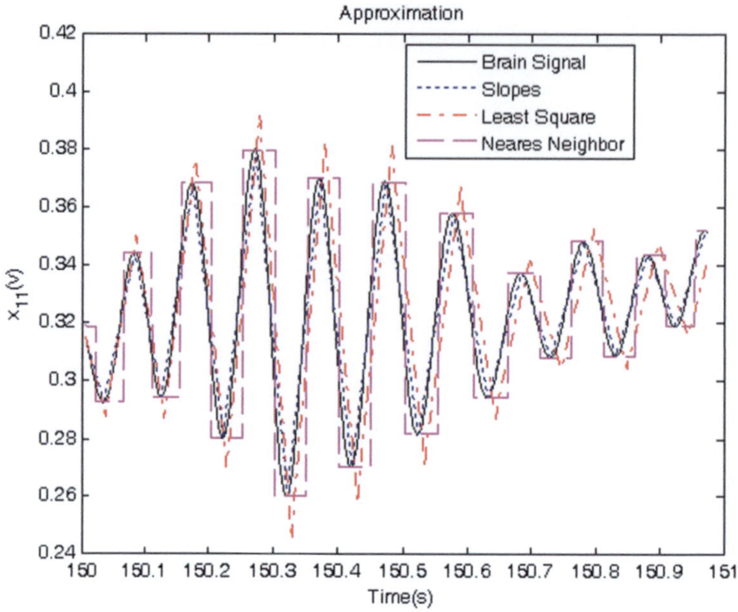

Fig. 10 Approximation results for example 2

Table 1 Comparison for RMSE

RMSE	Slopes	Least square	Nearest neighbor
Example 1	0.0336	0.1075	0.0894
Example 2	0.0058	0.0234	0.0204

From Figs. 11 and 12 and Table 1, it can be observed that the slopes algorithm achieves better performance when compared with both the least squares and nearest neighbor methods for approximation of the brain signals because the RMSE is smaller for the first than for the other two.

From [30], the elements considered for computation complexity in each iteration are the number of multiplications or the number of algebraic additions. The equations used each iteration for slopes algorithm are (5), (6), and (7). Table 2 shows the comparison of the computation complexity of the three algorithms where the multiplications number is denoted as M, the algebraic additions number is denoted as A, the equations used for each algorithm are denoted as E, the total algebraic additions or multiplications are denoted as To, and the elements number of each interval is m, $m > 1$.

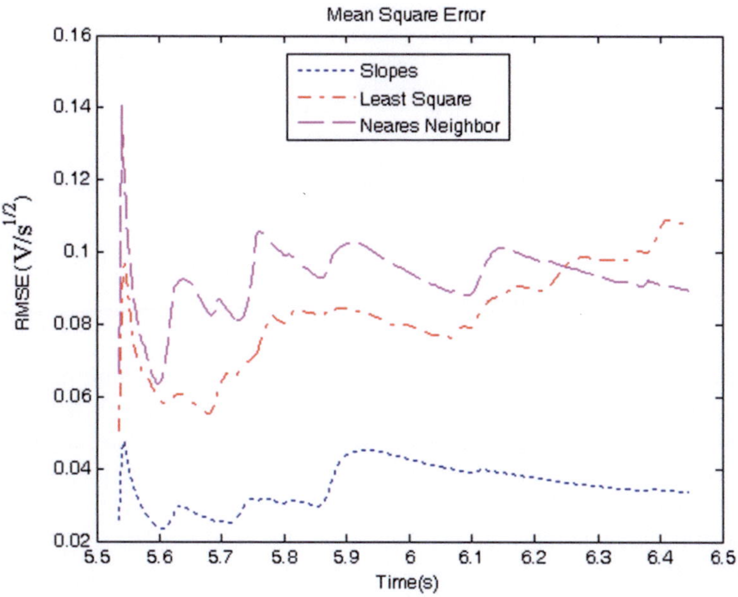

Fig. 11 The RMSE for example 1

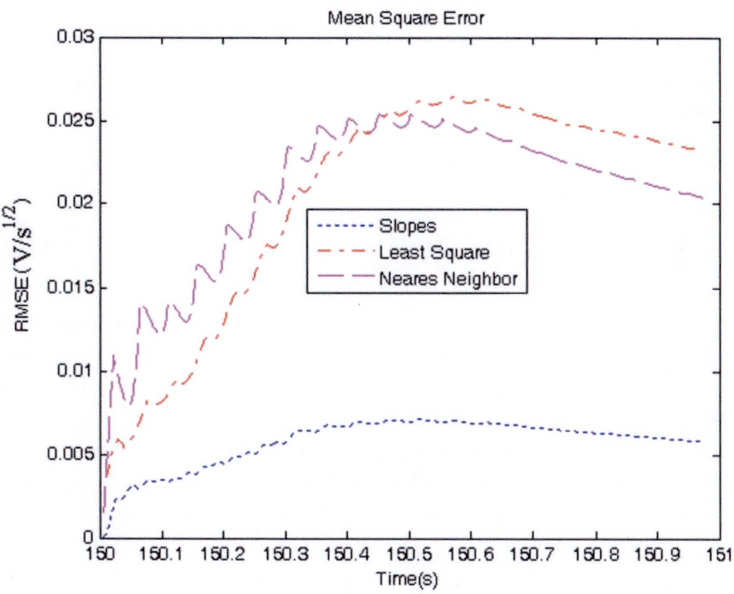

Fig. 12 The RMSE for example 2

Table 2 Computation complexity

Least square	A	M	Nearest neighbor	A	M	Slopes	A	M
Example 1	2	1		2	1		2	1
	1	1		10	6		2	2
	$2m+1$	2		2	2		2	1
	$6m+2$	$2m+4$						
To	$8m+6$	$2m+8$	To	14	9	To	6	4

From Table 2, it can be seen that for the least squares algorithm the algebraic additions number is $8m + 6$ and the multiplications number is $2m + 8$, for the nearest neighbor algorithm the algebraic additions number is 14 and the multiplications number is 9, and for the slopes algorithm the algebraic additions number is 6 and the multiplications number is 4. Thus, the slopes approach is the algorithm with the least computational complexity because it uses the least number of operations in each iteration.

Remark 4 It is difficult the existence of a benchmark signal because these signals are very variable, even for the same person, in different times, different signals are obtained, as can be seen from the signals of Figs. 9 and 10 which are obtained from the same person at different times; this depends on many factors such as the attitude, sense of humor, comfortability, and so on. This issue is greater for different persons than for one person.

5 Concluding Remarks

In this chapter, the slopes algorithm was proposed for the approximation of brain signals. The slopes algorithm was compared with the least squares and nearest neighbor algorithms for the approximation of brain signals, given that the proposed approach achieved better performance when compared with both the second and third algorithms because the RMSE for the first is the smallest one. The above method could be used on medical instrumentation for classification, recognition, prediction, detection, diagnosis, or control of epileptic seizures. As future research, the proposed acquisition system could be used to obtain other biological signals, or the slopes algorithm could be compared with some intelligent algorithms.

References

1. M. Amiri, F. Bahrami, M. Janahmadi, Functional modeling of astrocytes in epilepsy: a feedback system perspective. Neural Comput. Appl. **20**, 1131–1139 (2011)
2. A. Bertrand, M. Moonen, Distributed signal estimation in sensor networks where nodes have different interests. Signal Process. **92**, 1679–1690 (2012)
3. C. Chen, O. Bıro, Three-dimensional time-harmonic eddy current problems solved by the geometric multigrid preconditioned conjugate gradient method. IET Sci. Meas. & Technol. **6**(5), 319–323 (2012)
4. B. Jelfs, D.P. Mandic, S.C. Douglas, An adaptive approach for the identification of improper complex signals. Signal Process. **92**, 335–344 (2012)
5. J. Lei, S. Liu, X.Y. Wang, Dynamic inversion in electrical capacitance tomography using the ensemble Kalman filter. IET Sci. Meas. & Technol. **6**(2), 63–77 (2012)
6. J. Tang, F. Liu, X. Zhang, X. Liang, Q. Fan, Partial discharge recognition based on sf6 decomposition products and support vector machine. IET Sci. Meas. & Technol. **6**(4), 198–204 (2012)
7. S.T. Chong, W. Man, Adaptive approximate nearest neighbor search for fractal image compression. IEEE Trans. Image Process. **11**(6), (2002)
8. D.C. Dening, F.G. Gray, R.M. Haralick, Prosthesis control using a nearest neighbor electromyographic pattern classifier. IEEE Trans. Biomed. Eng. BME-30 (6), (1983)
9. E. Lughofer, Sigle pass active learning with conflict and ignorance. Evol. Syst. **3**, 251–271 (2012)
10. E. Lughofer, A dynamic split-and-merge approach for evolving cluster models. Evol. Syst. **3**, 135–151 (2012)
11. C. Mu, C. Sun, X. Yu, Internal model control based on a novel least square support vector machines for MIMO nonlinear discrete systems. Neural Comput. Appl. **20**, 1159–1166 (2011)
12. A.H. Phan, A. Cichocki, Seeking an appropriate alternative least squares algorithm for nonnegative tensor factorizations. Neural Comput. Appl. **21**, 623–637 (2012)
13. C. Martinez, B. Rojas, Tecnicas de Electroencefalografia, 2da edición, Secretaria de Educación Publica, Comunicaciones Científicas Mexicanas S.A. de C.V., México. ISBN: 968-7858-12-5, (1998)
14. J.B. Webster, *Medical Instrumentation, Application and Design*, 4th edn. (Jonh Wiley & Sons Inc, United States of America, 2010)
15. C. Ramirez, M. Hernandez, Procesamiento en tiempo real de variables fisiológicas, Universidad Nacional de Experimental de Táchira, Decanato de Investigación, Grupo de Biomédica
16. F. Gibbs, E. Gibbs, *Atlas of Electroencephalography, Changes Whit age, Asleep*, vol. 1 (Addison Wesley, Massachusetts, 1950), pp. 82–89
17. D. Klass, D. Daly, *Current Practice of clinical electroencephalography* (Raven Press, New York, 1975), pp.69–109. Chapter 5
18. S. De Castro, J. Perez, Manual de patología general, 6ta Edición, Masson Elsevier, Barcelona. ISBN: 978 84 458 1540 3, (2006)
19. L. Cost, *Low Power Instrumentation Amplifier AD620* (Analog Devices, USA, 1999)
20. R. Darraji, F.M. Ghannouchi, O. Hammi, Generic load-pull-based design methodology for performance optimisation of Doherty amplifiers. IET Sci. Meas. & Technol. **6**(3), 132–138 (2012)
21. A.S. Hussaini, I. Elfergani, J. Rodriguez, R.A. Abd-Alhameed, Efficient multi-stage load modulation radio frequency power amplifier for green radio frequency front end. IET Sci. Meas. & Technol. **6**(3), 117–124 (2012)
22. J.D. Bronzino, *Biomedical Signal Analysis, the Biomedical Engineering Handbook*, 3rd edn. (Tylor & Francis Group, Hartford, Connecticut, USA, 2006). ISBN: 0 8493 2121 2
23. R.L. Boylestad, L. Nashelsky, *Electronic Devices and Circuit Theory*, 10th edn. (Prentice Hall, 2008). ISBN 970-26-0436-2
24. *Ultralow Offset Voltage Operational Amplifier, OP07* (Analog Devices)
25. J.J. Rubio, D. Vazquez, J. Pacheco, V. Garcia, Mathematical model of low pass filters. Recent. Pat. Eng. **5**(2), 155–162 (2011). Bentham Science Publishers

26. 8th-Order, Lowpass, Bessel, Switched-Capacitor Filters, Max7401, Maxim, USA (1999)
27. J. Gutierrez, Detección del foco epiléptico y su ruta de propagación, Congreso Latinoamericano de Ingenieria Boimedica (2001)
28. R. Homan, Cerebral location of international 10–20 system electrode placement. Electroencephalogr. Clin. Neurophysiol. **66**(4), 376–382 (1987)
29. G.H. Klem, H.O. LuEders, H.H. Jasper, C. Elger, The ten-twenty electrode system of the International Federation. Recommendations for the Practice of Clinical Neurophysiology: Guidelines of the International Federation of Clinical Physiology (EEG Suppl. 52). International Federation of Clinical Neurophysiology. All rights reserved. International Federation of Clinical Neurophysiology. Elsevier, 1, (1999)
30. W. Khalil, J. Kleinfinger, M. Gautier, Reducing the computational burden of the dynamic models of robots, in *IEEE International Conference on Robotics and Automation* (1986), pp. 525–531

A Method for Online Pattern Recognition of Abnormal Eye Movements

Abstract In this chapter, a method for the pattern recognition is used to provide a better diagnosis for patients with abnormal eye movements. The real data of signals of two eye movements (up and down) of patients are obtained using a mindset ms-100 system. A new method which uses one intelligent algorithm for online pattern recognition is proposed. The difference between the proposed method and the previous works is that in other works, both behaviors (up and down) are trained with one intelligent algorithm, while in this work, up behavior is trained with one intelligent algorithm and down behavior is trained with other intelligent algorithm. This is because the multi-output system can always be decomposed into a collection of single-output systems with the advantage of using different parameters for each one if necessary. The comparison results of the proposed method using the adaline network, multilayer network, or the Sugeno fuzzy inference system are presented for online pattern recognition of two eye movements.

1 Introduction

There is some medical research such as [1–8]. The aforementioned research is interesting; the work of [1, 7] is related to cardiac signals, the work of [3, 8] is related to the image process, the work of [4, 6] is related to cancers, and the work of [2, 5] is related to diagnosis. The work of this chapter is related to diagnosis like the works of [2, 5], but the work of [2] is related to cardiac diagnosis, and the work of [5] is related to diagnosis based on X-rays, while the work of this chapter is related to abnormal eye movements. A normal eye movement is when the patient wants to move their eye up or down and the eye moves. An abnormal eye movement is when the patient wants to move their eye up or down and the eye does not move or it moves to another place.

Recent results show that the neural networks or fuzzy system techniques seem to be very effective for the pattern recognition of many real problems. There are some authors who have proposed some results in pattern recognition such as [9–22].

In [9], the detection of broken rotor bars and broken end-ring in three-phase squirrel cage induction motors using an artificial neural network is studied. In [10],

J. de J. Rubio et al., *Dynamic Models of Energy, Robotic, and Biological Systems*,
https://doi.org/10.1007/978-3-031-85438-5_9

the authors propose a real-time electromyographic (EMG) pattern recognition for the control of a multifunction myoelectric hand from four channel EMG signals. In [11], the authors develop an efficient feature-projection method for electromyographic (EMG) pattern recognition. In [12], a neural network model is introduced, which is based on nonlinear perturbed Duffing equation; the proposed model is then implemented for three different parameters of the Duffing map separately. The three different models have been used for binary pattern recognition. In [13], they present some of the classics pattern recognition methods such as are the Bayesian decision, the likelihood or the multilayer neural network. The investigation of [14] presents a system for the diagnosis of repairable technical objects with the use of an artificial neural network of a radial basis function. In [15], the authors present a novel pattern recognition framework by capitalizing on dimensionality increasing techniques. The study of [16] presents a new method for fault classification in a series-compensated transmission line using a multiclass support vector machine and a multiclass extreme learning machine. The research of [17] proposes a way of self-organizing feature mapping for recognizing a road sign. In [18], the authors propose a perimeter intruder detection system which uses radar effect and it carries out continuous perimeter patrol by performing sequential suveillance of detector outputs as well as distributed pattern recognition analysis. In [19], the authors give the comparison results between the back propagation, the fuzzy neural network without normalization and the fuzzy neural network with normalization algorithms for the case of abnormal neonatal cerebral doppler ultrasound waveforms. A novel flexible array self-organizing map algorithm is proposed in [20]; the algorithm is successfully applied in pattern recognition of two artificial data sets and red spotted stonecrop samples. In [21], a new two-dimensional supervised learning method is developed for face recognition. The investigation of [22] looks the application of the multi-layer perceptron to the task of categorizing texts based on their authors' style.

The first difference between the proposed method for online pattern recognition and the previous works is that in other works, both behaviors (Up and Down) are trained with one intelligent algorithm, while in this work, Up behavior is trained with one intelligent algorithm and Down behavior is trained with other intelligent algorithm. The second difference is that in the aforementioned works, there is not a pattern recognition application for the case of abnormal eye movements.

A doctor could say that a patient is sick while he/she is healthy or could mistakenly say that the patient is healthy while he/she is sick. So it is important to generate a system that can give a good diagnosis, in this case for abnormal eye movements.

In this chapter, a method for pattern recognition to provide a better diagnosis for the patients related to abnormal eye movements is proposed.

In [23], the authors propose a good communication system to give the electrooculograms (EOG) occurring as a result of eye movements and in [24] they found the optimum positions for the electrodes for the communication system. The aforementioned works are used as a guide to obtain the real data of eye movements of some patients.

This chapter is organized as follows. In Sect. 2, the mindset ms-100 and the communication systems are briefly reviewed. In Sect. 3, the logical combinations are briefly reviewed. In Sect. 4, the differences between the proposed method and previous works is presented, In Sect. 5, the intelligent algorithms used by the proposed method are explained in detail. In Sect. 6, the proposed method for online pattern recognition is described in detail. In Sect. 7, a numbered procedure of the proposed method is explained. In Sect. 8, experimental results of the proposed method applied to some persons is presented. Finally, in Sect. 9 the results and the possible future researches are explained.

2 The Communication System

The mindset ms-100 system is used to obtain the real signals of eye movements [25]. The features of the mindset ms-100 are shown in Fig. 1, where 1 is the Power Light, 2 is the SCSI Sampling Light, 3 is the Circuit Reference Ground, 4 are the EEG Input Channels, and 5 is the Expansion Connector.

Figure 2 shows a block diagram of the electro-oculograms (EOG) communication system obtained from the eye movements of a patient where Ch.V is the vertical

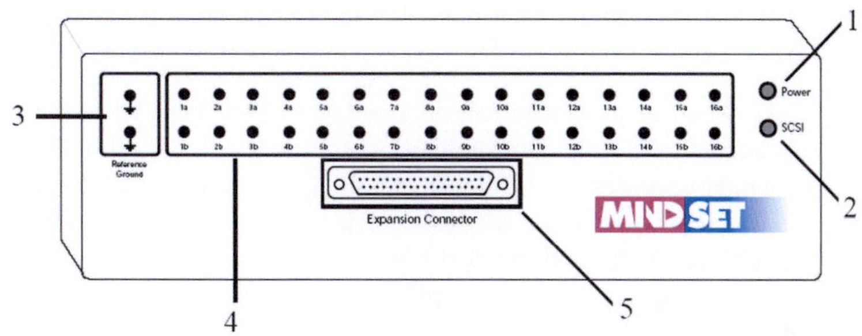

Fig. 1 Mindset front view

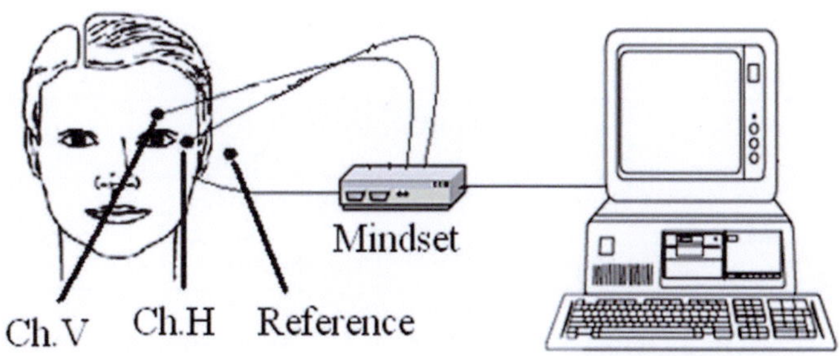

Fig. 2 Block diagram of the EOG communication system

channel signal, Ch.H is the horizontal channel signal, and Reference is the reference signal.

The EOG are the signals obtained as a result of the eye movements of a patient and these EOG are detected using three electrodes; one electrode on the temple, one above and other underneath of the eye. Usually, the detected signals are by direct current (DC) coupling to specify the direction of the gaze. In the experiments in this chapter, three electrodes are placed on the dominant side of the eye of the patient according to the optimum positions suggested by [23, 24].

3 The Logical Combinations

Figure 3 shows the relationship between real eye movements (input) and the EOG signals (output) of the system. Let us denoted the upper and lower thresholds of the vertical channel Ch.V as V1 and V2, respectively, and let us denote the upper and lower thresholds of the horizontal channel Ch.H as H1 and H2, respectively. When the EOG potential exceeds one of these thresholds, the output assumes ON, and when the EOG potential does not exceed one of these thresholds, the output assumes OFF. The process of transforming the EOG signals from the intention of the patient is as follows [23]:

1. Output Up is when an Up behavior is obtained, first, Threshold V1 of the vertical channel becomes ON while Threshold V2 is OFF, second, Threshold V2 of the vertical channel becomes ON while Threshold V1 becomes OFF; this behavior is denoted as Ch.V-Up. H1 and H2 of the horizontal channel remain OFF all the time; this behavior is denoted as Ch.H-Up.
2. Output Down is when a Down behavior is obtained, first, Threshold V2 of the vertical channel becomes ON while Threshold V1 is OFF, second, Threshold V1 of the vertical channel becomes ON while Threshold V2 becomes OFF; this behavior is denoted as Ch.V-Down. H1 and H2 of the horizontal channel remain OFF all the time; this behavior is denoted as Ch.H-Down.

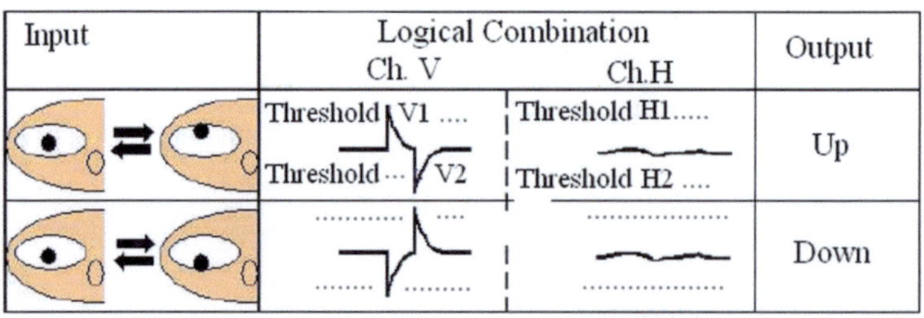

Fig. 3 Relationship between eye movements, the detected EOG signals, and intention input

4 Differences Between the Proposed Method for Online Pattern Recognition and Previous Works

The first difference between the proposed method for online pattern recognition and the previous works such as [9–22] is that in other works, both behaviors (Up and Down) are trained with one intelligent algorithm; please see Figs. 2, 3, and 4, where Ch.V-Up is the EOG signal of the vertical channel for the up behavior, Ch.H-Up is the EOG signal of the horizontal channel of the up behavior, Ch.V-Down is the EOG signal of the vertical channel for the down behavior, Ch.H-Down is the EOG signal of the horizontal channel of the down behavior, while in this work, Up behavior is trained with one intelligent algorithm and Down behavior is trained with other intelligent algorithm; please see Figs. 2, 3, and 5, where Ch.V-Up is the EOG signal of the vertical channel for the up behavior, and Ch.H-Up is the EOG signal of the horizontal channel of the up behavior, Ch.V-Down is the EOG signal of the vertical channel for the down behavior, Ch.H-Down is the EOG signal of the horizontal channel of the down behavior. In the proposed method, one intelligent algorithm is not used to learn both behaviors as in the previous works because the multi-output system can always be decomposed into a collection of single-output systems [26] with the advantage of using different parameters for each one if necessary. The second difference is that in the aforementioned works, there is not a pattern recognition application for the case of abnormal eye movements.

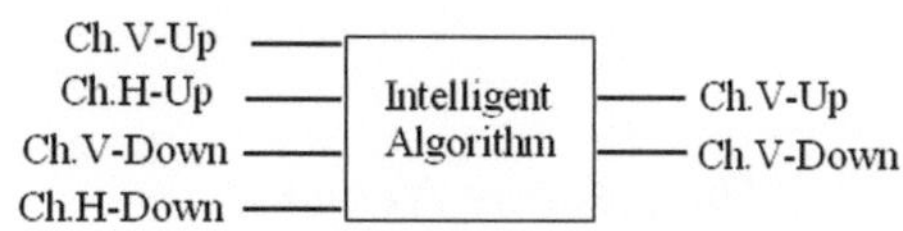

Fig. 4 Training with the previous works

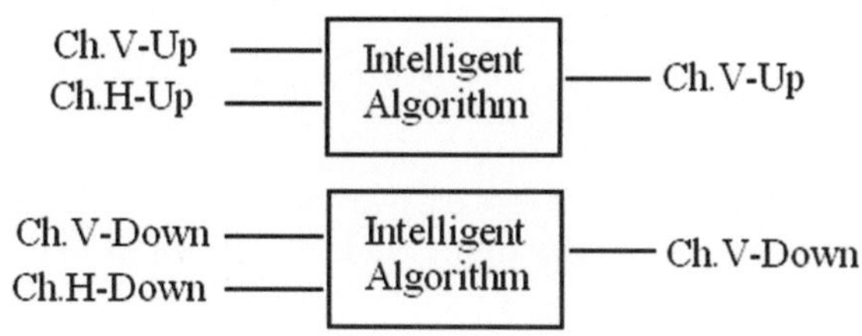

Fig. 5 Training with the proposed method

5 Intelligent Algorithms

In this section, the intelligent algorithms used by the proposed method for the online pattern recognition known as neural networks or fuzzy system are presented. Please see Figs. 2, 3, and 5 for the details of the proposed method. The neural networks are the multilayer neural network [13, 27–29], the Sugeno fuzzy inference system [26, 27, 29], or the adaline network [28]. The intelligent algorithms in this study are used to online approximate the Up and Down behaviors. The intelligent algorithms learn the up behavior considering the vertical and the horizontal real signals obtained from the vertical Ch.V and the horizontal channels Ch.H; the two inputs for each intelligent algorithm are denoted as $z_1(k) =$ Ch.V-Up and $z_2(k) =$ Ch.H-Up for the Up behavior, or $z_1(k) =$ Ch.V-Down and $z_2(k) =$ Ch.H-Down for the Down behavior. Please see Fig. 5. The output $y(k)$ for each of the intelligent algorithm is the average of the two input signals as follows:

$$y(k) = \frac{\sum_{i=1}^{2} z_i(k)}{2}, \tag{1}$$

so the output is obtained as $y(k) =$ (Ch.V-Up+Ch.H-Up)$/2$ for the Up behavior or $y(k) =$ (Ch.V-Down+Ch.H-Down)$/2$ for the Down behavior. Please see Fig. 5.

The intelligent algorithm used to learn the Down behavior in the same as that used to learn for the Up behavior.

5.1 *The Adaline Network*

The adaline network denoted as AN approximates the real output $y(k)$ as follows [28]:

$$\widehat{y}_1(k) = \phi\left(\sum_{i=1}^{2} w_i(k) z_i(k)\right), \tag{2}$$

where $z_1(k)$ and $z_2(k)$ are the two real inputs for one of the behaviors (up or down) and $w_i(k)$ are the weights of the hidden layer. ϕ is a sigmoid function given as follows:

$$\phi(x(k)) = \frac{1}{1 + e^{-x(k)}}, \tag{3}$$

where $x(k) = \sum_{i=1}^{2} w_i(k) z_i(k)$. The updating of the weights for the training is given as follows:

$$w_i(k+1) = w_i(k) - \eta_{w1} z_i(k) e_1(k), \tag{4}$$

where $0 < \eta_{w1} < 1$ is the constant learning speed, the initial weights $w_i(1)$ are selected as random number from 0 to 1, and $e_1(k)$ is the identification error defined as follows:

$$e_1(k) = \widehat{y}_1(k) - y(k), \tag{5}$$

The difference between this network and the classical one is that the second one uses a signum function that is used only for binary cases and the first one uses a sigmoid function that is used for the continuous case.

5.2 *The Multilayer Neural Network*

The multilayer neural network denoted as MNN approximates the real output $y(k)$ as follows [13, 27–29]:

$$\widehat{y}_2(k) = \sum_{j=1}^{m} v_j(k)\phi_j\left(\sum_{i=1}^{2} w_{ij}(k)z_i(k)\right), \tag{6}$$

where $z_1(k)$ and $z_2(k)$ are the two real inputs for one of the behaviors (up or down), $w_{ij}(k)$ and $v_j(k)$ are the weights of the hidden and output layer, respectively, m is the number of neuron in the hidden layer. ϕ_j is the sigmoid function given as follows:

$$\phi_j(x_j(k)) = \frac{1}{1 + e^{-x_j(k)}} \text{ for } j = 1, \ldots, m, \tag{7}$$

where $x_j(k) = \sum_{i=1}^{2} w_{ij}(k)z_i(k)$. The updating of the weights for the training is given as follows:

$$\begin{aligned} v_j(k+1) &= v_j(k) - \eta_{v2}\phi_j(x_j(k))e_2(k), \\ w_{ij}(k+1) &= w_{ij}(k) - \eta_{w2}z_i(k)v_j(k)\frac{e^{-x_j(k)}}{\left[1+e^{-x_j(k)}\right]^2}e_2(k), \end{aligned} \tag{8}$$

where $0 < \eta_{v2} < 1$ and $0 < \eta_{w2} < 1$ are the constant learning speeds, the initial weights $v_j(1)$ and $w_{ij}(1)$ are selected as random numbers from 0 to 1, and $e_2(k)$ is the identification error defined as follows:

$$e_2(k) = \widehat{y}_2(k) - y(k), \tag{9}$$

The difference between this network and the classical one is that the second one is more complex because uses signum functions in the hidden and in the output layer, while the first one is more simple because uses a sigmoid function only in the hidden layer.

5.3 The Sugeno Fuzzy Inference System

The Sugeno fuzzy inference system denoted as SFIS approximates the real output $y(k)$ as follows [26, 27, 29]:

$$\widehat{y}_3(k) = \frac{\sum_{j=1}^{m} v_j(k)\alpha_j\left(-\prod_{i=1}^{2}\frac{[z_i(k)-c_{ij}(k)]^2}{\sigma_{ij}^2(k)}\right)}{\sum_{j=1}^{m}\alpha_j\left(-\prod_{i=1}^{2}\frac{[z_i(k)-c_{ij}(k)]^2}{\sigma_{ij}^2(k)}\right)}, \tag{10}$$

where $z_1(k)$ and $z_2(k)$ are the two real inputs for one of the behaviors (up or down), $c_{ij}(k)$ and $\sigma_{ij}(k)$ are the centers and the widths of the input membership functions, and $v_j(k)$ are the centers of the output membership functions. m is the number of rules. α_j is the Gaussian function given as follows:

$$\alpha_j(x_j(k)) = \exp(x_j(k)), \tag{11}$$

where $x_j(k) = -\prod_{i=1}^{2}\frac{[z_i(k)-c_{ij}(k)]^2}{\sigma_{ij}^2(k)}$. The updating of the centers and the widths of the input membership functions and the centers of the output membership functions for the training is given as follows:

$$\begin{aligned}
v_j(k+1) &= v_j(k) - \eta_{v3}\frac{\alpha_j(x_j(k))}{\sum_{j=1}^{m}\alpha_j(x_j(k))}e_3(k),\\
c_{ij}(k+1) &= c_{ij}(k) - \eta_{c3}\beta_c(k)e_3(k),\\
\sigma_{ij}(k+1) &= \sigma_{ij}(k) - \eta_{\sigma 3}\beta_\sigma(k)e_3(k),\\
\beta_c(k) &= \frac{2\alpha_j(x_j(k))[z_i(k)-c_{ij}(k)][v_j(k)-\widehat{y}_3(k)]}{\left(\sum_{j=1}^{m}\alpha_j(x_j(k))\right)\sigma_{ij}^2(k)},\\
\beta_\sigma(k) &= \frac{2\alpha_j(x_j(k))[z_i(k)-c_{ij}(k)]^2[v_j(k)-\widehat{y}_3(k)]}{\left(\sum_{j=1}^{m}\alpha_j(x_j(k))\right)\sigma_{ij}^3(k)},
\end{aligned} \tag{12}$$

where $0 < \eta_{v3} < 1, 0 < \eta_{c3} < 1$ and $0 < \eta_{\sigma 3} < 1$ are the constant learning speeds, the initial weights $v_j(1)$, $c_{ij}(1)$, and $\sigma_{ij}(1)$ are selected as random numbers from 0 to 1, and $e_3(k)$ is the identification error defined as follows:

$$e_3(k) = \widehat{y}_3(k) - y(k), \tag{13}$$

The difference between this fuzzy system and the classical one is that the second one could uses a summarizing of the Gaussian functions and the first one uses a product.

6 Description of the Proposed Method for Online Pattern Recognition

Please see the earlier sections for a detailed description of the preliminaries of the proposed method.

Figure 6 shows one example of the 7770 real data of Up and Down behaviors of eye movements that are obtained from the vertical channel Ch.V of the above described system for each one of 7 different persons. Please note that the data are normalized and filtered; the filter is a tool box of Matlab. These data are used for the training and for the testing of the intelligent algorithms.

The proposed method for online pattern recognition uses one intelligent algorithm. The intelligent algorithm used by the proposed method could be any of the following: the adaline network denoted as AN [28], the multilayer neural network denoted as MNN [13, 27–29], or the Sugeno fuzzy inference system denoted as SFIS [26, 27, 29].

One intelligent algorithm is used to learn the up behavior and another one is used to learn the down behavior of the eye movements. Please see Fig. 5. One intelligent algorithm is not used to learn both behaviors because the multi-output system can always be decomposed into a collection of single-output systems [26] with the advantage of using different parameters for each one if necessary.

3330 data are used to train each intelligent algorithm. 4440 data are used for 8 testing, so 555 data are used for each testing. The root mean square error (RMSE) used in [30] is used for the testing of each intelligent algorithm. The RMSE is as follows:

$$RMSE = \left(\frac{1}{N} \sum_{k=1}^{N} e_i^2(k) \right)^{\frac{1}{2}}, \tag{14}$$

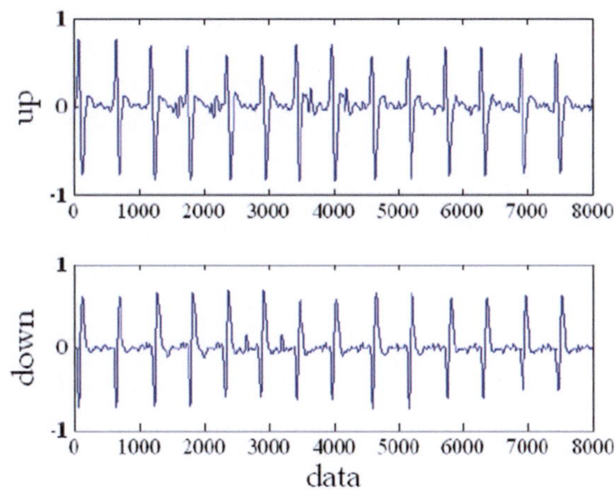

Fig. 6 7770 data of up and down behaviors of eye movements

where $e_i(k)$ is the identification error of the intelligent algorithms defined in Eq. (5) for $i = 1$ (AN), Eq. (9) for $i = 2$ (NN), or Eq. (13) for $i = 3$ (FS), and N is the number of data used for the testing.

Table 1 describes the training of the intelligent algorithms which learn the up and the down behaviors.

Where *NNup* is the multilayer neural network which learns the up behavior, *NNdown* is the multilayer neural network which learns the down behavior, *ANup* is the adaline network which learns the up behavior, *ANdown* is the adaline network which learns the down behavior, *SFup* is the Sugeno fuzzy inference system which learns the up behavior, and *SFdown* is the Sugeno fuzzy inference system which learns the down behavior.

Table 2 describes the comparison results between the intelligent algorithm which learned the up behavior and the intelligent algorithm which learned the down behavior using up data.

Where *RMSENNup*, *RMSEANup*, or *RMSESFup* is the RMSE for one testing of the intelligent algorithm that learned the up behavior, *RMSENNdown*, *RMSEANdown*, or *RMSESFdown* is the RMSE for one testing of the intelligent algorithm that learned the down behavior, *TT* indicates that the intelligent algorithm obtained a true test, and *FT* indicates that the intelligent algorithm obtained a false test.

Table 3 describes the comparison results between the intelligent algorithm which learned the up behavior and the intelligent algorithm which learned the down behavior using down data.

If *NNup*, *ANup*, or *SFup* obtain a true test, a counter denoted as ClassNN1, ClassAN1, or ClassSF1 is increased by 1 and if *NNdown* network obtain a true test, a counter denoted as ClassNN2, ClassAN2, or ClassSF2 is increased by 1.

Table 1 Training of both behaviors

NNup learns the Up behavior with up data
NNdown learns the Down behavior with down data
ANup learns the Up behavior with up data
ANdown learns the Down behavior with down data
SFup learns the Up behavior with up data
SFdown learns the Down behavior with down data

Table 2 One testing with up data

IF ($RMSENNup \leq RMSENNdown$) then (*TT* for *NNup*)
IF ($RMSENNup > RMSENNdown$) then (*FT* for *NNup*)
IF ($RMSEANup \leq RMSEANdown$) then (*TT* for *ANup*)
IF ($RMSEANup > RMSEANdown$) then (*FT* for *ANup*)
IF ($RMSESFup \leq RMSESFdown$) then (*TT* for *SFup*)
IF ($RMSESFup > RMSESFdown$) then (*FT* for *SFup*)

Table 3 One testing with down data

IF (*RMSENNdown* ≤ *RMSENNup*) then (*TT* for *NNdown*)
IF (*RMSENNdown* > *RMSENNup*) then (*FT* for *NNdown*)
IF (*RMSEANdown* ≤ *RMSEANup*) then (*TT* for *ANdown*)
IF (*RMSEANdown* > *RMSEANup*) then (*FT* for *ANdown*)
IF (*RMSESFdown* ≤ *RMSESFup*) then (*TT* for *SFdown*)
IF (*RMSESFdown* > *RMSESFup*) then (*FT* for *SFdown*)

Table 4 One example of the 8 testing

RMSENNup		*RMSENNdown*	
0.0221	0.0228	0.0213	0.0208
0.0221	0.0228	0.0213	0.0208
0.0220	0.0228	0.0215	0.0211
0.0220	0.0228	0.0215	0.0211
ClassNN1 = 4		ClassNN2 = 4	

Table 4 shows one example of the 8 testing for the case of the multilayer neural networks.

Where the first column is the RMSE of the up behavior and the second column is the RMSE of the down behavior, for the adaline network *RMSENNup* and *RMSENNdown* are changed by *RMSEANup* and *RMSEANdown*, respectively, for the Sugeno fuzzy inference system *RMSENNup* and *RMSENNdown* are changed by *RMSESFup* and *RMSESFdown*, respectively, for the adaline network ClassNN1 and ClassNN2 are changed by ClassAN1 and ClassNN2, respectively, and for the Sugeno fuzzy inference system ClassNN1 and ClassNN2 are changed by ClassSF1 and ClassSF2, respectively.

From Table 4, it can be seen for the first four lines that the RMSE of the first column is smaller than the RMSE of the second column, using Table 2 the Class1 is increased until 4 because the tests are true tests *TT*.

From Table 4, it can be seen for the last four lines that the RMSE of the first column is bigger than the RMSE of the second column, using Table 3 the Class2 is increased until 4 because the tests are true tests *TT*.

In the example described in Table 4, *TT* is 8 because all the tests are true *TT*.

Let us define the accuracy of the intelligent algorithms denoted as *AccuracyNN*, *AccuracyaAN* or *AccuracySF* as follows:

$$\begin{aligned} AccuracyNN &= \frac{TTNN}{TTNA}(100)\%, \\ AccuracyAN &= \frac{TTAN}{TTDAN}(100)\%, \\ AccuracySF &= \frac{TTSF}{TTDSF}(100)\%, \end{aligned} \tag{15}$$

where the *TTNN*, *TTAN*, or *TTSF* is the number of true tests which is the addition of the ClassNN1, ClassAN1, or ClassSF1 for the up behavior and ClassNN2, ClassAN2, or ClassSF2 for the down behavior, and the *TTDNN*, *TTDAN*, or *TTDSF* is the total number of tests obtained as the addition of the true and the false tests (*TTDNN* =

$TTNN + FTNN$, $TTDAN = TTAN + FTAN$, or $TTDSF = TTSF + FTSF$) which is 8 for this chapter.

Remark 1 The proposed method is not a simple if else algorithm, as Table 3 denotes, note that this if else rules use the RMSE errors of the different intelligent algorithms.

7 The Proposed Method for Online Pattern Recognition

The proposed method for online patter recognition is as follows:

1. Obtain the noisy data of the up and down behaviors with the mindset ms-100 system; please see Figs. 2, 3, and 5 for the details.
2. Filter the data obtained data to obtain the up and down behaviors; please see Fig. 6.
3. Learn the up and the down behaviors using Eqs. (2)–(5) for the adaline network, Eqs. (6)–(9) for the multilayer neural networks, or Eqs. (10)–(13) for the Sugeno fuzzy inference system. Please see Table 1.
4. Obtain the RMSE of the testing identification error with Eq. (14).
5. Obtain the true tests for up behavior. Please see Table 2. Obtain the true tests for the down behavior. Please see Table 3.
6. Obtain the number of true tests of ClassNN1, ClassAN1, or ClassSF1 for the up behavior and ClassNN2, ClassAN2, or ClassSF2 for the down behavior. Please see Table 4.
7. Obtain the accuracy of the intelligent algorithm using Eq. (15).

8 Experimental Results

In this section, the comparison results of the proposed method using each of the intelligent algorithms for online pattern recognition of two real eye movements are presented. Table 5 shows the pattern recognition results of the adaline network (AN) of Eqs. (2)–(5), the multilayer neural network (NN) of Eqs. (6)–(9), or the Sugeno fuzzy system (SF) of Eqs. (10)–(13) applied for 7 persons. For the adaline network, there is only one neuron. For the multilayer neural network, m is selected as 10 because it provides the best testing behavior. For the Sugeno fuzzy inference system, m is selected as 10 because it provides the best testing behavior.
Where AN is the adaline network, NN is the multilayer neural network, and the SF is the Sugeno fuzzy inference system.

From Table 5, it can be seen that when the proposed method uses the AN and the NN, it gives better behavior than when the proposed method uses the SF.

Remark 2 The work of this chapter is related to diagnosis, similar to the work of [2, 5], but the work of [2] is related to the cardiac diagnosis, the work of [5] is related to diagnosis based on X-ray, and the work of this chapter is related to abnormal eye movements.

Table 5 Pattern recognition results

	AN	NN	SF
TT for Noe	8	8	7
TT for Ricardo	8	8	7
TT for JorgeC	8	8	7
TT for JorgeZ	8	8	7
TT for Erick	8	8	7
TT for Ulises	8	8	7
TT for Monica	8	8	7
Accuracy	100%	100%	83.93%

Remark 3 In the work of [2], the authors' findings demonstrated that a 90% correct classification rate was obtained from the multilayer neural network, and a 88.33% correct classification rate was obtained from the neuro-fuzzy system; since they had a limited number of patients, there is no significant performance difference observed between the two methods. In this chapter, the adaline network and the multilayer neural network give a 100% correct classification rate, while the Sugeno fuzzy inference system gives a 83.93% correct classification rate with the proposed method.

Remark 4 The difficulty for doctors in using the proposed method is that they have to know how to use the mindset ms-100 system and this system is expensive, Fig. 7 shows when the system is used to obtain the real data of the eye movements.

Fig. 7 The mindset system used to obtain the data of the eye movements

9 Concluding Remarks

In this chapter, the signals of two eye movements (up and down) were obtained with the mindset ms-100 system. A new method which uses one intelligent algorithm for online pattern recognition was proposed for abnormal eye movements. The adaline network, the multilayer neural network, and the Sugeno fuzzy inference system were compared using the proposed method for online pattern recognition of two eye movements, given that the adaline network and the multilayer neural network have the best behavior. As future work, the mixing of the proposed method with other more sophisticated systems such as the evolving systems will be considered to look for a better result, i.e., to obtain a result that needs fewer iterations, while for other future work, the result will extended from two movements (up and down) to four movements (up, down, left, and right), and one circuit will be designed to avoid the use of the mindset ms-100 system because it is expensive making it undesirable.

References

1. D. Ertel, T. Pflederer, S. Achenbach, W.A. Kalendera, Real-time determination of the optimal reconstruction phase to control ECG pulsing in spiral cardiac CT. Phys. Med. **25**(3), 122–127 (2009)
2. F. Hardalac, N. Barisci, U. Ergun, Classification of aorta insufficiency and stenosis using MLP neural network and neuro-fuzzy system. Phys. Med. XX (4), (2004)
3. K. Imai, M. Ikeda, Y. Enchi, T. Niimi, A detection method for streak artifacts and radiological noise in a non-uniform region in a CT image. Phys. Med. **26**(3), 157–165 (2010)
4. A. Keshtkar, A. Mesbahi, S.H. Rastaa, A. Keshtkar, The feasibility of computational modelling technique to detect the bladder cancer. Phys. Med. **26**(1), 34–37 (2010)
5. K. Kisielewicza, A. Truszkiewicz, S. Wach, M. Wasilewska-Radwanska, evaluation of dose area product vs. patient dose in diagnostic X-ray units. Phys. Med. **27**(2), 117–120 (2011)
6. R. Prabhakar, M.A. Laviraj, K.P. Haresh, P.K. Julka, G.K. Rath, Impact of patient setup error in the treatment of head and neck cancer with intensity modulated radiation therapy. Phys. Med. **26**(1), 26–33 (2010)
7. R. Zannoli, I. Corazza, A. Branzi, Mechanical simulator of the cardiovascular system. Phys. Med. **25**(2), 94–100 (2009)
8. A. Zeinali, B. Hashemi, S. Akhlaghpoor, Noninvasive prediction of vertebral body compressive strength using nonlinear finite element method and an image based technique. Phys. Med. **26**(2), 88–97 (2010)
9. H. Arabacı, O. Bilgin, Automatic detection and classification of rotor cage faults in squirrel cage induction motor. Neural Comput. Appl. **19**, 713–723 (2010)
10. J.U. Chu, I. Moon, M.S. Mun, A real-time EMG pattern recognition system based on linear-nonlinear feature projection for a multifunction myoelectric hand. IEEE/ASME Trans. Mechatron. **12**(3), 282–290 (2007)
11. J.U. Chu, I. Moon, Y.J. Lee, S.K. Kim, M.S. Mun, A feature-projection-based real-time EMG pattern recognition for multifunction myoelectric hand A real-time EMG pattern recognition system based on linear-nonlinear feature projection for a multifunction myoelectric hand. IEEE Trans. Biomed. Eng. **53**(11), 2232–2239 (2006)
12. M. Daneshyari, Chaotic neural network controlled by particle swarm with decaying chaotic inertia weight for pattern recognition. Neural Comput. Appl. **19**, 637–645 (2010)

13. R.O. Duda, P.E. Hart, D.G. Stork, *Pattern Classification* (John Wiley and Sons, New York, 2001). ISBN: 0-471-05669-3
14. S. Duer, Diagnostic system for the diagnosis of a reparable technical object, with the use of an artificial neural network of RBF type. Neural Comput. Appl. **19**, 691–700 (2010)
15. C. Liu, Capitalize on dimensionality increasing techniques for improving face recognition grand challenge performance. IEEE Trans. Pattern Anal. Mach. Intell. **28**(5), 725–737 (2006)
16. V. Malathi, N.S. Marimuthu, S. Baskar, A comprehensive evaluation of multicategory classification methods for fault classification in series compensated transmission line. Neural Comput. Appl. **19**, 595–600 (2010)
17. Y. Nguwi, S. Cho, Emergent self-organizing feature map for recognizing road sign images. Neural Comput. Appl. **19**, 601–615 (2010)
18. J.O. Peralta, M. de Paralta, Security PIDS with physical sensors, real time pattern recognition, and continuous patrol. IEEE Trans. Sytems Man Cybern. Part C Appl. Rev. **32**(4), 340–346 (2002)
19. H. Seker, H. Evans, N. Aydin, E. Yazgan, Compensatory fuzzy neural networks-based intelligent detection doppler ultrasound waveforms. IEEE Trans. Inf. Technol. Biomed. **5**(3), 187–194 (2001)
20. X. Song, P. Wang, Flexible array self-organizing map neural network and its application in complex pattern recognition. Neural Comput. Appl. **20**, 9–16 (2011)
21. N. Sun, Z. Ji, C. Zou, L. Zhao, Two-dimensional canonical correlation analysis and its application in small sample size face recognition. Neural Comput. Appl. **19**, 377–382 (2010)
22. N. Tsimboukakis, G. Tambouratzis, A comparative study on authorship attribution classification tasks using both neural network and statistical methods. Neural Comput. Appl. **19**, 573–582 (2010)
23. K. Yamagishi, J. Hori, M. Miyakama, Development of EOG-based communication system controlled by eight-directional eye movements, in *Proceedings of the 28th IEEE EMBS Annual International Conference* (2006), pp. 2574–2577
24. J. Hori, K. Sakano, Y. Saitoh, Development of a communication support device controlled by eye movements and voluntary eye blink. IEICE Trans. Inf. Syst. E89-D (6), 1790–1797 (2006)
25. Owners Manual for the MINDSET, Nolan Computer Systems (1997–2000)
26. L.X. Wang, *A Course in Fuzzy Systems and Control* (Prentice Hall, Englewood Cliffs, NJ, 1997)
27. S. Haykin, *Neural Networks—A Comprehensive Foundation* (Macmillan, New York, 1994)
28. J.R. Hilera, V.J. Martinez, Redes Neuronales Artificiales, Fundamentos, Modelos y Aplicaciones (Adison Wesley Iberoamericana, USA, 1995). ISBN: 0-201-87895-X
29. J.S.R. Jang, C.T. Sun, *Neuro-Fuzzy and Soft Computing* (Prentice Hall, NJ, 1996)
30. J.J. Rubio, SOFMLS: online self-organizing fuzzy modified least-squares network. IEEE Trans. Fuzzy Syst. **17**(6), 1296–1309 (2009)

A Method with Neural Networks for the Classification of Fruits and Vegetables

Abstract In this chapter, a novel method for the classification of fruits and vegetables is introduced. This technique is divided into two parts: the electronic nose and classification method. First, an electronic nose is designed with an arduino microcontroller and with some electronic sensors to obtain real data of the smells of fruits or vegetables. Second, a classification method is introduced with a neural network to detect between three kind of objects: fruits or vegetables. The introduced strategy is validated by three experiments with the adaline, multilayer, and radial basis function neural networks.

1 Introduction

Humans employ the senses such as taste, smell, or touch to perceive their environment. In particular, the olfactory system detects and classifies some kind of fruits such as papaya, orange, apple, guava, lemon, and banana, or vegetables such as onion and garlic. The smells of some elements are pleasant, but there smells of other elements exist which could be nasty or dangerous for the people; thus, an electronic nose could be employed in these cases.

There is some research about electronic noses. In [1], an artificial perception model based on multi-sensor data fusion to analyze the quality of tea is introduced. The electronic nose sensor of the classification in four pattern recognition algorithms is investigated in [2]. In [3], six approaches for the recognition of four tomato juice groups are considered. An adaptive neuro-fuzzy inference system of the concentration estimation in organic compounds is evaluated in [4]. In [5], the combination of the electronic tongue and nose to predict the rice type is addressed. Electronic nose technologies to characterize individuals are researched in [6]. In [7], a novel sensor selection using the pattern recognition technique in an electronic nose is developed. From the above research, the electronic noses are well applied as sensors for the classification of objects based on their smells.

There are some works about classification. In [8], a collection of methods for evolving classification models are considered. A pattern recognition method for the online monitoring of processes is described in [9]. In [10], a constrained optimization

J. de J. Rubio et al., *Dynamic Models of Energy, Robotic, and Biological Systems*,
https://doi.org/10.1007/978-3-031-85438-5_10

model for classification with kernels is addressed. The computer user behaviors are classified in [11]. In [12], a two-stage algorithm of the application in industrial plants is introduced. In [13], evolving fuzzy classifiers to handle the classification are considered. A novel active learning strategy of data-driven classifiers is designed in [14]. In [15], an enhanced version of the evolving participatory learning is suggested. A novel algorithm for the classification is described in [16]. In [17], an evolving neural fuzzy modeling approach is introduced. A class of hybrid-fuzzy models is presented in [18]. In [19], a novel methodology to create classification techniques is utilized. A novel evolving fuzzy-rule-based classifier is proposed in [20]. In [21], a novel meta-cognitive-based scaffolding classifier is considered. The classification in the context pervasive computing is focused in [22]. In [23], the evolving modeling processes in a regression context is explained. An evolution feature selection for extraction in biomedical texts is proposed in [24]. In [25], a hybrid dynamic classifier able to monitor a process is focused. A support vector machine for the classification with noise is detailed in [26]. In [27–29], important evolving classifiers are discussed. The aforementioned works show that the neural networks are often used for classification.

In this chapter, an alternative method for the classification of fruits or vegetables is introduced. This technique is divided into two parts; the electronic nose and classification method. First, an electronic nose is designed to obtain real data of the smells of three objects: papaya, orange, and apple in experiment 1, or onion, guava, and banana in experiment 2, or lemon, garlic, and onion in experiment 3. Later, a classification method is introduced to detect between the three kind of objects. The proposed technique is employed for the comparison of the functioning between the adaline, multilayer, and radial basis function neural networks.

This chapter is organized as follows. In Sect. 2, the electronic nose is described. In Sect. 3, the concentrations of the objects are showed. In Sect. 4, the adaline, multilayer, and radial basis function neural networks are described, each of them will be used in the classification method. In Sect. 5, the final intelligent algorithms are described by steps. In Sect. 6, the novel classification method is explained in detail. In Sect. 7, the proposed strategy is applied for the detection of three objects. Finally, in Sect. 8, the results and the possible future research options are explained.

2 Electronic Nose

In this chapter, an electronic nose is constructed with an array of 5 gas sensors that would classify the smell of 3 objects. With the array of sensors, it is possible to detect a large amount of smells due to the sensitivity of different chemical compounds from each of the sensors.

2.1 Sensors

In this section, the sensors used in the electronic nose are described. Table 1 shows the list of gas sensors used in the construction of the sensor array of the electronic nose considered in this research.

The MQ-2 is a gas sensor that is composed of the micro ceramic tube Al_2O_3, the tin dioxide (SnO_2) sensitive layer, the measuring electrode, and the heater are set in a crust made by plastic mesh stainless steel. The heater provides necessary working conditions for the functioning of sensitive components. The MQ-2 system has 6 pins; 4 of them are used to look for signs and the other 2 are used to provide a heating current. This sensor obtains concentrations of H_2, C_3H_8, and C_4H_{10} gases.

The sensitive material of the gas sensor MQ-3 is SnO_2 which has lower conductivity in clean air. When alcohol target gas exists, the conductivity sensor is higher along with increasing gas concentration. This sensor obtains concentrations of C_6H_6, and C_2H_{60} gases.

The MQ-135 is used for equipment control air quality for buildings or offices, and it is suitable for the detection of NH_3, NO_x, alcohol, benzene, smoke, CO_2, etc. This sensor obtains the concentrations of CO_2, NH_3, and N_2 gases.

The TGS-2610 is a type of semiconductor gas sensor that combines high sensitivity to liquefied petroleum gas (LP) with low power consumption and long life. This sensor obtains concentrations of C_3H_8, C_4H_{10}, CH_4, H_2, and C_2H_{60} gases.

The TGS-2611 is a type of semiconductor gas sensor that combines very high sensitivity with the methane gas power consumption and long life low. This sensor obtains the concentration of CH_4 gas.

These sensors were placed on a plate to form the arrangement with the electronic configuration of Fig. 1.

Each sensor is coupled to a variable resistor or potentiometer pin electrode to create an output voltage. This resistor is adjusted to set the sensitivity of the sensor to detect different compounds or gases.

The output voltage adjusting resistance of each sensor varies between 0 and 5 volts and the data acquisition board (arduino) collects the values of each sensor in the presence of the object. The 5 sensors are processed in the arduino to record all variations and build a data table on the computer concerning each of the objects.

Table 1 Gas sensors of the electronic nose

Sensors	Chemicals
MQ-2	H_2, LPG, CH_4, CO
MQ-3	Alcohol, Benzene, CH_4, Hexane
MQ-135	CO_2, NH_3, NO_x, CO, Alcohol, Benzene
TGS2610	LPG, Methane, Hydrogen, Isobutane, Propane
TGS2611	Methane, Isobutane, Methanol

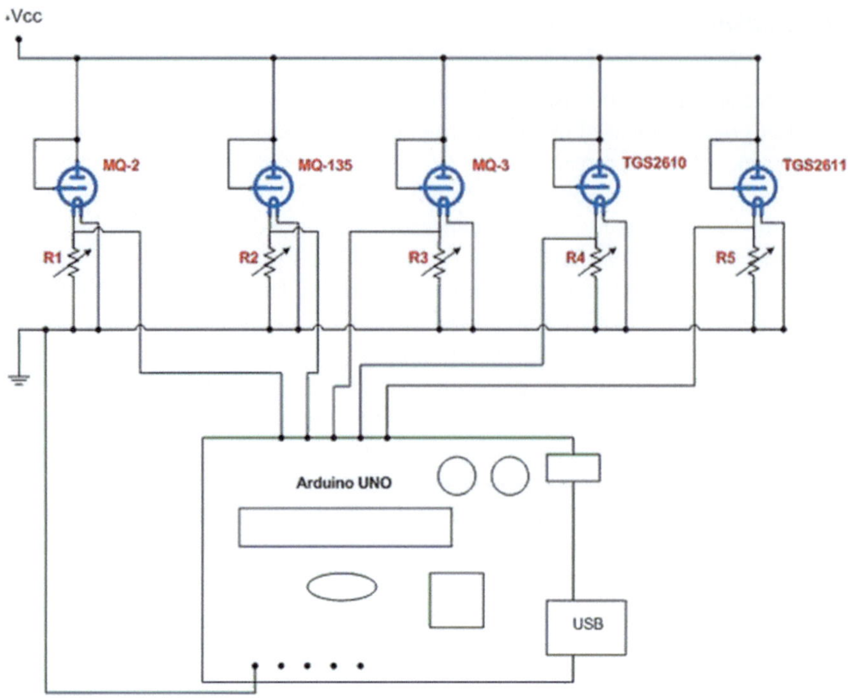

Fig. 1 Diagram of the electronic nose

In the arduino voltages obtained in the analog inputs are amplified and mapped to integer values ranging from 0 to 1023, representing a value of 4.9 mV per unit. The response of the device is of 100 microseconds to read the analog inputs.

2.2 Microcontroller

Arduino is a device used in this chapter, first, to amplify the signals obtained by the sensors and, second, to send the data from the amplification stage to a personal computer. Figure 2 shows the arduino microcontroller.

3 Concentrations for the Objects

The values obtained in the process of detecting scents represent 5 inputs for the learning algorithm and are denoted as $x_1(k) = \text{MQ-135}, x_2(k) = \text{TGS-2610}, x_3(k) = \text{MQ-2}$, $x_4(k) = \text{TGS-2611}$, and $x_5(k) = \text{MQ-3}$.

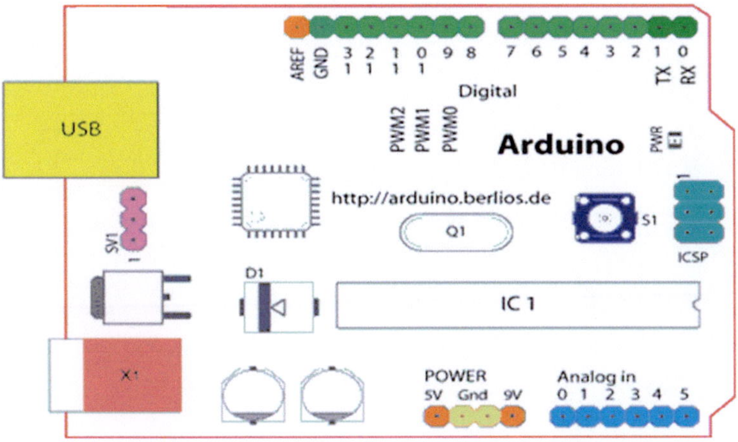

Fig. 2 Arduino microcontroller

Figures 3, 4, and 5 show the electronic signals of the objects employed in experiment 1: papaya, orange, and apple concentrations.

Figures 6, 7, and 8 show the electronic signals of the objects utilized in experiment 2: onion, guava, and banana concentrations.

Figures 9, 10, and 11 show the electronic signals of the objects utilized in experiment 3: lemon, garlic, and onion concentrations.

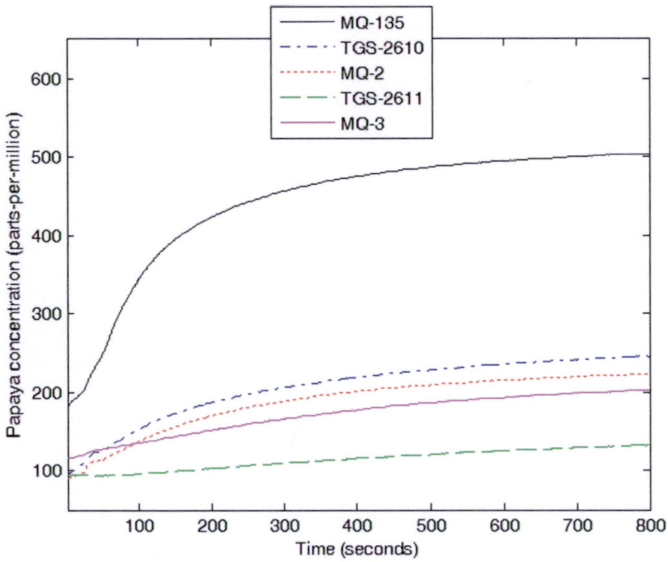

Fig. 3 Papaya concentrations

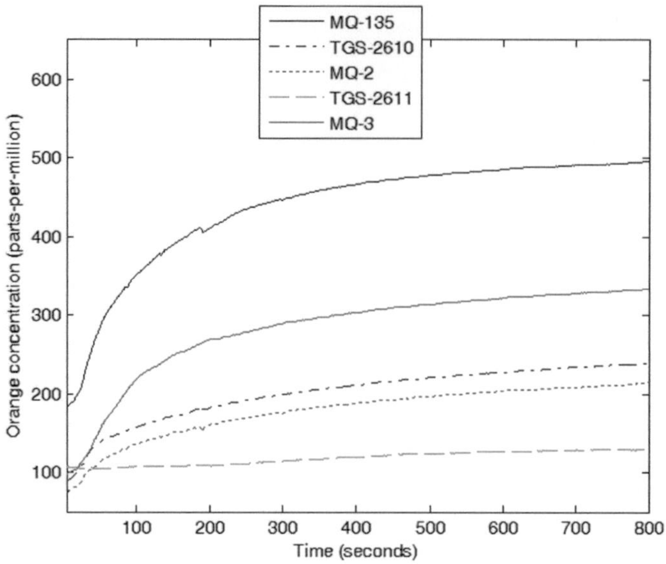

Fig. 4 Orange concentrations

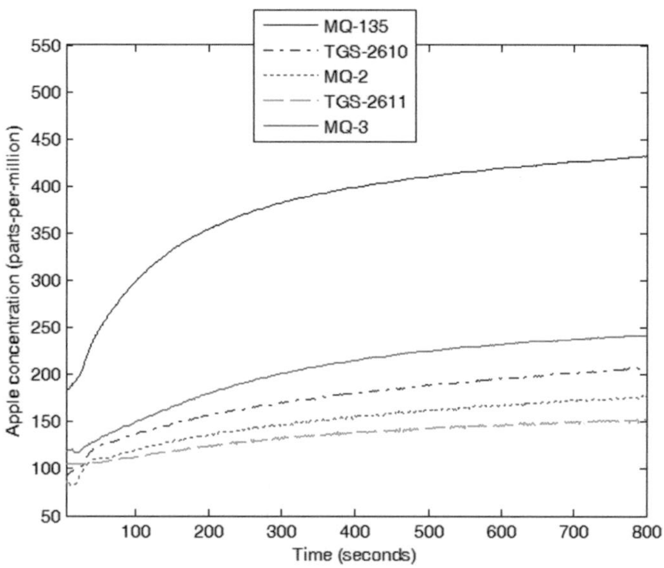

Fig. 5 Apple concentrations

Remark 1 The importance of Figs. 3, 4, 5, 6, 7, 8, 9, and 10 is to show that the behaviors of the concentrations vary slowly over time and they rise.

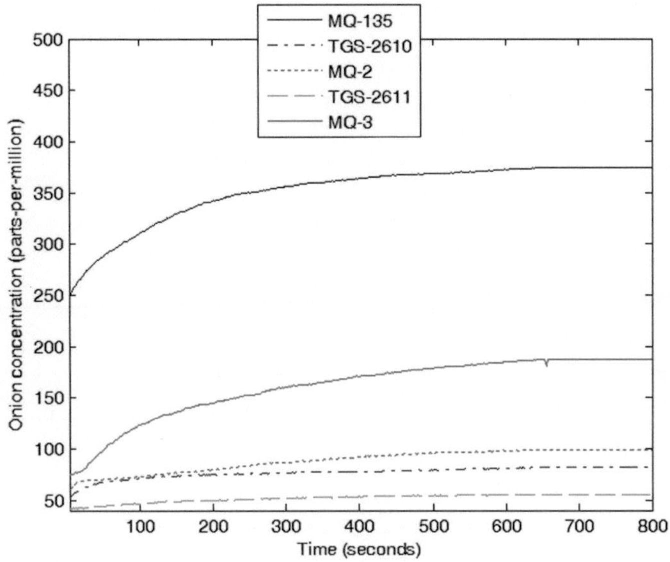

Fig. 6 Onion concentrations

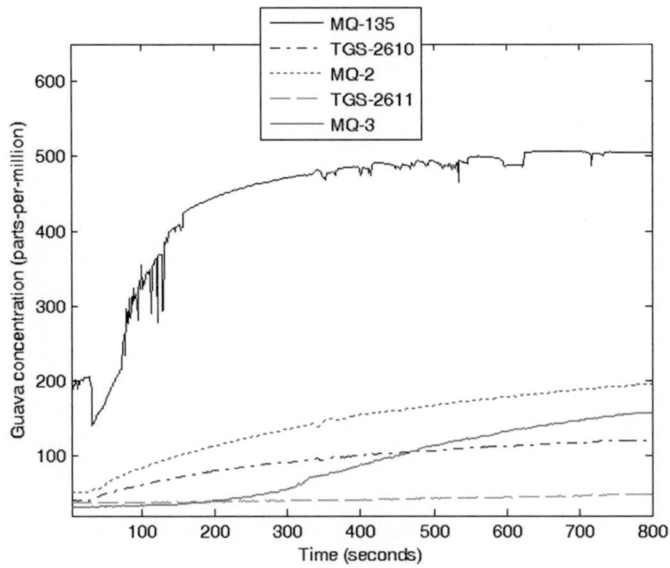

Fig. 7 Guava concentrations

Remark 2 Since the behaviors of the concentrations vary slowly over time, the signals are repeatable. For example, in 10 experiments, the variance of the signal is 0.01%.

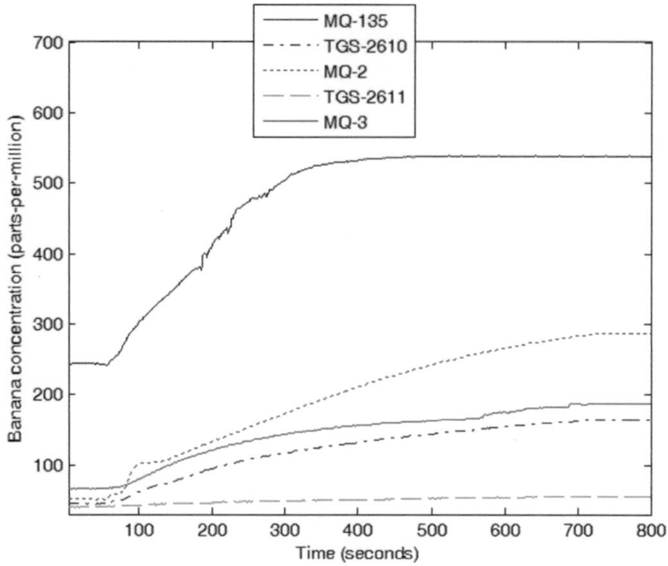

Fig. 8 Banana concentrations

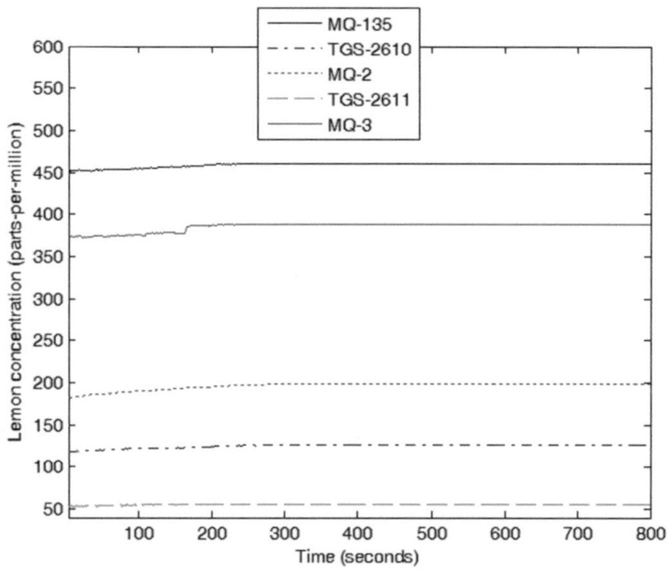

Fig. 9 Lemon concentrations

For data recording process smell detection is established with the electronic nose to take samples of the 3 objects.

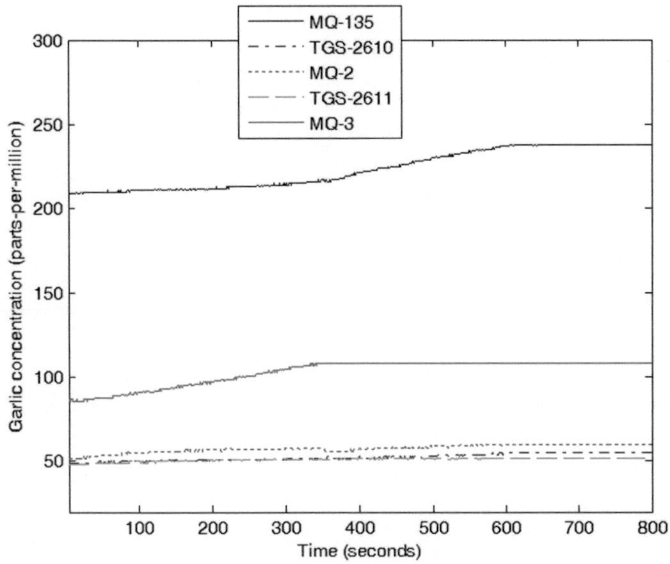

Fig. 10 Garlic concentrations

The data are obtained as follows. Initially the electronic nose is allowed to stand for 10 minutes. Then add the object 1, and take readings for 3 minutes; subsequently, release the aroma of this object, leaving the device for 3 minutes. Once this time has finished, the object 2 is incorporated and samples are taken continuously releasing the scent of this object for 3 minutes; next, release the aroma of this object leaving the device for 3 minutes. And finally, object 3 is incorporated into the electronic nose to make data records for 3 minutes. This method yields approximately 800 sample points for each object. In the range of 800 data obtained for each object, values vary according to the concentration of smell over time.

4 Intelligent Algorithms

In this section, the neural networks to be used by the classification technique are presented. The neural networks are the adaline, multilayer, and radial basis function neural networks. Five inputs for each intelligent algorithm are denoted as $x_1(k) =$ MQ-135, $x_2(k) =$ TGS-2610, $x_3(k) =$ MQ-2, $x_4(k) =$ TGS-2611, and $x_5(k) =$ MQ-3, which have different values for the concentrations of the three objects. The outputs for each intelligent algorithm are as follows:

$$o_1(k) = 1,\\ o_2(k) = 0,\\ o_3(k) = 0, \tag{1}$$

$$o_1(k) = 0,\\ o_2(k) = 1,\\ o_3(k) = 0, \tag{2}$$

$$o_1(k) = 0,\\ o_2(k) = 0,\\ o_3(k) = 1, \tag{3}$$

where (1) are for object 1, (2) are for object 2, and (3) are for object 3.

4.1 Adaline Neural Network

The adaline network approximates the real outputs $o_l(k)$ as follows:

$$\widehat{o_l}(k) = v_{li}(k)\alpha_i\left(u_i(k)\right), \tag{4}$$

where $u_i(k) = x_i(k)$, $i = 1, \ldots, 5$, $l = 1, \ldots, 3$, $x_i(k)$ are the five real inputs with different values for the three objects, $\widehat{o_l}(k)$ are the outputs, and α_i are the sigmoid functions given as follows:

$$\alpha_i(u_i(k)) = \frac{1}{1 + e^{-u_i(k)}}. \tag{5}$$

The updating of the weights for the training is given as follows:

$$v_{li}(k+1) = v_{li}(k) - \rho_a x_i(k)\widetilde{o_l}(k), \tag{6}$$

where $0 < \rho_a < 1$ is the constant learning speed and a is adaline, the initial weights $v_{li}(1)$ are selected as a random number from 0 to 1, and $\widetilde{o_l}(k)$ are the identification errors defined as follows:

$$\widetilde{o_l}(k) = \widehat{o_l}(k) - o_l(k). \tag{7}$$

The difference between this network and the classical one is that the second one uses a signum function, while the first one uses a sigmoid function.

4.2 Multilayer Neural Network

The multilayer neural network approximates the real outputs $o_l(k)$ as follows:

$$\widehat{o_l}(k) = \sum_{j=1}^{m} v_{li}(k)\beta_j\left(u_j(k)\right), \tag{8}$$

where $i = 1, \ldots, 5, l = 1, \ldots, 3, j = 1, \ldots, m, \widehat{o_l}(k)$ are the outputs, $v_{lj}(k)$ are the weights of the output layer, m is the neurons number in the hidden layer, and β_i are sigmoid functions given as follows:

$$\beta_j(u_j(k)) = \frac{1}{1 + e^{-u_j(k)}}, \tag{9}$$

where $u_j(k) = \sum_{i=1}^{5} w_{ij}(k)x_i(k)$, $x_i(k)$ are the five real inputs with different values for the three objects, and $w_{ij}(k)$ are the weights of the hidden layer. The updating of the weights for the training is given as follows:

$$\begin{aligned} v_{lj}(k+1) &= v_{lj}(k) - \rho_m\beta_j(u_j(k))\widetilde{o_l}(k), \\ w_{ij}(k+1) &= w_{ij}(k) - \rho_m x_i(k)v_{lj}(k)\frac{e^{-u_j(k)}}{\left[1+e^{-u_j(k)}\right]^2}\widetilde{o_l}(k), \end{aligned} \tag{10}$$

where $0 < \rho_m < 1$ is the constant learning speed and m is multilayer, the initial weights $v_{lj}(1)$ and $w_{ij}(1)$ are selected as random numbers from 0 to 1, and $\widetilde{o_l}(k)$ are the identification errors defined as:

$$\widetilde{o_l}(k) = \widehat{o_l}(k) - o_l(k). \tag{11}$$

The difference between this network and the classical one is that the second one uses signum functions in the hidden and output layers, while the first one uses sigmoid functions only in the hidden layer.

4.3 Radial Basis Function Neural Network

The radial basis function neural network approximates the real outputs $o_l(k)$ as follows:

$$\widehat{o}_l(k) = \frac{\sum_{j=1}^{m} v_{lj}(k)\gamma_j(u_j(k))}{\sum_{j=1}^{m} \gamma_j(u_j(k))}, \tag{12}$$

where $i = 1, \ldots, 5, l = 1, \ldots, 3, j = 1, \ldots, m, \widehat{o}_l(k)$ are the outputs, $v_{lj}(k)$ are the outputs weights, m is the neurons number in the hidden layer, and γ_j are the Gaussian functions given as follows:

$$\gamma_j(u_j(k)) = \exp(u_j(k)), \tag{13}$$

where $u_j(k) = -\sum_{i=1}^{5} \frac{[x_i(k)-c_{ij}(k)]^2}{\sigma_{ij}^2(k)}$, $c_{ij}(k)$ and $\sigma_{ij}(k)$ are the centers and the widths of the input Gaussian functions, and $x_i(k)$ are the five real inputs with different values for the three objects. The updating of the weights of the Gaussian functions and output weights for the training is given as follows:

$$\begin{aligned} v_{lj}(k+1) &= v_{lj}(k) - \rho_{rbf} \frac{\gamma_j(u_j(k))}{\sum_{j=1}^{m} \gamma_j(u_j(k))} \widetilde{o}_l(k), \\ c_{ij}(k+1) &= c_{ij}(k) - \rho_{rbf} \xi_c(k) \widetilde{o}_l(k), \\ \sigma_{ij}(k+1) &= \sigma_{ij}(k) - \rho_{rbf} \xi_\sigma(k) \widetilde{o}_l(k), \\ \xi_c(k) &= \frac{2\gamma_j(u_j(k))[x_i(k)-c_{ij}(k)][v_{lj}(k)-\widehat{o}_l(k)]}{\left(\sum_{j=1}^{m} \gamma_j(u_j(k))\right) \sigma_{ij}^2(k)}, \\ \xi_\sigma(k) &= \frac{2\gamma_j(u_j(k))[x_i(k)-c_{ij}(k)]^2[v_{lj}(k)-\widehat{o}_l(k)]}{\left(\sum_{j=1}^{m} \gamma_j(u_j(k))\right) \sigma_{ij}^3(k)}, \end{aligned} \tag{14}$$

where $0 < \rho_{rbf} < 1$ is the constant learning speed and rbf is the radial basis function, the initial weights $v_{lj}(1)$, $c_{ij}(1)$, and $\sigma_{ij}(1)$ are selected as random numbers from 0 to 1, and $\widetilde{o}_l(k)$ are the identification errors defined as follows:

$$\widetilde{o}_l(k) = \widehat{o}_l(k) - o_l(k). \tag{15}$$

The difference between this radial basis function and the classical one is that the second one uses the product of the Gaussian functions, while the first one uses the addition.

Remark 3 The objective of the updating of the weights of Eqs. (6), (10), and (14) is to find their optimal values. The parameters ρ_a, ρ_m, and ρ_{rbf}, represent the learning steps: if these parameters are small, maybe the weights will delay to find their optimal value, but if these parameters are big, maybe the weights will jump their optimal value. Thus, these parameters should be correctly selected.

5 Final Intelligent Algorithms

In this section, the steps for computing in the learning of the intelligent algorithms are explained.

5.1 Adaline Neural Network

The adaline neural network is as follows:

(1) Obtain the outputs of the nonlinear system $o_l(k)$ with Eqs. (1), (2), and (3). The outputs number $l = 1, \ldots, 3$ is selected according to this nonlinear system.
(2) Select the following parameters; ρ_a with a value between 0 and 1; $v_{lj}(1)$ as random numbers between 0 and 1; $i = 1, \ldots, 5$; obtain the outputs of the neural network as $\widehat{o}_l(1)$ with Eqs. (4) and (5).
(3) For each iteration k, obtain the neural network outputs $\widehat{o}_l(k)$ with Eqs. (4) and (5), obtain the identification errors $\widetilde{o}_l(k)$ with Eq. (7), and update the parameters $v_{lj}(k+1)$ with Eq. (6).
(4) Note that the behavior of the algorithm could be improved by changing the values of $v_{lj}(1)$ or ρ_a.

5.2 Multilayer Neural Network

The multilayer neural network is as follows:

(1) Obtain the outputs of the nonlinear system $o_l(k)$ with Eqs. (1), (2), and (3). The outputs number $l = 1, \ldots, 3$ is selected according to this nonlinear system.
(2) Select the following parameters; ρ_m with a value between 0 and 1; $v_{lj}(1)$ and $w_{ij}(1)$ as random numbers between 0 and 1; $i = 1, \ldots, 5$, $j = 1, \ldots, m$, m as an integer number; obtain the outputs of the neural network as $\widehat{o}_l(1)$ with Eqs. (8) and (9).
(3) For each iteration k, obtain the neural network outputs $\widehat{o}_l(k)$ with Eqs. (8) and (9), obtain the identification errors $\widetilde{o}_l(k)$ with Eq. (11), and update the parameters $v_{lj}(k+1)$ and $w_{ij}(k+1)$ with Eq. (10).
(4) Note that the behavior of the algorithm could be improved by changing the values of m, $v_{lj}(1)$, $w_{ij}(1)$, or ρ_m.

5.3 Radial Basis Function Neural Network

The radial basis function neural network is as follows:

(1) Obtain the outputs of the nonlinear system $o_l(k)$ with Eqs. (1), (2), and (3). The outputs number $l = 1, \ldots, 3$ is selected according to this nonlinear system.
(2) Select the following parameters; ρ_{rbf} with a value between 0 and 1; $v_{lj}(1)$, $c_{ij}(1)$, $\sigma_{ij}(1)$ as random numbers between 0 and 1; $i = 1, \ldots, 5$, $j = 1, m$, m as an integer number; obtain the outputs of the neural network as $\widehat{o}_l(1)$ with Eqs. (12), (13).
(3) For each iteration k, obtain the neural network outputs $\widehat{o}_l(k)$ with Eqs. (12), (13), obtain the identification errors $\widetilde{o}_l(k)$ with Eq. (15), and update the parameters $v_{lj}(k+1)$, $c_{ij}(k+1)$, and $\sigma_{ij}(k+1)$ with Eq. (14).
(4) Note that the behavior of the algorithm could be improved by changing the values of m, $v_{lj}(1)$, $c_{ij}(1)$, $\sigma_{ij}(1)$, or ρ_{rbf}.

Remark 4 A radial basis function neural network can be seen as a fuzzy inference system [30].

6 Classification Method with the Neural Networks

In this section, the proposed method for the classification of objects is detailed. The total number of data is divided into two parts; the first is for the training, and the second is for the testing.

6.1 Training

The training data is divided into three parts; the first part is used for learning the behavior in object 1, the second part is used for the learning of the behavior in object 2, and the third part is used for the learning of the behavior in object 3.

6.2 Testing

The testing data is divided into 16 parts; for each of these parts, the root mean square error (RMSE) is used for the evaluation and is given as follows:

$$RMSE = \left(\frac{1}{T} \sum_{k=1}^{T} \sum_{l=1}^{3} \widetilde{o}_l^2(k) \right)^{\frac{1}{2}}, \tag{16}$$

where $\widetilde{o}_l(k)$ are the errors of Eq. (7) for the adaline neural network, Eq. (11) for the multilayer neural network, or Eq. (15) for the radial basis function neural network, T is the iterations number, and 3 is the number of outputs.

If the following criterion is satisfied:

$$RMSE < \varepsilon, \tag{17}$$

where $0 < \varepsilon < 1$ is the success parameter selected by the designer, then a success in the classification is obtained, and the parameter called True Testing (TT) is increased as follows:

$$TT = TT + 1. \tag{18}$$

Later, the parameter called the Average of True Testing (ATT) is obtained as follows:

$$ATT = \frac{TT}{16} * 100, \tag{19}$$

where 16 is the total number of testing.

Now, all the testing data is also divided into three parts; the first part is employed for the testing of the behavior in object 1, the second part is employed for the testing of the behavior in object 2, and the third part is employed for the testing of the behavior in object 3.

In the first of the three parts, the input data of the concentration in object 1 is utilized for the testing, and the output data of the concentrations in the three objects are utilized for the testing. Then, the TT of Eq. (18) for the object 1 should be increased, while the TT of Eq. (18) of the other objects should not be increased. Thus, the ATT of Eq. (19) of object 1 should be the highest.

In the second of the three parts, the input data of the concentration in object 2 is utilized for the testing, and the output data of the concentrations in the three objects are utilized for the testing. Then, the TT of Eq. (18) for object 2 should be increased, while the TT of Eq. (18) of the other objects should not be increased. Thus, the ATT of Eq. (19) of object 2 should be the highest.

In the third of the three parts, the input data of the concentration of object 3 is utilized for the testing, and the output data of the concentrations in the three objects are utilized for the testing. Then, the TT of Eq. (18) for the object 3 should be increased, while the TT of Eq. (18) of the other objects should not be increased. Thus, the ATT of Eq. (19) of the object 3 should be the highest.

The three previous paragraphs build the confusion matrix for the testing of the concentrations. The percentage of the system efficiency of the data which is classified correctly, and it is obtained as the percentages addition for the terms in the main diagonal of the confusion matrix.

Remark 5 The success parameter ε should be selected small to be compared with the $RMSE$, and to determine a success or a mistake in the classification.

Remark 6 The True Testing (TT) is important because it is a counter which describes the number of successes and mistakes in the classifications. If a success in the classification is obtained, TT is increased. If a mistake in the classification is obtained, TT is not increased.

7 Experimental Results

In this section, the results of the comparison between the three neural networks for the classification of three objects are shown by two experiments. The objective is that the data is classified correctly for the three objects: fruits in experiment 1, fruits or vegetables in experiment 2, and fruits and vegetables in experiment 3.

Figure 11 shows the electronic nose used in this chapter to obtain the concentrations of the objects.

7.1 *Experiment 1*

This section presents the confusion matrix of the three neural networks for the classification of the concentrations in the three objects: object 1 as papaya, object 2 as orange, and object 3 as apple. 400 iterations of data are used for the learning and 400 iterations of data are used for the testing.

Fig. 11 Electronic nose

7.1.1 Adaline Neural Network

The adaline neural network of Eqs. (1)–(3), (4)–(7), and (16)–(19) is employed with its parameters described as $v_{lj}(1) = \text{rand}$, $\varepsilon = 1 \times 10^{-10}$, $\rho_a = 0.25$. rand is a random number between 0 and 1. Table 2 shows the $RMSE$ comparisons, Table 3 shows the true testing numbers, and Table 4 shows the confusion matrix of the adaline neural network with the electronic nose.
where P is the papaya, O is the orange, and A is the apple.

7.1.2 Multilayer Neural Network

The multilayer neural network of Eqs. (1)–(3), (8)–(11), and (16)–(19) is employed with parameters $v_{lj}(1) = \text{rand}$, $w_{ij}(1) = \text{rand}$, $m = 10$, $\varepsilon = 1 \times 10^{-10}$, $\rho_m = 0.25$. rand is a random number between 0 and 1. Table 5 shows the $RMSE$ comparisons, Table 6 shows the true testing numbers, and Table 7 shows the confusion matrix of the multilayer neural network with the electronic nose.
where P is the papaya, O is the orange, and A is the apple.

Table 2 RMSE for the comparisons with $\varepsilon = 1 \times 10^{-10}$

	First part	Second part	Third part
Object 1	3.8309×10^{-17}	0.1706	0.1089
Object 2	0.2425	2.7060×10^{-17}	0.1089
Object 3	0.2425	0.1706	1.7272×10^{-17}
Object 1	5.2595×10^{-17}	0.2670	0.2171
Object 2	0.3333	4.2365×10^{-17}	0.2171
Object 3	0.3333	0.2670	3.4447×10^{-17}
Object 1	6.2697×10^{-17}	0.3317	0.2828
Object 2	0.3974	5.2619×10^{-17}	0.2828
Object 3	0.3974	0.3317	4.4874×10^{-17}
Object 1	7.0564×10^{-17}	0.3816	0.3327
Object 2	0.4472	6.0538×10^{-17}	0.3327
Object 3	0.4472	0.3816	5.2779×10^{-17}
Object 1	7.6991×10^{-17}	0.4224	0.3733
Object 2	0.4880	6.7023×10^{-17}	0.3733
Object 3	0.4880	0.4224	5.9226×10^{-17}
Object 1			0.4077
Object 2			0.4077
Object 3			6.4689×10^{-17}

Table 3 True testing of the adaline neural network

	Inputs			
Outputs		P	O	A
	P	5	0	0
	O	0	5	0
	A	0	0	6

Table 4 Results of the adaline neural network

	Inputs			
Outputs		P	O	A
	P	31.25	0	0
	O	0	31.25	0
	A	0	0	37.5

Table 5 RMSE for the comparisons with $\varepsilon = 1 \times 10^{-10}$

	First part	Second part	Third part
Object 1	3.8309×10^{-17}	0.1706	0.1089
Object 2	0.2425	2.7060×10^{-17}	0.1089
Object 3	0.2425	0.1706	1.7272×10^{-17}
Object 1	5.2650×10^{-17}	0.2670	0.2171
Object 2	0.3333	4.2365×10^{-17}	0.2171
Object 3	0.3333	0.2670	3.4447×10^{-17}
Object 1	6.2764×10^{-17}	0.3317	0.2828
Object 2	0.3974	5.2619×10^{-17}	0.2828
Object 3	0.3974	0.3317	4.4874×10^{-17}
Object 1	7.0638×10^{-17}	0.3816	0.3327
Object 2	0.4472	6.0538×10^{-17}	0.3327
Object 3	0.4472	0.3816	5.2779×10^{-17}
Object 1	7.7072×10^{-17}	0.4224	0.3733
Object 2	0.4880	6.7023×10^{-17}	0.3733
Object 3	0.4880	0.4224	5.9226×10^{-17}
Object 1			0.4077
Object 2			0.4077
Object 3			6.4689×10^{-17}

Table 6 True testing of the multilayer neural network

	Inputs			
Outputs		P	O	A
	P	5	0	0
	O	0	5	0
	A	0	0	6

Table 7 Results of the multilayer neural network

	Inputs			
		P	O	A
Outputs	P	31.25	0	0
	O	0	31.25	0
	A	0	0	37.5

7.1.3 Radial Basis Function Neural Network

The radial basis function neural network of Eqs. (1)–(3), (12)–(15), and (16)–(19) is employed with parameters $v_{lj}(1) = \text{rand}$, $c_{ij}(1) = \text{rand}$, $\sigma_{ij}(1) = \text{rand}$, $m = 20$, $\varepsilon = 1 \times 10^{-1}$, $\rho_{rbf} = 0.25$. rand is a random number between 0 and 1. Table 8 shows the $RMSE$ comparisons, Table 9 shows the true testing numbers, and Table 10 shows the confusion matrix of the radial basis function neural network with the electronic nose.
where P is the papaya, O is the orange, and A is the apple.

Table 8 RMSE for the comparisons with $\varepsilon = 1 \times 10^{-1}$

	First part	Second part	Third part
Object 1	0.0060	0.1646	0.1069
Object 2	0.2377	0.0059	0.1051
Object 3	0.2373	0.1676	0.0038
Object 1	0.0082	0.2578	0.2133
Object 2	0.3268	0.0093	0.2096
Object 3	0.3262	0.2624	0.0075
Object 1	0.0098	0.3202	0.2778
Object 2	0.3895	0.0115	0.2730
Object 3	0.3889	0.3259	0.0098
Object 1	0.0110	0.3683	0.3267
Object 2	0.4384	0.0132	0.3211
Object 3	0.4376	0.3750	0.0116
Object 1	0.0120	0.4078	0.3666
Object 2	0.4783	0.0147	0.3603
Object 3	0.4775	0.4151	0.0130
Object 1			0.4005
Object 2			0.3936
Object 3			0.0142

Table 9 True testing of the radial basis function neural network

	Inputs			
		P	O	A
Outputs	P	5	0	0
	O	0	5	0
	A	0	0	6

Table 10 Results of the radial basis function neural network

	Inputs			
		P	O	A
Outputs	P	31.25	0	0
	O	0	31.25	0
	A	0	0	37.5

7.1.4 Description of the Obtained Results

From Tables 4, 7, and 10, it can be seen that the three neural networks yield equal results for the classification of fruits using an electronic nose because the confusion matrix of the three neural networks shows a system efficiency of 100%. The first difference is that the radial basis function required a higher value for the parameter ε; therefore, this neural network is less accurate than the other two. The second difference is that while the adaline network uses 1 neuron, the multilayer neural network uses 10 neurons, and the radial basis function uses 20 neurons. Thus, the adaline and multilayer neural networks are more convenient for the proposed classification strategy in the case of fruits because they are more compact and more accurate.

7.2 Experiment 2

This section presents the confusion matrix of the three neural networks for the classification of the concentrations of three objects: object 1 as onion, objects 2 as guava, and objects 3 as banana. 400 iterations of data are used for the learning and 400 iterations of data are used for the testing.

7.2.1 Adaline Neural Network

The adaline neural network of Eqs. (1)–(3), (4)–(7), and (16)–(19) is employed with parameters $v_{lj}(1) = \text{rand}$, $\varepsilon = 1 \times 10^{-10}$, $\rho_a = 0.25$. rand is a random number between 0 and 1. Table 11 shows the $RMSE$ comparisons, Table 12 shows the

Table 11 RMSE for the comparisons with $\varepsilon = 1 \times 10^{-10}$

	First part	Second part	Third part
Object 1	3.8197×10^{-17}	0.1706	0.1089
Object 2	0.2425	3.0771×10^{-17}	0.1089
Object 3	0.2425	0.1706	1.7272×10^{-17}
Object 1	5.2497×10^{-17}	0.2670	0.2171
Object 2	0.3333	4.8174×10^{-17}	0.2171
Object 3	0.3333	0.2670	3.4447×10^{-17}
Object 1	6.2581×10^{-17}	0.3317	0.2828
Object 2	0.3974	5.9835×10^{-17}	0.2828
Object 3	0.3974	0.3317	4.4874×10^{-17}
Object 1	7.0432×10^{-17}	0.3816	0.3327
Object 2	0.4472	6.8839×10^{-17}	0.3327
Object 3	0.4472	0.3816	5.2779×10^{-17}
Object 1	7.6848×10^{-17}	0.4224	0.3733
Object 2	0.4880	7.6213×10^{-17}	0.3733
Object 3	0.4880	0.4224	5.9226×10^{-17}
Object 1			0.4077
Object 2			0.4077
Object 3			6.4689×10^{-17}

Table 12 True testing of the adaline neural network

	Inputs
Outputs	$\begin{array}{cccc} & O & G & B \\ O & 5 & 0 & 0 \\ G & 0 & 5 & 0 \\ B & 0 & 0 & 6 \end{array}$

Table 13 Results of the adaline neural network

	Inputs
Outputs	$\begin{array}{cccc} & O & G & B \\ O & 31.25 & 0 & 0 \\ G & 0 & 31.25 & 0 \\ B & 0 & 0 & 37.5 \end{array}$

true testing numbers, and Table 13 shows the confusion matrix of the adaline neural network with the electronic nose.

where O is the onion, G is the guava, and B is the banana.

7.2.2 Multilayer Neural Network

The multilayer neural network of Eqs. (1)–(3), (8)–(11), and (16)–(19) is employed with parameters $v_{lj}(1) = \text{rand}$, $w_{ij}(1) = \text{rand}$, $m = 10$, $\varepsilon = 1 \times 10^{-10}$, $\rho_m = 0.25$. rand is a random number between 0 and 1. Table 14 shows the $RMSE$ comparisons, Table 15 shows the true testing numbers, and Table 16 shows the confusion matrix of the multilayer neural network with the electronic nose.
where O is the onion, G is the guava, and B is the banana.

Table 14 RMSE for the comparisons with $\varepsilon = 1 \times 10^{-10}$

	First part	Second part	Third part
Object 1	3.8151×10^{-17}	0.1706	0.1089
Object 2	0.2425	2.7060×10^{-17}	0.1089
Object 3	0.2425	0.1706	1.7272×10^{-17}
Object 1	5.2433×10^{-17}	0.2670	0.2171
Object 2	0.3333	4.2365×10^{-17}	0.2171
Object 3	0.3333	0.2670	3.4447×10^{-17}
Object 1	6.2504×10^{-17}	0.3317	0.2828
Object 2	0.3974	5.2619×10^{-17}	0.2828
Object 3	0.3974	0.3317	4.4874×10^{-17}
Object 1	7.0346×10^{-17}	0.3816	0.3327
Object 2	0.4472	6.0538×10^{-17}	0.3327
Object 3	0.4472	0.3816	5.2779×10^{-17}
Object 1	7.6754×10^{-17}	0.4224	0.3733
Object 2	0.4880	6.7023×10^{-17}	0.3733
Object 3	0.4880	0.4224	5.9226×10^{-17}
Object 1			0.4077
Object 2			0.4077
Object 3			6.4689×10^{-17}

Table 15 True testing of the multilayer neural network

	Inputs
	O G B
Outputs	O 5 0 0 G 0 5 0 B 0 0 6

Table 16 Results of the multilayer neural network

	Inputs			
		O	G	B
Outputs	O	31.25	0	0
	G	0	31.25	0
	B	0	0	37.5

7.2.3 Radial Basis Function Neural Network

The radial basis function neural network of Eqs. (1)–(3), (12)–(15), and (16)–(19) is employed with parameters $v_{lj}(1) = \text{rand}, c_{ij}(1) = \text{rand}, \sigma_{ij}(1) = \text{rand}, m = 20, \varepsilon = 1 \times 10^{-1}, \rho_{rbf} = 0.25$. rand is a random number between 0 and 1. Table 17 shows the $RMSE$ comparisons, Table 18 shows the true testing numbers, and Table 19 shows the confusion matrix of the radial basis function neural network with the electronic nose.
where O is the onion, G is the guava, and B is the banana.

Table 17 RMSE for the comparisons with $\varepsilon = 1 \times 10^{-1}$

	First part	Second part	Third part
Object 1	0.0048	0.1646	0.1069
Object 2	0.2385	0.0059	0.1051
Object 3	0.2393	0.1676	0.0038
Object 1	0.0066	0.2577	0.2133
Object 2	0.3277	0.0093	0.2096
Object 3	0.3288	0.2625	0.0076
Object 1	0.0078	0.3201	0.2778
Object 2	0.3907	0.0115	0.2730
Object 3	0.3920	0.3260	0.0098
Object 1	0.0088	0.3683	0.3267
Object 2	0.4397	0.0133	0.3211
Object 3	0.4412	0.3750	0.0116
Object 1	0.0096	0.4078	0.3666
Object 2	0.4797	0.0147	0.3603
Object 3	0.4814	0.4152	0.0130
Object 1			0.4005
Object 2			0.3936
Object 3			0.0142

Table 18 True testing of the radial basis function neural network

	Inputs			
		O	G	B
Outputs	O	5	0	0
	G	0	5	0
	B	0	0	6

Table 19 Results of the radial basis function neural network

	Inputs			
		O	G	B
Outputs	O	31.25	0	0
	G	0	31.25	0
	B	0	0	37.5

7.2.4 Description of the Obtained Results

From Tables 13, 16, and 19, it can be seen that the three neural networks yield equal results for the classification of fruits and vegetables using an electronic nose because the confusion matrix of the three neural networks shows a system efficiency of 100%. The first difference is that the radial basis function required a higher value for the parameter ε; therefore, this neural network is less accurate than the other two. The second difference is that while the adaline network uses 1 neuron, the multilayer neural network uses 10 neurons, and the radial basis function uses 20 neurons. Thus the adaline and multilayer neural networks are more convenient for the proposed classification strategy in the case of fruits or vegetables because they are more compact and more accurate.

7.3 Experiment 3

This section presents the confusion matrix of the three neural networks for the classification of the concentrations of three objects: object 1 as lemon, objects 2 as garlic, and objects 3 as onion. 400 iterations of data are used for the learning and 400 iterations of data are used for the testing.

7.3.1 Adaline Neural Network

The adaline neural network of Eqs. (1)–(3), (4)–(7), and (16)–(19) is employed with parameters $v_{lj}(1) = \text{rand}$, $\varepsilon = 1 \times 10^{-10}$, $\rho_a = 0.25$. rand is a random number between 0 and 1. Table 20 shows the $RMSE$ comparisons, Table 21 shows the true testing numbers, and Table 22 shows the confusion matrix of the adaline neural network with the electronic nose.

Table 20 RMSE for the comparisons with $\varepsilon = 1 \times 10^{-10}$

	First part	Second part	Third part
Object 1	3.8309×10^{-17}	0.1706	0.1089
Object 2	0.2425	2.7060×10^{-17}	0.1089
Object 3	0.2425	0.1706	1.7272×10^{-17}
Object 1	5.2650×10^{-17}	0.2670	0.2171
Object 2	0.3333	4.2365×10^{-17}	0.2171
Object 3	0.3333	0.2670	3.4447×10^{-17}
Object 1	6.2764×10^{-17}	0.3317	0.2828
Object 2	0.3974	5.2619×10^{-17}	0.2828
Object 3	0.3974	0.3317	4.4874×10^{-17}
Object 1	7.0638×10^{-17}	0.3816	0.3327
Object 2	0.4472	6.0538×10^{-17}	0.3327
Object 3	0.4472	0.3816	5.2779×10^{-17}
Object 1	7.7072×10^{-17}	0.4224	0.3733
Object 2	0.4880	6.7023×10^{-17}	0.3733
Object 3	0.4880	0.4224	5.9226×10^{-17}
Object 1			0.4077
Object 2			0.4077
Object 3			6.4689×10^{-17}

Table 21 True testing of the adaline neural network

	Inputs			
		L	G	O
Outputs	L	5	0	0
	G	0	5	0
	O	0	0	6

Table 22 Results of the adaline neural network

	Inputs			
		L	G	O
Outputs	L	31.25	0	0
	G	0	31.25	0
	O	0	0	37.5

where L is the lemon, G is the garlic, and O is the onion.

7.3.2 Multilayer Neural Network

The multilayer neural network of Eqs. (1)–(3), (8)–(11), and (16)–(19) is employed with parameters $v_{lj}(1) = \text{rand}$, $w_{ij}(1) = \text{rand}$, $m = 10$, $\varepsilon = 1 \times 10^{-10}$, $\rho_m = 0.25$. rand is a random number between 0 and 1. Table 23 shows the $RMSE$ comparisons,

Table 23 RMSE for the comparisons with $\varepsilon = 1 \times 10^{-10}$

	First part	Second part	Third part
Object 1	3.8098×10^{-17}	0.1706	0.1089
Object 2	0.2425	2.7060×10^{-17}	0.1089
Object 3	0.2425	0.1706	1.7272×10^{-17}
Object 1	5.2360×10^{-17}	0.2670	0.2171
Object 2	0.3333	4.2365×10^{-17}	0.2171
Object 3	0.3333	0.2670	3.4447×10^{-17}
Object 1	6.2418×10^{-17}	0.3317	0.2828
Object 2	0.3974	5.2619×10^{-17}	0.2828
Object 3	0.3974	0.3317	4.4874×10^{-17}
Object 1	7.0249×10^{-17}	0.3816	0.3327
Object 2	0.4472	6.0538×10^{-17}	0.3327
Object 3	0.4472	0.3816	5.2779×10^{-17}
Object 1	7.6648×10^{-17}	0.4224	0.3733
Object 2	0.4880	6.7023×10^{-17}	0.3733
Object 3	0.4880	0.4224	5.9226×10^{-17}
Object 1			0.4077
Object 2			0.4077
Object 3			6.4689×10^{-17}

Table 24 True testing of the multilayer neural network

	Inputs			
Outputs		L	G	O
	L	5	0	0
	G	0	5	0
	O	0	0	6

Table 25 Results of the multilayer neural network

	Inputs			
Outputs		L	G	O
	L	31.25	0	0
	G	0	31.25	0
	O	0	0	37.5

Table 24 shows the true testing numbers, and Table 25 shows the confusion matrix of the multilayer neural network with the electronic nose.
where L is the lemon, G is the garlic, and O is the onion.

7.3.3 Radial Basis Function Neural Network

The radial basis function neural network of Eqs. (1)–(3), (12)–(15), and (16)–(19) is employed with parameters $v_{lj}(1) = \text{rand}, c_{ij}(1) = \text{rand}, \sigma_{ij}(1) = \text{rand}, m = 20, \varepsilon = 1 \times 10^{-1}, \rho_{rbf} = 0.25$. rand is a random number between 0 and 1. Table 26 shows the $RMSE$ comparisons, Table 27 shows the true testing numbers, and Table 28 shows the confusion matrix of the radial basis function neural network with the electronic nose.

where L is the lemon, G is the garlic, and O is the onion.

Table 26 RMSE for the comparisons with $\varepsilon = 1 \times 10^{-1}$

	First part	Second part	Third part
Object 1	0.0053	0.1646	0.1069
Object 2	0.2386	0.0059	0.1051
Object 3	0.2376	0.1676	0.0038
Object 1	0.0073	0.2577	0.2133
Object 2	0.3280	0.0093	0.2096
Object 3	0.3265	0.2624	0.0075
Object 1	0.0087	0.3201	0.2778
Object 2	0.3909	0.0115	0.2730
Object 3	0.3893	0.3259	0.0098
Object 1	0.0097	0.3683	0.3267
Object 2	0.4400	0.0133	0.3211
Object 3	0.4381	0.3749	0.0116
Object 1	0.0106	0.4077	0.3666
Object 2	0.4801	0.0147	0.3603
Object 3	0.4780	0.4151	0.0130
Object 1			0.4005
Object 2			0.3936
Object 3			0.0142

Table 27 True testing of the radial basis function neural network

	Inputs
Outputs	L G O L 5 0 0 G 0 5 0 O 0 0 6

Table 28 Results of the radial basis function neural network

	Inputs			
		L	*G*	*O*
Outputs	*L*	31.25	0	0
	G	0	31.25	0
	O	0	0	37.5

7.3.4 Description of the Obtained Results

From Tables 22, 25, and 28, it can be seen that the three neural networks yield equal results for the classification of fruits and vegetables using an electronic nose because the confusion matrix of the three neural networks show a system efficiency of 100%. The first difference is that the radial basis function required a higher value for the parameter ε; therefore, this neural network is less accurate than the other two. The second difference is that while the adaline network uses 1 neuron, the multilayer neural network uses 10 neurons, and the radial basis function uses 20 neurons. Thus the adaline and multilayer neural networks are more convenient for the proposed classification strategy in the case of fruits or vegetables because they are more compact and more accurate.

8 Concluding Remarks

In this chapter, a novel method for classification of fruits or vegetables was introduced. This technique was proven with the adaline, multilayer, and radial basis function neural networks. The three neural networks gave a system efficiency of 100%, but the adaline and multilayer neural networks were more convenient for the proposed classification strategy in the case of fruits or vegetables because they were more compact and more accurate. The proposed technique could be used for the classification of several objects such as the fruits, vegetables, liquids, foods, or garbage. In future research, this method could be combined with the evolving systems or could be applied for the classification of other objects.

References

1. R.B. Roy, P. Chattopadhyay, B. Tudu, N. Bhattacharyya, R. Bandyopadhyay, Artificial flavor perception of black tea using fusion of electronic nose and tongue response: a Bayesian statistical approach. J. Food Eng. **142**, 87–93 (2014)
2. P.S. Gromski, E. Correa, A.A. Vaughan, D.C. Wedge, M.L. Turner, R. Goodacre, A comparison of different chemometrics approaches for the robust classification of electronic nose data. Anal. Bioanal. Chem. **406**, 7581–7590 (2014)

3. X. Hong, J. Wang, S. Qiu, Authenticating cherry tomato juices-discussion of different data standardization and fusion approaches based on electronic nose and tongue. Food Res. Int. **60**, 173–179 (2014)
4. S.K. Jha, K. Hayashi, R. Yadava, Neural, fuzzy and neuro-fuzzy approach for concentration estimation of volatile organic compounds by surface acoustic wave sensor array. Measurement **55**, 186–195 (2014)
5. L. Lu, S. Deng, Z. Zhu, S. Tian, Classification of rice by combining electronic tongue and nose. Food Anal. Methods **8**(8), 1893–1902 (2015)
6. X. Rosalind-Wang, J.T. Lizier, A.Z. Berna, F.G. Bravo, S.C. Trowell, Human breath-print identification by e-nose, using information-theoretic feature selection prior to classification. Sens. Actuators B Chem. **217**, 165–174 (2015)
7. L. Zhang, F. Tian, G. Pei, A novel sensor selection using pattern recognition in electronic nose. Measurement **54**, 31–39 (2014)
8. F. Gomide, E. Lughofer, Recent advances on evolving intelligent systems and applications. Evol. Syst. **5**, 217–218 (2014)
9. L. Hartert, M. Sayed-Mouchaweh, Dynamic supervised classification method for online monitoring in non-stationary environments. Neurocomputing **126**, 118–131 (2014)
10. J.A. Iglesias, I. Skrjanc, Applications, results and future direction. Evol. Syst. **5**, 1–2 (2014)
11. J.A. Iglesias, A. Ledezma, A. Sanchis, Evolving classification of UNIX users' behaviors. Evol. Syst. **5**, 231–238 (2014)
12. B.S.J. Costa, P.P. Angelov, L.A. Guedes, Fully unsupervised fault detection and identification based on recursive density estimation and self-evolving cloud-based classifier. Neurocomputing **150**, 289–303 (2015)
13. E. Lughofer, O. Buchtala, Reliable all-pairs evolving fuzzy classifiers. IEEE Trans. Fuzzy Syst. **21**(4), 625–641 (2013)
14. E. Lughofer, Hybrid active learning for reducing the annotation effort of operators in classification systems. Pattern Recognit. **45**, 884–896 (2012)
15. L. Maciel, F. Gomide, R. Ballini, Enhanced evolving participatory learning fuzzy modeling: an application for asset returns volatility forecasting. Evol. Syst. **5**, 75–88 (2014)
16. K. Manimala, I.G. David, K. Selvi, A novel data selection technique using fuzzy c-means clustering to enhance SVM-based power quality classification. Evol. Syst. **19**, 3123–3144 (2015)
17. A.M. Silva, W. Caminhas, A. Lemos, F. Gomide, A fast learning algorithm for evolving neo-fuzzy neuron. Appl. Soft Comput. **14**, 194–209 (2014)
18. A. Nuñez, B.D. Schutter, D. Saez, I. Skrjanc, Hybrid-fuzzy modeling and identification. Appl. Soft Comput. **17**, 67–78 (2014)
19. M.M. Pozo, J.A. Iglesias, A.I. Ledezma, Intelligent promotions recommendation system for instaprom platform. Lecture Notes on Computational Systems, vol. 8669 (2014), pp. 231–238
20. M. Pratama, S.G. Anavatti, M.J. Er, E.D. Lughofer, pClass: an effective classifier for streaming examples. IEEE Trans. Fuzzy Syst. **23**(2), 369–386 (2015)
21. M. Pratama, S.G. Anavatti, J. Lu, Recurrent classifier based on an incremental meta-cognitive-based scaffolding algorithm. IEEE Trans. Fuzzy Syst. **23**(6), 2048–2066 (2015)
22. M. Prossegger, A. Bouchachia, Multi-resident activity recognition using incremental decision trees. Lecture Notes in Artificial Intelligence, vol. 8779 (2014), pp. 182–191
23. A. Shaker, E. Lughofer, Self-adaptive and local strategies for a smooth treatment of drifts in data streams. Evol. Syst. **5**, 239–257 (2014)
24. U.K. Sikdar, A. Ekbal, S. Saha, MODE: multiobjective differential evolution for feature selection and classifier ensemble. Evol. Syst. **19**, 3529–3549 (2015)
25. H. Toubakh, M. Sayed-Mouchaweh, Hybrid dynamic classifier for drift-like fault diagnosis in a class of hybrid dynamic systems: application to wind turbine converters. Neurocomputing **171**, 1496–1516 (2016)
26. X. Yang, L. Han, Y. Li, L. He, A bilateral-truncated-loss based robust support vector machine for classification problems. Soft Comput. **19**, 2871–2882 (2015)

27. E. Lughofer, M. Sayed-Mouchaweh, Autonomous data stream clustering implementing split-and-merge concepts—towards a plug-and-play approach. Inf. Sci. **304**, 54–79 (2015)
28. M. Sayed-Mouchaweh, E. Lughofer, *Learning in Non-Stationary Environments: Methods and Applications* (Springer, New York, 2012)
29. A.V. Uriarte-Arcia, I. Lopez-Yañez, C. Yañez-Marquez, J. Gama, O. Camacho-Nieto, Data stream classification based on the gamma classifier. Math. Probl. Eng. **2015**, 1–17 (2015)
30. J.-S. Roger-Jang, C.-T. Sun, E. Mitzutani, *Neuro-Fuzzy and Soft Computing, A Computational Approach to Learning and Machine Intelligence*. ISBN: 0-13-261066-3 (1997)

MIX
Papier aus verantwortungsvollen Quellen
Paper from responsible sources
FSC® C105338

If you have any concerns about our products,
you can contact us on
ProductSafety@springernature.com

In case Publisher is established outside the EU,
the EU authorized representative is:
Springer Nature Customer Service Center GmbH
Europaplatz 3, 69115 Heidelberg, Germany

Printed by Libri Plureos GmbH
in Hamburg, Germany